The French Socialist Experiment

Edited by
JOHN S. AMBLER

A Publication of the
Institute for the Study of Human Issues
Philadelphia

Manufactured in the United States of America

1 2 3 4 5 6   89 88 87 86 85

Library of Congress Cataloging in Publication Data

Main entry under title:

The French socialist experiment.

Bibliography: p.
Includes index.
1. Socialism—France—Addresses, essays, lectures.
2. France—Economic policy—1945–   —Addresses, essays,
lectures.   3. France—Social policy—Addresses, essays,
lectures.   4. France—Politics and government—1981–
—Addresses, essays, lectures.   I. Ambler, John S.
HX264.F73   1984   335′.00944   84-707
ISBN 0-89727-057-6
ISBN 0-89727-065-7 (pbk.)

For information, write:

Director of Publications
ISHI
3401 Science Center
Philadelphia, PA 19104

Contributors

John S. Ambler is Professor of Political Science at Rice University. He is the author of a number of articles on French politics and of *The French Army in Politics, 1945–1962* (1966) and *The Government and Politics of France* (1971).

Douglas E. Ashford is Andrew W. Mellon Professor of Comparative Politics at the University of Pittsburgh. Professor Ashford has written numerous books and articles on local politics and policy in Britain and France, including *British Dogmatism and French Pragmatism: Central-Local Relations in the Welfare State* (1982). His recent book on policy-making in France is *Policy and Politics in France: Living with Uncertainty* (1982).

Gary Freeman is Associate Professor of Government at the University of Texas and has taught at the University of Pennsylvania. He is the author of *Immigrant Labor and Racial Conflict in Industrial Societies: The French and British Experiment, 1945–76,* and of articles on social policy in Europe and America. His research on comparative social security has been supported by grants from the National Endowment for the Humanities and the German Marshall Fund of the United States.

Jane Jenson is Associate Professor of Political Science at Carleton University, Ottawa, Ontario, and Research Associate at the Harvard Center for European Studies. She is the co-author of *Political Choice in Canada,* with Harold Clarke et al. (1979); *Crisis, Challenge and Change: Party and Class in Canada,* with Janine Brodie (1980) and *Lives in a Cell: Rank-and-File Communism in France,* with George Ross (1983).

John T. S. Keeler is Assistant Professor of Political Science and Chairman of the School of International Studies' West European Studies Committee at the University of Washington. He has contributed articles on various aspects of French politics and policy to *The Fifth Republic at Twenty* (1981), *Organizing Interests in Western Europe* (1981), *France* *in the Troubled World Economy* (1982), *French Politics and Public Policy* (2nd edition, 1983) and *Soviet Policy Toward Western Europe* (1983), as well as to *Peasant Studies.*

George Ross is Professor of Sociology at Brandeis University and Senior Research Associate at the Harvard Center for European Studies. He is the author of *Workers and Communists in France* (1982) as well as co-author of *Unions, Crisis and Change,* with Peter Lange and Maurizio Vannicelli (1982) and *Lives in a Cell: Rank-and-File Communism in France,* with Jane Jenson (1983).

Martin Schain is Associate Professor of Politics at New York University. He is co-author of *French Politics and Public Policy* (1980) and author of *French Communism in Power: Urban Politics and Political Change* (1981).

Preface

JOHN S. AMBLER

In May and June of 1981, for the first time in French history, a
government representing the egalitarian strand in the French revolutionary tradition took power with a reliable parliamentary majority.[1]
Like earlier representatives of this tradition, from Babeuf to Léon
Blum, François Mitterrand believed that the ideals of "liberty, equality, fraternity" call for more than political equality: they require much
greater economic and social equality as well. Influenced in part by a
desire to enlist the help of the Communist Party in ending conservative domination of the Fifth Republic, the French Socialist Party
adopted a Marxist language of class struggle. It viewed the society
which it inherited as one designed primarily to serve the interests of
"le grand capital." In his introduction to the socialist version of the
common program adopted in 1972 by the Communist and Socialist
parties, Mitterrand promised a broad-scale attack upon "the economic and political system . . . on which is built an unjust and decadent society."[2] The Party, he continued, addresses its appeal to "the
immense majority of Frenchmen," but added, "it does not seek the
approval of the privileged, the exploiters, the profiteers: there can be
no truce between the enemies of the people and the people themselves."[3] Mitterrand was aware that the rapid expansion of the service
sector of the economy and more than two decades of unprecedented
prosperity had produced a society very different from the one Marx
had envisaged. The French Socialists addressed their appeal not only
to industrial workers (who make up little more than a third of the
population), but also to white-collar workers, professionals and managerial personnel. Yet Mitterrand insisted that "enemies of the people" were seeking to defend "an unjust and decadent society."

The Marxist strain in the pronouncements of the French Socialists, as well as their commitment to nationalize banks and a series of major industrial firms, distinguishes them from most other European socialist parties. Elsewhere, despite occasional radical pronouncements—usually when they are in the opposition—socialist parties in the postwar period generally have sought to extend the welfare state without seriously challenging the capitalist structure of the economy. The "deradicalization" process, which in the nineteenth and early twentieth centuries converted revolutionary Marxist movements into evolutionary, democratic socialist parties, continued to operate in the 1950s and 1960s, as social democratic parties shed most remaining attachments to Marxist doctrine.[4]

The French socialist experiment clearly is unique in the history of France; indeed, it is virtually unique in the history of Europe, with the closest approximation being the British Labour Party government of 1945–1951. The French socialist program represented a return to the traditional meaning of socialism: government ownership of the basic means of production. To the surprise of the skeptics, the Mitterrand government proceeded in the first year to enact large portions of its program. Then in June 1982, an expansionary economic policy gave way, at least temporarily, to a policy of austerity. The municipal elections of March 1983, in which the Left lost control of 31 cities of over 30,000 population, served as a warning that public support was weakening. In the spring of 1983, as travel agents, students, farmers, small businessmen and other groups took to the streets in protest, the government tightened the screws on private spending with increased taxes, exchange controls and a compulsory savings plan. The two phases of rapid reform, then retrenchment, offer a fascinating case study of the possibilities and limits of democratic socialism in Europe.

The economic reversals of the first two years of socialist government brought into clearer relief tensions within the French Left. The sharpest potential conflict, between the *Parti Socialiste* (PS) and the *Parti Communiste Français* (PCF), was muted, at least for the moment, by the PCF's awareness that its electoral losses of 1981 were due in part to the Party's repeated attacks upon the Socialists. More serious in the short run is the problem of reconciling incompatible socialist goals. As George Ross and Jane Jenson show in Chapter 2, the PS is an alliance of diverse ideological factions. Its preferred alternative to bureaucratic state controls—self-management in the workplace and in local government—is not easily reconciled with other party goals, such as national economic planning, increased productivity and greater equality.[5] Policies designed to improve the competitive posture of French industry may increase unemployment and widen the gap between efficient and inefficient firms. The tension between competing socialist objectives is a theme which appears frequently in the chapters to follow.

This book will focus on what seems most important to the Mitterrand government: the attempt to reshape French society. It will not deal with foreign and defense policy, where socialism has brought little change of direction, despite the presence of four communist ministers in the government. In their commitment to a French nuclear striking force, in their continued international sale of armaments, and in their vigorous opposition to Soviet positions on Afghanistan, Poland and disarmament, the Socialists have adhered to established policies. Only in French policy toward the Third World, and particularly in their greater sympathy toward leftist movements in Central America, have the Socialists altered somewhat the perspectives of Georges Pompidou and Valéry Giscard d'Estaing. Even here, the expedition of troops to Chad in 1983 followed a tradition of French intervention in that former colony. On the central issues of East-West relations, the commitment of the Mitterrand government to the Atlantic Alliance is at least as strong as that of its predecessor.

Most of the chapters to follow deal with policy more than with political institutions. There has been only one major institutional reform, which is the subject of Douglas Ashford's chapter on decentralization. After objecting bitterly in earlier years to the strong presidency created by General de Gaulle, the Socialists seem to have accepted the institutions of the Fifth Republic, recognizing that they are admirably suited to reformist purposes. After less than two months in office, President Mitterrand told a journalist, "The institutions were not created for me. But they suit me extremely well."[6] Indeed, never before in French republican history has the constitutional framework been so widely accepted. Such changes as have occurred since 1981 in the functioning of the national political institutions of the Fifth Republic are due in large measure to the rare French phenomenon of single-party control of both the executive and the National Assembly.

Between the first and last chapters, which place the French socialist experiment in historical and comparative perspective, this book focuses on six areas of domestic policy: the economy, agriculture, social security, education, decentralization and immigrants. George Ross and Jane Jenson examine factional debates behind the Socialist government's initial economic policy, the reasons why it failed and the fallback to a centrist policy. John Keeler describes the confrontation between a Socialist minister of agriculture, bent on reform, and a conservative farmers' association. Gary Freeman explores the Socialists' attempt to expand and democratize a complex social security system in the face of serious political and financial obstacles. John Ambler shows how the Socialist objective of greater equality in education, which was acclaimed in the abstract by the major teachers' unions, drew skepticism, then opposition as the principle was translated into proposals for specific change. Douglas Ashford describes the extended preparations for governmental decentralization and analyzes the likely effects of the transformation of the traditional perfect into a *commissaire*. Martin Schain studies the increasingly important issue of immigrants concentrated in certain urban areas and the widespread policy of setting quotas for them. In each chapter the author examines the intentions of the Socialist Party, the situation which the Socialists inherited in May 1981, the obstacles which have been encountered in the pursuit of their goals, and the extent to which they have succeeded in overcoming these obstacles.

Earlier versions of some of the chapters were presented to the annual meeting of the American Political Science Association in September 1982. We are indebted to John Woolley, of Washington University, and to Gaston Rimlinger, of Rice University, for their helpful comments on several chapters. An earlier version of Chapter 2 has appeared in *Studies in Political Economy*. Other chapters appear here for the first time.

Notes

1. On the "social strand" in the revolution, see David Thomson, *Democracy in France* (Oxford: Oxford University Press, 1969).
2. Parti Socialiste, *Changer la Vie: Programme de Gouvernement du Parti Socialiste* (Paris: Flammarion, 1972), p. 8. All translations from the French are by the author.
3. *Changer la Vie*, p. 9.
4. Robert Tucker, "The Deradicalization of Marxist Movements," *The American Political Science Review*, Vol. 61, No. 2 (June, 1967), pp. 343–358; Adam Przeworski, "Social Democracy as a Historical Phenomenon," *New Left Review*, No. 122 (July–August, 1980), pp. 27–58; and Otto Kirchheimer, "The Transformation of the Western European Party Systems," in *Political Parties and Political Development*, Joseph LaPalombara and Myron Weiner, eds. (Princeton: Princeton University Press, 1966), pp. 177–200.
5. On "autogestion," see Michel Rocard, "La social-démocratie et nous," in *Qu'est-ce que la social-démocratie?* (Paris: Seuil, 1979); Jean-Pierre Cot, "Autogestion and Modernity in France," in *Eurocommunism and Eurosocialism*, B. E. Brown, ed. (New York: Cyrco, 1979), pp. 67–103; and Bernard E. Brown, *Socialism of a Different Kind: Reshaping the Left in France* (Westport, Conn.: Greenwood, 1982), Chapter 4.
6. *Le Monde*, July 2, 1981.

Contents

1

Is the French Left Doomed to Fail?

JOHN S. AMBLER

The French Socialists confirmed their victory in the presidential election of May 1981 with a sweep of the legislative elections in June, then proceeded at a dizzying pace to enact their program. In the year beginning that May they nationalized all of those large banks which remained in private hands. They established a dominant state role in the chemical, steel and electronics industries, among others, by nationalizing five giant industrial groups and purchasing a controlling state interest in four more. They increased the minimum wage by 25 percent. They established national guidelines, to be implemented by local negotiation, to reduce the work week from 40 to 39 hours without a cut in pay, to give employees a fifth week of paid vacation, and to reduce the age at which workers are entitled to retirement from 65 to 60. They increased the old age pension minimum by 38 percent, rent allocations by 50 percent, and family allowances by 25 percent (and by 50 percent for those with two children).[1] They passed initial legislation to decentralize power from Paris to local governments. They abolished the death penalty and limited discretionary powers of the police and courts granted by the previous government. Rarely has an elected government enacted so many changes in so brief a time.

After a year in office, faced with an inflation rate of 13.9 percent, a serious deficit in trade relations, and loss of over half of the foreign reserves of the Bank of France in a losing battle to defend the franc,

1

despite a devaluation in September 1981, the government changed course. Suffice it to say that the new policy of wage and price restraints, fiscal conservatism and postponement of costly social programs brought with it a much warmer public attitude toward private entrepreneurs. In early January 1983, the architect of the policy of "rigeur," Minister of Economy Jacques Delors, told an interviewer that "We must get away from the idea that the state alone can produce an industrial leap forward in France. Its task is to guide a macroeconomic policy which allows enterprises to develop. . . . I consider it to be one of my duties to try to win acceptance for the phenomenon of the enterprise in our society, which, by its traditions and culture, has not so far assimilated it."[2] We are far from the campaign rhetoric of class struggle and from the popular socialist slogan "capital will pay." The policy of "rigeur" of François Mitterrand and Prime Minister Pierre Mauroy was reminiscent of the policy of "austérité" sponsored by their immediate predecessors, Valéry Giscard d'Estaing and Raymond Barre.

The retreat from the ambitious policy of "Year 1" revived a century-old debate among European socialists: Is democratic socialism within a capitalist environment doomed to failure? Will socialist reforms inevitably be sabotaged, either by the internal business community or by the power of international capitalism? The flight of French capital in the spring and early summer of 1981 and the reluctance of the private sector to contribute to economic growth through investment were viewed by many on the French Left as evidence that big capital was determined to destroy the Mitterrand government, just as the "200 families" and the "wall of money" were thought to have brought down the Popular Front governments of the 1930s. International speculation against the franc brought to mind the machinations of ITT and other multinational corporations which were said to have contributed to the economic troubles and ultimate overthrow of the Marxist government of Allende in Chile. This example was very much in the mind of Jean Poperen, a prominent member of the National Secretariat of the Socialist Party, when he warned in April 1983 that the government was losing popular support and that right-wing extremists and their allies in industry, the press, banking and the state bureaucracy would, "if they could," carry out "their own style Chilean coup" against the Left.[3] To be sure, parties which still adhere to the Socialist International have headed stable governments in a number of European countries, notably in Britain, Scandinavia, Germany and Austria; but they have made little effort to extend public ownership of industry. The Swedish Meidner Plan (discussed in

Chapter 8) is still only a potential exception to this pattern. Is it the case that the socialist parties succeed only by abandoning socialism?[4] Is their objective role simply to administer capitalism, indeed to save it by rendering it more humane?

The classical Marxist view on this question holds that the state is an instrument of class oppression, controlled ultimately by that class which owns the means of production. As early as the 1870s, before the era of universal suffrage in most continental countries, Marx foresaw the possibility that in certain exceptional circumstances, notably in England and America, "the workers can attain their goal by peaceful means."[5] Yet in the main he was contemptuous of "bourgeois democracy," critical of social democrats who sought cooperation with elements of the bourgeoisie, and insistent upon the historical necessity of a dictatorship of the proletariat to crush the bourgeoisie as a class and secure the transition from capitalism to socialism.[6] By whatever means a socialist government might come to power, it was inconceivable from a Marxist perspective that it could achieve its historical mission without quickly establishing public ownership of the basic means of production.

The German Social Democratic Party, founded in 1875 in the merger of two small parties, adopted a practice of reformism which Eduard Bernstein subsequently elevated to a theory of evolutionary socialism.[7] For evolutionary socialists the task of socialist parties is to force enactment of irreversible reforms, leading inexorably toward a socialist society. As Jean Jaurès told the Fifth Congress of the French Section of the Workers International (SFIO) at Toulouse in 1908, "Precisely because it is a party of revolution, precisely because its incessant demands are not stopped by outmoded capitalist and bourgeois property law, the Socialist Party is the most absolutely, the most actively reformist party, the only one which can give full effect to each of the demands of the workers."[8] The debate between evolutionary and revolutionary socialists underlay the split between European socialist and communist parties in 1920. It continues to the present day, now dividing communist as well as socialist parties.[9] Proponents of a strategy of class struggle argue today, as they did a century ago, that reformism will never lead to a socialist society. The extent and permanence of the reforms accomplished by socialists in other European countries will be assessed in the final chapter. Our task here is to examine the historical record of the French Left in power, particularly in the Popular Front of 1936–38 and the tripartite government of 1945–47, in search of evidence bearing upon the hypothesis that democratic socialism is a futile endeavor.

A Divided Left

From 1928 until 1958, political parties which identified themselves as being of the Left—Socialists, Communists and Radicals—won a majority of votes in every single election.[10] And yet for most of this period France was governed from the Center or Center-Right. The explanation is quite simple: parties of the Left either failed to unite in elections or, once elected, as in 1924, 1932, 1936, 1945 and 1946, failed to form stable coalition governments. Again the explanation is relatively simple. The French Left is divided over at least three basic issues which dissect it at different angles. The first issue is the economic role of the government, or, more precisely, the extent to which the state should intervene in the economy to redistribute income, regulate the allocation of resources, and absorb private industries into the public sector. A second divisive issue, which has plagued reformers in most of the Catholic countries, is the church-state question. Its principal contemporary manifestations are conflicts over state subsidies to Catholic schools and state regulation of such moral issues as divorce, contraception and abortion. Thirdly, attitudes of the Left vary on the legitimacy of liberal, or pluralistic, democracy.[11] In the period between the wars, Radical Socialists regularly allied with the Socialists in defense of the secular republic against its critics on the Right, only to split over socialist proposals for social and economic reforms which the Radicals viewed as inconsistent with property rights. The Communists and the Socialists, in turn, could agree on the principle of anticlericalism as well as on the need for social and economic reform. They parted ways, as in 1947, when the central issue became loyalty to established democratic institutions.[12] At the end of the Second World War, the Socialists found a promising new coalition partner in the Popular Republican Movement (MRP), a new Christian Democratic party which was committed both to the Republic and to social reform. The Barangé Law of 1951, which provided indirect subsidies to private schools, contributed to the rupture of that alliance. A coalition founded upon a commonality of views on any subset of these issues—economic policy, secularism and democracy—soon foundered when the policy agenda shifted, or when a new cross-cutting issue—usually foreign and colonial policy—forced its way to the front.

The Popular Front

The Popular Front government which emerged from the electoral victory of the Radicals, Socialists and Communists in 1936 is a striking example of the difficulties of coalition building on the Left.[13] The Left assumed power at a time when the French "nation of patriots" seemed in process of disintegration.[14] The passionate social and political animosities of the 1930s made the France of 1981 appear, in comparison, to be a consensual society. A deadlocked parliament and a series of short-lived governments in the early and mid-1930s proved incapable of dealing effectively with the problems of depression, political scandal and the rising threat of fascism both across the Rhine and at home.[15] The stormtroops of the enemies of the Republic, including communists as well as members of such right-wing groups as *Action Française, Jeunesses Patriotes* and *Solidarité Française,* came frighteningly close to taking over the Chamber of Deputies and creating a new provisional government in the bloody riots of February 6, 1934, on the Place de la Concorde.[16]

The political hatred expressed in the riots of February 6 continued to be fed by the rightist press. In one of a series of attacks on the Socialist leader Léon Blum, Charles Maurras, leader of the *Action Française,* wrote in April 1935, "This naturalized German Jew, or son of a naturalized citizen, who told the French, in open Chamber, that he hated them, is not to be treated as a natural person. He a monster of the democratic Republic. . . . He is a man to be shot, but in the back."[17] The following October he spelled out his advice: "You have somewhere an automatic pistol, a revolver or even a kitchen knife? This weapon, whatever it may be, should be used against the murderers of peace, whose names you have."[18] As if in response to these words, on February 14, 1936, a crowd of *Action Française* supporters attending the funeral of the conservative historian, Jacques Bainville, stopped an automobile in which Léon Blum was returning home from the Chamber down the Boulevard Saint-Germain, smashed its windows, dragged out Blum and beat him nearly to death. Political passion was not confined to the Far Right. France in the 1930s seemed increasingly polarized between enemy camps, each fearful that Bolshevism or fascism was about to take control.

The Left was slow to unite against the threat of fascism. Until May 1935, the PCF continued to denounce the Socialists as "social fascists" and oppose any preparation for a war between capitalist societies. The Popular Front was born, not in Paris, but in Moscow. In late May, as the Soviet leadership finally became alarmed by German Nazism, *Pravda* called for a united front of Socialists and Communists against fascism. The PCF quickly filled the streets of Paris with posters announcing *"STALINE A RAISON"* ("STALIN IS RIGHT.")[19]

The Popular Front program of January 10, 1936, was purposefully moderate in order to accommodate the Radical Socialists and to attract as broad a segment of French society as possible into the anti-fascist campaign.[20] The armaments industry was the only industry targeted for nationalization. Léon Blum, who emerged as the first socialist prime minister in French history in June 1936, cautioned his party followers that "There is no socialist majority. There is no proletarian majority. There is a majority of the Popular Front, whose program is the geometrical center. Our mandate, our duty, is to enact and to execute this program."[21] Blum had little choice. Unlike Mitterrand in 1981, his party could govern only with coalition partners. The SFIO declined slightly in popular votes from 17.6 percent of the first ballot vote in 1932 to 16.9 percent in 1936, but gained 16 seats as a result of cooperation among parties of the Left in runoff elections.[22] Its 147 seats represented less than a quarter of the votes in the Chamber of Deputies. The PCF, which chose to support the Blum government without joining it, was the biggest winner in the 1936 election, rising from 6.8 percent of the vote and 11 seats in 1922 to 12.5 percent of the vote and 72 seats in 1936. The combined socialist and communist seats were approximately equal to the strength of the conservative opposition. Blum was dependent for a majority upon the 106 Radical Socialists, self-declared representatives of the petite bourgeoisie.[23]

The Popular Front victory of May 3 created high expectations among jubilant workers. In the transition period before the formation of the Blum government on June 4, their impatience and new self-confidence were expressed in a massive strike movement. In the last half of May, strikes broke out in the metal industry, the automobile industry and the ports, then spread on to two million strikers in 12,000 separate strikes, 9000 of them involving the new tactic of sit-ins. The strikes appeared to confirm conservative fears that a Bolshevik revolution was at hand. In fact the strike movement was largely spontaneous and intended to improve wages and working conditions rather than to overthrow the Republic. It was most widespread in those industries like metals, textiles and food processing, where union membership was under five percent.[24] Indeed, against the outraged protests of radical revolutionaries who believed that a revolutionary opportunity was being lost, the PCF, the SFIO and the General Confederation of Labor (CGT) all sought to contain the agitation.[25]

Six years later, when placed on trial by the Vichy government on the charge of having undermined national defense, Blum spoke of the "social explosion" of May 1936, "which had come to strike the government in the face as soon as it arrived."[26] Yet in that same trial

Blum recognized that the strikes, while they increased social tensions, also greatly augmented his political leverage. He told his accusers:

> But I must say to you that at that moment, in the bourgeoisie and particularly in the world of employers, I was considered to be, expected to be, hoped to be a savior. The circumstances were so agonizing, we were so close to something which resembled a civil war, that all that was left was to hope for a sort of providential intervention, I mean the arrival in power of a man believed to have sufficient power of persuasion, sufficient ascendancy over the working class to make it listen to reason, and to convince it not to use, not to abuse its strength.[27]

If Blum overstates the hopes which conservatives had for him, he is correct in saying that the business community sought his help in ending the strikes. Shortly after the formation of his government, Blum was told that the major employers' association, the *Confédération Générale de la Production Française* (CGPF) would like him to arrange a meeting between representatives of employers and workers. Blum met first with CGPF representatives, then with officials of the CGT and finally, on June 7, with the two groups together at the prime minister's Matignon Palace. Out of these negotiations, which René Duchemin, a CGPF representative, characterized as "courteous, difficult and painful," came the Matignon Agreements.[28] The parties agreed to seven articles, including wage increases of 7 to 15 percent, with an average increase of 12 percent and more substantial raises for the lowest-paid workers; the establishment of collective labor contracts; "full and complete freedom for unions"; and the election of worker representatives in all firms with more than ten employees.

The Matignon Agreements were insufficient to end the strikes. Indeed the numbers of striking workers peaked in the week of June 8, before gradually receding over the course of the summer. Many employers, particularly in smaller firms, bitterly resented the summit agreements and resisted their implementation.[29] With social tension continuing to mount, CGT membership swelled from less than a million at the beginning of 1936 to four million in 1937.

Blum proceeded quickly to push reform legislation through parliament. A bill reducing the work week to 40 hours without a decrease in salary was adopted by the Chamber of Deputies on June 12, by the more conservative Senate on June 18, and was promulgated on June 21. An avalanche of legislation followed. A law establishing a right of all workers in industry and commerce to a two-week paid vacation was promulgated on June 20, one establishing the right to collective labor contracts on June 24, and on July 14 another providing for a reform of the statutes of the Bank of France, leaving ownership in private hands, but replacing the old Council of Regents (controlled by the Bank's 200 largest stockholders) with a General Council representing the government and consumers, as well as all stockholders. On August 12, the school-leaving age was extended to 14 and several armament manufacturers were nationalized with compensation. The creation of *l'Office du Blé,* designed to regulate farm production and to protect the small farmer from speculators and overproduction, was created on August 15. A public works plan, designed to create jobs, was promulgated on August 18.

These reform laws, along with a host of other laws and decrees on subjects such as the dissolution of the fascist leagues, social insurance, farm debts, temporary loans to businesses, retirement plans for miners and prosecution of tax evaders, represented substantial fulfillment of the program of the Popular Front. Indeed this enacted legislation surpassed that program in some respects. Guaranteed paid vacations were not part of the program of the Popular Front, although they were a long-standing demand of the socialist and communist parties. The Popular Front called simply for a reduction in the work week; Blum decided that it should be reduced substantially from an average of 44.5 hours in firms with over 100 workers to 40 hours.[30]

The Blum government was guided by no elaborate economic theory. When Léon Jouhaux, Secretary General of the CGT, urged Blum to implement that union's plan, the Prime Minister replied, "That which inspires me at the present time is the Roosevelt example, not his whole policy, but a part of his policy and especially that part where his boldness allowed him to change methods when he recognized that the expected results were not being attained. . . . Consequently, nothing is final."[31] Unlike Roosevelt, who was guaranteed four years in office (and later Mitterrand, who had seven), Blum could be deposed at any time. There was too little time for problem solving by trial and error.

Nationalization of private industries—apart from armaments—was out of the question. Blum had neither the votes in parliament nor the will to pursue such a divisive policy.[32] Hence he had no choice but to reply upon private industry to take France out of the depression. For fear of further alarming the business community, Blum long delayed imposing currency controls to halt the flight of capital, devaluing the franc and imposing price controls to slow inflation.

Two of the government's primary objectives in the early months were to create jobs and to increase purchasing power on the assumption that recovery would follow. The primary justification for the 40-

hour week and the subsequent decree which prohibited overtime, even at higher pay, was the expectation that work could be and would be shared with the unemployed. The early results were disappointing. The index of industrial production, with 1928 production equal to 100, stood at 87 in May 1936. By September it had dipped to 81. A 29 percent devaluation of the franc on October 1 contributed to a rise in industrial production to 91 in December and 94 in March 1937, before it dipped again to 89 in May, a month before the Blum government resigned.

Historians and economists often have noted that the Popular Front governments might have produced better economic results had they devalued earlier and focused more on production.[33] The franc clearly was overvalued, even after devaluation, with the results being a chronic trade deficit and repeated assaults on the franc, which were met by massive sales of gold reserves amounting to 600 to 800 million gold francs per week in September 1936.[34] The Matignon Agreements, combined with paid vacations and, beginning in the fall of 1936, the 40-hour week, sharply increased the cost of labor without increasing production. By September the cost of living had risen 7 percent since May, compared to a rise of 3 percent in Britain. By June 1937, inflation had essentially eaten up the salary increases of a year before. The Popular Front, as well as the trade unions, thought more in terms of sharing the wealth than increasing it. The prohibition of overtime beyond the 40-hour week had the effect of limiting production in the many firms which could not find skilled employees to fill out the established work week. In agriculture as in industry and commerce, the governments of the Popular Front tended not to sweep away traditional restrictions and privileges, but rather to protect the numerous marginal enterprises which belonged to "static France." The expansion of chain stores and *prisunics* was blocked by new legislation in defense of the small merchant, but at the expense of the consumer and of the economy as a whole.

In contrast to the later Mitterrand government, which faced no major foreign crises in its first years in office, Blum and his Popular Front government were confronted soon after taking office with the outbreak of the Spanish Civil War.[35] The instinctive reaction of the French socialists and communists was to help defend a sister Popular Front government against General Franco's assault. The charges leveled against the Spanish Republicans by Franco's forces—Bolshevism, atheism, and chaos—were painfully familiar to the French Left. And yet, after some hesitation, the Blum government decided to adopt a policy of nonintervention, refusing the loyalists both arms and volunteers. Blum followed the wishes of the British in this policy, even though Mussolini and Hitler provided important military aid to Franco's Nationalist forces. Blum, who still hoped to avoid war with Germany, was reluctant to risk setting off such a war in Spain. More important, he was aware that prominent Radical Party leaders were opposed to intervention and that the survival of the Popular Front government might be at stake. In foreign policy as in economic policy, the price of survival for this coalition government was caution, and caution sometimes looked very much like timidity.

In June 1936, with the franc still under pressure, the treasury almost depleted and production only slightly above the level of a year before, Blum asked for delegated powers to impose new taxes and to deal with the continuing flight of capital. His proposal was approved by the Chamber of Deputies but rejected in the Senate where the Radicals failed to support the government. Blum promptly resigned and proposed as his successor Camille Chautemps, a Radical who twice before had served as Prime Minister. Although Blum stayed on as Vice-President of the Council of Ministers, along with eight other socialist ministers, the Popular Front clearly was in decline. The creation, in August 1937, of the National Railroad Corporation (SNCF), with 51 percent government ownership, was prompted more by the financial difficulties of private railroads than by socialist zeal. Chautemps' austerity policy was sufficient to antagonize the communists, but inadequate to solve the government's financial problems or to set off an economic recovery. Amid a renewal of strike activity, bickering between socialists and communists, and an intensification of conservative and fascist pressure, the SFIO brought down the Chautemps cabinet in January 1938, supported a new government under the same leadership, then forced its resignation in March. Blum then re-emerged as Prime Minister on March 13, only to resign on April 6, when the Chamber rejected his request for special powers to deal with persisting financial, monetary and economic problems. The Radicals, following a well-rehearsed script, made an about-face and formed a government with the conservatives.

Tripartite Government, 1945–47

The mystique of '36, in which many on the Left had lost faith in the declining days of the Third Republic, reappeared in the Resistance stronger than before. In France as in Britain, the shared hardships of war increased the sensitivity of the middle classes to the social injustices of prewar society.[36] Conservative forces emerged from the war, moreover, badly weakened by the association of a number of conservative politicians and captains of industry with Vichy and the Nazi occupiers. Meeting in Algiers in March 1944, the National Council of the Resistance adopted a program which called for "the establishment of a true social and economic democracy, implying the eviction of the great economic and financial feudalities from control of the economy," "the intensification of national production along the lines of a plan decided upon by the state" and "the return to the nation of the great means of production held by monopolies, fruit of the common labor, of energy sources, of underground riches, of insurance companies and large banks."[37] Even conservative members of the Council agreed, although with misgivings, to a program which went well beyond the Popular Front in its commitment to state control over key "levers of command" in industry and finance.

Charles de Gaulle, the acknowledged leader of *la France résistante* at the time of liberation, was aware that the political strength and international prestige which he sought for his country were unattainable without social and economic reform. Touring Lille in the early fall of 1944, he confirmed his view that France needed a "profound social transformation." In his memoirs he writes, "Either there would be an official and rapid move to institute a marked change in the conditions of the working people, and profound limitations upon financial privilege, or the embittered and suffering mass of workers would founder upon those disturbances which risked depriving France of what remained of her substance."[38] To the crowd assembled in Lille's Place de la République, he promised "State control of the nation's economic resources" and "security and dignity assured to each worker."[39] As prime minister of the provisional government, De Gaulle reorganized social insurance into a more coordinated system, although numerous separate funds survived. He mandated the creation of elected plant committees, giving them extensive authority in social welfare matters, but no access to information which the firm might choose to withold as "trade secrets."[40] His government nationalized the Bank of France, which issues bank notes, the four largest deposit banks, holding 55 percent of the country's total bank deposits, several coal mines in the north of France, and Air France, in which the state already had partial ownership. A new public corporation was created to manage the Renault automobile company, which was seized by the state upon the death of Louis Renault, who had been awaiting trial on charges of collaboration with the Germans.

The results of the October 1945 elections promised further extension of the public sector. The Communists surged to 26.1 percent of the vote and 148 seats in the Constituent Assembly. Together with the Socialists, who won 23.8 percent of the vote and 134 seats, they controlled 54 percent of the seats. The new Popular Republican

Movement (MRP), which also was committed to further nationalization, swelled the coalition to 423 out of 522 seats.[41] De Gaulle was
confirmed as chief executive by the new Assembly, but after two
months of bickering with leaders of the revitalized parties in parliament, resigned in protest against the re-emerging "régime des partis"
and was replaced by a socialist, Félix Gouin. In April 1946, in the last
month of its life, the First Constituent Assembly passed a large number of economic and social reform measures—35 of them in the final
24 hours.[42] The larger insurance companies were nationalized and
giant public firms were created in gas (GDF), electricity (EDF) and
coal (Charbonnages de France) in the course of this flurry of legislative activity. In keeping with a formula first proposed by the CGT in
1919, each industry was placed under the authority of a tripartite
council representing government, employees and consumers. The
social security system was strengthened and its coverage broadened to
encompass the great majority of citizens. The powers of the new plant
committees were extended, and the rights of sharecroppers against
eviction reinforced. All forms of forced labor in the empire were
abolished and the rights of natives expanded. The influence of the
new MRP was exerted in the abolition of licenced brothels following a
lengthy debate over social hygiene, the sanctity of family, and the
wartime politics of brothel owners.[43] This burst of reformist energy
was short-lived, but of lasting importance. France henceforth was
endowed with a mixed economy. Moreover, the early efforts at "indicative" economic planning, guided by Jean Monnet, whose first plan
appeared in December 1946, established a pattern of broad consultation, coordination, exhortation to invest and manipulation of incentives which may well have contributed to the economic boom of the
1950s and 1960s.[44]

The Second Constituent Assembly, required by the electorate's
rejection of the first proposed constitution, enacted no new structural
reforms but wrote its faith in nationalization into the preamble of the
second proposed constitution, which was adopted by referendum in
October 1946. The statement of purpose reads: "Any property, or
any firm, which possesses or acquires the character of a national
public service or of a de facto monopoly must come under common
ownership."[45] The Second Constituent Assembly's most important
achievements, other than the drafting of a second constitution, were
the creation of a fund for the reconstruction of war-damaged structures and the standardization of appointment, promotion and salaries
within the civil service.

The first regular parliament of the Fourth Republic, elected in
November 1946, and soon torn by conflict between the coalition part-

ners, focused primarily upon fighting inflation at home and coping with rebellion in Indochina. Léon Blum came out of retirement to serve briefly as prime minister from December 16, 1946 to January 16, 1947. He devoted his major effort to an economic stabilization program. His all-socialist government was replaced by a broad coalition government including radicals and conservatives, but headed by another socialist, Paul Ramadier. Again, as in 1937 and 1938, reform gave way to a policy of austerity and wage restraints as inflation emerged as a threat to economic recovery. Moreover, unanimity on further nationalization had weakened, as in 1937. The MRP was unwilling to expand the public sector at a time when it perceived the newly nationalized industries to be in a state of chaos. As relations between the Soviet Union and the West deteriorated into a state of cold war, the PCF became increasingly estranged from its partners. It opposed them on Indochina, where the National Liberation Front was led by communists. It finally refused to risk alienating its working-class supporters by defending the government's wage restraint policy and opposing the strike which broke out at Renault in the spring of 1947. Ultimately, in May 1947, communist deputies voted against the government on wage policy, communist ministers were dismissed, and the second popular front was at an end.

Henceforth until the mid-1960s, the PCF was isolated in permanent opposition, leaving the Left divided and ineffective. Until the 1951 parliamentary elections, and again after the 1956 elections, the SFIO was a regular participant in coalitions. Under the leadership of Guy Mollet, it clung to a Marxist doctrine of class struggle, yet cooperated with conservative parties and administered conservative policies—including the use of reservists to defend French Algeria—in highly opportunistic fashion.[46] In the process its electorate shrunk from a postwar peak of 23.8 percent in the legislative elections of 1945 to approximately 15 percent in the elections of 1951, 1956 and 1958, then to a low of 5 percent in the presidential election of 1969.

The Record of Accomplishments

In both instances, 1936–38 and 1945–47, the Left failed to retain control of the government for more than two years. Yet in each of these periods, governments of the Left established policies and institutions which have become imbedded in French society. Were they then successful as reformers? The answer seems to be the familiar one given by Finance Minister Giscard d'Estaing when asked if he would follow the lead of President De Gaulle: "Yes, but." In a European environment of growing affluence and expanding social rights, the

French welfare state very likely would have developed, but more gradually, had the Left never come to power. A number of the nationalized industries no doubt would have remained predominantly in private hands had there been no governments of the Left; yet, as we shall see, they have not always served the purposes for which they were created.

If the sizeable wage increases of 1936, like those of 1945–46, were largely erased by inflation, the social reforms of the Blum government, even when amended temporarily by the Daladier government and the Vichy regime, altered permanently the predominant French conception of rights. Paid vacations (with subsidized rail fare for travel), a shorter work week, collective labor contracts and union rights all date from the Popular Front. French employers have fought to the present day to maintain full control over their workers, yet Blum was correct when he told the Riom Trial that as a consequence of the Popular Front, "The divine right employer is dead."[47]

Social insurance in France antedates the Popular Front. The first general, compulsory old age insurance plan (which was only partially implemented) dates from 1910. It was expanded in 1930 to include health, maternity, disability and old age insurance for workers below a certain income level, and in 1932 to provide family allowances.[48] Disparate social insurance plans were coordinated to create the present social security system (although administration remains in the hands of locally elected councils) by the ordinances of October 4 and 19, 1945, prior to the first postwar elections. The tripartite governments of 1945 to 1947 nonetheless played an important role in expanding the coverage of these programs and increasing benefit levels. That expansion continued after 1947, with the eventual coverage of virtually the whole population and the addition of housing subsidies and allowances for mothers at home among others.

Perhaps no objective was more important for the Left than the construction of a more egalitarian society. The governments of the Popular Front and of the immediate postwar period helped to keep that idea alive. Their success in achieving it was modest. The extension of the school-leaving age to 14 and promotion of the comprehensive school (Jean Zay's "*école unique,*" then ahead of its time, but since partially implemented) pushed along a process of democratization of French education which offers today's working-class youth a somewhat greater chance for upward social mobility. The number who climb, however, is still very limited. Enhanced rights for workers and unions did not guarantee effective bargaining power, given the divided nature of the union movement and low levels of union membership. Even the growth of the welfare state has had only a mildly redistributive effect. It is well known that if the working class benefits from cash payments or services like subsidized housing, which in France is largely restricted to lower income groups, it makes much less use of such services as higher education and health insurance than does the middle class.[49] When programs are funded, as is the case in France, largely by payroll contributions by workers and by employers (some of which otherwise could go to workers in salary), rather than by general state revenues from a progressive income tax, as is more often the case in Scandinavia, the welfare state offers greater security without a great increase in equality. Although workers in programs offering higher than average benefits would have resisted any tendency toward leveling, it is possible that had the Left remained in power, funding of social insurance eventually would have become less regressive.

Wages increased significantly in the prosperous decades of the 1950s and 1960s. Yet the gap between the rich and the poor appears to have widened during this period, leaving France with the greatest income disparity among the wealthy democracies. In a widely cited study published in 1976, Malcolm Sawyer compared post-tax family income in twelve OECD countries.[50] He calculated seven measures of income inequality. France ranked highest—that is, most unequal—on all seven. The ratio of income share for the wealthiest decile, as compared to the poorest, was 21.7 in France, 17.7 in the United States, 10.8 in Germany and under 10 in Japan, Sweden, Norway and the United Kingdom.[51] A number of other studies, all using data from approximately 1970, reached similar conclusions.[52]

More recent data, reported by the *Centre d'Etudes des Revenus et des Coûts* (CERC) reveal a narrowing of the spread of French incomes in the 1970s as the result of rapid increases in the minimum wage and in industrial wages generally after May 1968, and of the rise of social transfer payments from 20.1 percent of disposable family income in 1970 to 33.7 percent in 1980.[53] The massive strikes of May 1968 were similar to those of 1936 in that they were largely spontaneous, set off by no union or political party.[54] They also resulted in a wage increase negotiated by labor, management and the government. This time the economy was sufficiently strong that the gains were not quickly wiped away by inflation. Built-in increases in social security benefits also bolstered low-income families. Although comparable data have not been collected for other countries, it seems likely that the pattern of French income distribution, like the distribution of wealth, was approaching that of the Federal Republic of Germany, while still clearly less egalitarian than that of Sweden, at the time Giscard d'Estaing left office. The parties of the Left had little to do with this reversal of the

trend other than through offering electoral competition which made
conservatives reluctant to hold back social security expenditures.[55]

The French Left appears, at least on first glance, to have been
more successful in extending the public sector. The division and
weakness of the parties of the Left after 1947 did not produce a
powerful demand for denationalization, as occurred in Britain after
the Conservatives replaced Labor in 1951. On the contrary, the great
public corporations created in 1946 remained public and were joined
by hundreds of additional firms in transportation, aircraft, petroleum
and other industries in which the government acquired a controlling
interest, or which were acquired by other nationalized firms like Renault, EDF and the insurance companies. Unlike the firms
nationalized immediately after the war, these typically were mixed
public-private firms, but often with a high level of government control. The special *rapporteur* of the Assembly's finance committee estimated that in 1971 the state directly or indirectly owned at least 30
percent of the shares of some 600 firms.[56] The vigor of the public
sector, even under conservative governments, is not surprising in
view of a very old French tradition of state regulation and control. If
the Popular Front popularized the idea of government-controlled
firms, it did not originate the idea. The state tobacco monopoly was
created by Louis XIV's minister, Jean-Baptiste Colbert, in 1674. Beginning in 1878, when the state assumed the administration of several
bankrupt railroads, public authorities intervened periodically to
create partially or wholly government-owned firms in the fields of rail
transport (1908), navigation (1912, 1921, 1924 and 1925), ports
(1920–24) and petroleum (1924).[57]

On the whole public enterprises are perceived by the French to
have performed well in the postwar period, despite early problems
with political favoritism in the coal industry, which initially was placed
under a Communist minister and managed largely by CGT representatives, and with poor management in both coal and in a newly
nationalized aircraft firm.[58] Nationalized firms have drawn some of
the nation's finest managerial talent, recruited out of the *grandes écoles*
and the civil service.[59] Some nationalized firms have been treated as
public services used by the government to serve policy objectives
other than profits, such as low fares in the case of the railroads, low
electricity rates to industrial customers in the case of EDF, and the
costly prestige of the Concorde and unprofitable lines in the case of
Air France. Others, like Renault, Gaz de France, and more recently
the oil firm Elf-Aquitaine, have been allowed great independence to
seek profits in whatever manner they choose. The performance of
nationalized industries has attracted broad, if generally unen-

thusiastic public support for the idea of government ownership. Public opinion polls conducted in the 1970s regularly showed that a majority of those respondents offering an opinion approved of further nationalization in such fields as automobile construction, iron and steel, pharmaceuticals, aircraft construction and banking.[60]

The continued vigor of the public sector was no proof that the Left had succeeded in the immediate postwar years in its objective of reshaping French society. The purpose of nationalization was not only to stimulate economic growth, but also to promote social justice. Under the guidance of more conservative governments, the nationalized firms could be used to restrain income redistribution rather than to promote it, to serve goals such as national defense or national prestige; or they could be left to operate like private firms. Indeed, under management imbued with the profit motive, they could serve as privileged spokesmen for the business community. In short the public sector in France, as in Britain after 1951, looked at least as much like state capitalism as socialism. To be sure Renault led the way—against government protest—in offering a third, then a fourth week of paid vacation to its employees. Yet in the main worker-management relations were little better in the public sector than in the private. For a new generation of French socialists the example of state capitalism in France and state socialism in Eastern Europe demonstrated that state ownership was not enough; worker control or "autogestion" was essential to insure that the workers would not once again be cheated out of the fruits of their labors.[61] Once in power, however, the Socialist government elected in 1981 moved very slowly on workplace democracy in public enterprises as in private, fearful of disrupting corporate life and delaying recovery from the crisis.

The economy which the Socialists inherited in 1981 was still predominantly a market economy. After the expansion of the public sector in 1981–82, nationalized firms represented one-third of the value added by French industry.[62] Rapid nationalization of all basic means of production was not a realistic option. The Left would not have been elected on such a program, nor would it be likely to win re-election after such a revolution. Moreover, the economic risks would be enormous in an international market which is essentially capitalist. Mitterrand, like Léon Blum, was required to enlist the cooperation of the private sector in order to meet his economic objectives.

For the French Left, the prospect of relations with private business brought back bitter memories of the capital flight and enmity of business which helped to bring down the Popular Front. The socialist dilemma in 1981 was the dilemma of all reformist governments in liberal democracies. Elected officials need a strong economy in order to win re-election. In order to promote economic growth, government needs the cooperation of business to produce desired investment, to limit price increases and to create jobs in areas of high unemployment. In order to win that cooperation, government must make concessions—in taxes, privileges, subsidies, credits and freedom from regulation—which may run counter to the objectives of a reform government.[63] Viewed in this light the problem of government is to structure incentives in such a way that business will contribute to the government's economic objectives, with the minimum possible damage to other objectives, such as increased economic and social equality and protection of the environment. The Swedish Social Democratic Party has demonstated over its more than four decades in office that it is not impossible to create a prosperous and relatively egalitarian society under socialist leadership, even when industry remains in private hands.

The veteran of the Popular Front might object that in France, at least, business will sabotage whatever a government of the Left may attempt. There is little doubt that most leaders in the business community hoped that the Popular Front experiment would terminate quickly and in failure. Yet it seems unlikely that most businessmen were prepared to take large financial losses, or forego promising opportunities to make money, in order to punish the Left. If they sent capital abroad, delayed industrial development at home, illegally held on to their gold and cut production to 40 hours, their primary motives are likely to have been fear, caution and greed, rather than sabotage.

Those leaders who emerged from the Resistance hoped to have found in economic planning a mechanism for strengthening the hand of government in its role as guarantor of prosperity. Indeed, from the late 1940s until the late 1970s, when global planning declined in importance under Giscard d'Estaing, the government regularly enticed, cajoled and threatened business into assisting in the fulfillment of targeted growth levels. Yet economic planning, like certain of the nationalized industries, also proved to be a means for business to increase its influence over government, rather than vice versa. Andrew Shonfield, one of the more sympathetic observers of French indicative planning, concludes "there is no doubt that the activity of planning, as it is practiced in France, has reinforced the systematic influence exerted by large-scale business on economic policy."[64] Among the 4500 people who were involved in the consultations out of which emerged the Sixth Plan (1971–76), businessmen and officials of employers' associations outnumbered trade union representatives three to one. The French Democratic Confederation of Labor

(CFDT) withdrew from the planning commissions in September 1970, charging that the plan was an exercise controlled by private industrialists.[65] From a socialist perspective, planning must seek social reform as well as economic growth. French experience with planning suggests that it is unlikely to serve that purpose unless socialists retain control of the government and resist pressure to view the world exclusively in terms of efficiency and profit opportunities.

Resistance from the business community is not the only obstacle confronting a government of the Left. There are powerful vested interests—including many within the state bureaucracy—that will struggle vigorously to prevent any change which threatens their status or authority. Even such staunch supporters of the Left as the major trade unions and teachers' associations can pose formidable obstacles to change. Despite the rapid economic growth of the postwar period, in some sectors France still exhibits the characteristics of a "blocked society."[66]

The vigor with which Frenchmen defend their *droits aquis,* including status and pay differentials, suggests a second obstacle to socialist reform. Is a citizen who manifests his abstract desire for a more egalitarian society by helping to elect a government of the Left likely to accept implementation of that goal when it means allowing those a notch below him on the income hierarchy to close the gap?

A third obstacle to reform, one which already has been mentioned, is the tension between socialist objectives, between a drive for productivity and centralized planning on the one hand and full employment, self-management and equality on the other. If pressures of international competition drive the socialists to abandon the last three, socialism in France could mean little more than the reinforcement of state capitalism.

There are some striking similarities between the two earlier experiences of government by the Left and the first two years of the Mitterrand presidency. In all three cases the Left came to power at a time of economic distress. Indeed the plight of the French Left has been to win elections only in times of economic crisis when it lacks the resources necessary to carry out its program. In 1936–38, as in 1945–47 and 1981–82, a wave of reform was followed quickly by inflation and an attack on the franc, to which the government responded with a policy of austerity. In 1936 and 1981, in particular, a serious trade deficit increased pressure on the franc. In each case an initial increase in purchasing power failed to produce economic recovery.

The differences between the circumstances in which Mitterrand and Blum took power are equally striking. The French economy in

1981 was far stronger and more competitive than in 1936 or 1945. In 1936, banks and major industries were all under private control; by 1982, domestic banks and a substantial portion of industry were publicly owned. Social and political tensions were far less intense in 1981 than in 1936, and the constitutional question was essentially settled.

No political force of consequence opposed the institutions of the Fifth Republic, as did the authoritarian and fascist leagues in the 1930s. There were no divisive international crises in 1981 comparable to the rise of Nazi Germany and the Spanish Civil War in 1936, or the uprisings in Madagascar and Indochina in 1946. Most important by far, the Socialist Party in 1981 won a solid, one-party majority in the National Assembly to pair with its control of the presidency. With the Senate deprived of its absolute veto over legislation, the Socialists could be certain of control over the government for five years unless the party itself should split. Unlike their socialist predecessors, Mitterrand and his government had time to change course and recover.

In sum, earlier French governments of the Left have contributed to a permanent expansion of social rights and to the development of the public sector. Their failure to stay in power and their limited achievements in the redistribution of income stem as much from the internal disunity of the Left as from the hostility of the business community. Their experience points up some obstacles to be overcome; it does not prove that they are insurmountable.

Notes

1. These figures are from Bela Belassa, "The First Year of the Socialist Government in France," *The Tocqueville Review*, Vol. 4, No. 2 (Fall–Winter 1982), pp. 337–358. They differ slightly from those in the following chapter, which relate to the first wave of reforms.
2. *L'Express*, January 7, 1983, p. 29.
3. From a document of "reflections," sent to President Mitterrand, as cited in *Le Monde*, April 28, 1983. For three differing views of the Allende experience, see Paul Sigmund, *The Overthrow of Allende and the Politics of Chile, 1964–1976* (Pittsburgh: University of Pittsburgh Press, 1977); Stefan De Vylder, *Allende's Chile: The Political Economy of the Rise and Fall of the Unidad Popular* (Cambridge: Cambridge University Press, 1976); and Arturo Valenzuela, *The Breakdown of Democratic Regimes: Chile* (Baltimore: Johns Hopkins University Press, 1978).
4. This is the thesis of Adam Przeworski's perceptive analysis in "Social Democracy as a Historical Phenomenon," *New Left Review*, No. 122 (July–August 1980).
5. See his speech to the First International in Amsterdam, September 8, 1872, in Robert C. Tucker, ed., *The Marx-Engels Reader* (New York: Norton, 1978), p. 523.
6. For one of Marx's most famous assaults upon reformism, see his "Circu-

lar Letter to Bebel, Liebknecht, Bracke and others," in *The Marx-Engels Reader,* pp. 549–555.

7. Eduard Bernstein, *Evolutionary Socialism: A Criticism and Affirmation* (London: Independent Labour Party, 1909).

8. Jean-Jacques Fiechter, *Le Socialisme Français: de l'affaire Dreyfus à la Grande Guerre* (Geneva: Droz, 1965), p. 163.

9. On the reconciliation of "Eurocommunism" with reformism and pluralistic democracy, see Bernard E. Brown, ed., *Eurocommunism and Eurosocialism* (New York: Cyrco, 1979); R. W. Johnson, *The Long March of the French Left* (New York: St. Martin's, 1981); and Alexandre Alder, Francis Cohen, Maurice Décaillot, Claude Frioux, and Léon Robel, *L'U.R.S.S. et Nous* (Paris: Editions Sociales, 1978).

10. Peter Campbell, *French Electoral Systems* (Hamden, Conn.: Archon Books, 1965), pp. 99, 100, 101, 107, 111, 113, 121, 125, and 131.

11. On the historical "pileup" of issues, see Seymour Martin Lipset, *Political Man* (New York: Doubleday, 1963), Chapter 3; and Philip Williams, *Crisis and Compromise: Politics in the Fourth Republic* (Hamden, Conn.: Archon Books, 1964), p. 4. On division over these issues in the Fourth Republic, see also Duncan Macrae, Jr., *Parliament, Parties, and Society in France, 1946–1958* (New York: St. Martin's, 1967).

12. A related and underlying issue in 1947 was the dependence of the PCF on the Soviet Union. See Ronald Tiersky, *French Communism, 1920–1972* (New York: Columbia University Press, 1974).

13. Among the many works on the Popular Front, the following are particularly useful: Georges Dupeux, *Le Front Populaire et les Elections de 1936,* Cahiers de la Fondation Nationale des Sciences Politiques, No. 99 (Paris: Armand Colin, 1959); Cahiers de la F.N.S.P., No. 155, *Léon Blum, Chef de Gouvernement, 1936–1937* (Paris: Armand Colin, 1967); Jacques Delperrié de Bayac, *Histoire du Front Populaire* (Paris: Fayard, 1972); Louis Bodin and Jean Touchard, *Front Populaire: 1936* (Paris: Armand Colin, 1972); William L. Shirer, *The Collapse of the Third Republic* (New York: Simon and Schuster, 1969); and Joel Colton, *Léon Blum, Humanist in Politics* (New York: Knopf, 1966).

14. A book by the noted historian, Carlton J. Hayes, depicts an underlying French unity which shortly was to be broken. *France, A Nation of Patriots* (New York: Columbia University Press, 1930).

15. On the minimal republican consensus of the 1920s and its destruction in the 1930s, see the classic essay by Stanley Hoffmann, "Paradoxes of the French Political Community," in *In Search of France* (Cambridge, Mass.: Harvard University Press, 1963), especially pp. 1–34.

16. William L. Shirer, who was an eyewitness of this event, gives a vivid account in *The Collapse of the Third Republic,* pp. 213–220.

17. In *L'Action Française,* April 9, 1935, as quoted in Bodin and Touchard, *Front Populaire: 1935,* pp. 31–32. Maurras alludes to an occasion in the Chamber of Deputies when Blum angrily denounced deputies of the Right who were continuously interrupting his speech.

18. *L'Action Française,* October 13, 1935, in Bodin and Touchard, *Front Populaire, 1936,* p. 32.

19. Shirer, pp. 233–234.

20. The program is reprinted in Dupeux, *Le Front Populaire,* pp. 179–183.

21. Delperrié de Bayac, *Histoire du Front Populaire,* p. 203.

22. These and other figures for the 1936 election are from Georges Dupeux, *Le Front Populaire*, pp. 126 and 139.

23. See the statement by Edouard Daladier in Shirer, *The Collapse of the Third Republic*, p. 235.

24. Antoine Prost, "Les grèves de juin 1936," in *Léon Blum, Chef de Gouvernement*, p. 73. See also Prost's book, *La C.G.T. à l'époque du Front Populaire, 1934–1939*, Cahiers de la F.N.S.P., No. 129 (Paris: Armand Colin, 1964).

25. Among those who believed that the situation was genuinely revolutionary were Marceau Pivert, "Tout est possible," *Le Populaire*, May 27, 1936, reprinted in *Léon Blum, Chef de Gouvernement*, pp. 178–180; and Leon Trotsky, "The French Revolution has Begun," in *Whither France* (New York: Pioneer, 1936).

26. *L'Oeuvre de Léon Blum*, Vol. 5, 1940–1945 (Paris: Albin Michel, 1955), p. 321.

27. *L'Oeuvre de Léon Blum*, pp. 263–264.

28. Delperrié de Bayac, p. 245.

29. Henry W. Ehrmann, *Organized Business in France* (Princeton, N.J.: Princeton University Press, 1957), pp. 32–42.

30. Jean-Marcel Jeanneney, "La Politique Economique de Léon Blum," in *Léon Blum, Chef de Gouvernement*, p. 226.

31. Quoted in Delperrié de Bayac, p. 214.

32. When members of the Conseil National Socialiste told Blum on May 10, 1936 that broad nationalization was the policy to follow, Blum replied, "Comment pourrions-nous vouloir jeter le pays dans le chaos et dans une bagarre furibonde? Notre succès suppose la confiance." Delperrié de Bayac, pp. 204–205.

33. Jeanneney, in *Léon Blum, Chef de Gouvernement*, pp. 224–232; Delperrié de Bayac, pp. 205–209; Gordon Wright, *France in Modern Times* (Chicago: Rand McNally, 1960), pp. 486–491; and François Goguel, *La Politique des Partis sous la IIIe République* (Paris: Seuil, 1946), pp. 341–362.

34. Jeanneney, in *Léon Blum, Chef de Gouvernement*, p. 218.

35. On the government's policy on this issue, see Pierre Renouvin, "La Politique Extérieure du Premier Gouvernement Léon Blum," in *Léon Blum, Chef de Gouvernement*, pp. 329–353.

36. Richard M. Titmuss, *Essays on "The Welfare State"* (London: Allen & Unwin, 1958).

37. Jacques Fauvet, *La IVe République* (Paris: Fayard, 1959), pp. 35–36.

38. Charles de Gaulle, *The Complete War Memoirs of Charles de Gaulle* (New York: Simon & Schuster, 1968), p. 688.

39. De Gaulle, p. 688.

40. Gordon Wright, *The Reshaping of French Democracy* (New York: Reynal & Hitchcock, 1948), p. 62.

41. Peter Campbell, *French Electoral Systems*, p. 107.

42. Gordon Wright, pp. 168–169.

43. "Abolitionists charged that the Gestapo had found the *maisons de tolérance* a fertile field for their investigations after 1940; partisans of licensed regulation retorted that the prewar abolitionist leaders in Alsace (where the movement then centered) had turned out to be pro-Nazi." Wright, p. 173.

44. On French planning, see Pierre Bauchet, *La Planification Française*,

Quinze Ans d'Expérience (Paris: Seuil, 1962); Pierre Massé, *Le Plan ou l'Anti-hasard* (Paris: Gallimard, 1965); Stephen S. Cohen, *Modern Capitalism Planning: The French Model* (Berkeley: University of California Press, 1977); Andrew Shonfield, *Modern Capitalism* (New York: Oxford University Press, 1965), Chapters 7 and 8; and Jack Hayward and Michael Watson, eds., *Planning, Politics and Public Policy* (New York: Cambridge University Press, 1975), Chapter 1 and Conclusion.

45. This preamble was reaffirmed in the constitution of the Fifth Republic and hence offers a constitutional support for the nationalizations of 1981–82.

46. Philip Williams, *Crisis and Compromise: Politics in the Fourth Republic* (Hamden, Conn.: Archon Books, 1964), pp. 88–102; Frank L. Wilson, *The French Democratic Left: Towards a Modern Party System* (Stanford, Cal.: Stanford University Press, 1971); and Harvey G. Simmons, *French Socialists in Search of a Role, 1956–1967* (Ithaca, N.Y.: Cornell University Press, 1970).

47. Léon Blum, *Oeuvres*, Volume 5, p. 325.

48. Roger Jambu-Merlin, *La Sécurité Sociale* (Paris: Armand Colin, 1970), especially pp. 14–23.

49. Julian LeGrand, *The Strategy of Equality: Redistribution and the Social Services* (Boston: Allen & Unwin, 1982).

50. Malcolm Sawyer, "Income Distribution in OECD Countries," *OECD Economic Outlook: Occasional Studies*, July 1976, pp. 3–36.

51. Calculated from Sawyer, Table 4, p. 14.

52. Centre d'Etudes des Revenus et des Coûts (CERC), *Dispersion et Disparités de Salaires à l'Etranger; Comparaisons avec la France, Documents du C.E.R.C.*, No. 29–30, 1976; G. Banderier, "Les Revenus fiscaux des ménages en 1970 et leur évolution depuis 1962," *Economie et Statistiques*, No. 52, 1974, pp. 15–28; Jacques Méraud, *Rapport de la Commission Inégalités Sociales* (Paris: La Documentation Française, 1975).

53. CERC, *Les Revenus des Français: troisième rapport de synthèses, Documents du C.E.R.C.*, No. 58, 1981, pp. 35, 45, 46; Jean Fourastié and Béatrice Bazil, *Le Jardin du Voisin: les inégalités en France* (Paris: Librairie Générale Française, Collection Pluriel, 1980); and Pierre Cohen-Tanugi and Christian Morrisson, *Salaires intérêts profits dans l'industrie française, 1968–1976* (Paris: F.N.S.P., 1979), pp. 219, 221, 257–263.

54. A critical view of the restraining role of the CGT in May, by a former CGT official, is offered by André Barjonet, *La C.G.T.* (Paris: Seuil, 1968), pp. 145–166. For a sampling of the extensive literature on the "Events of May," see Raymond Aron, *La Révolution Introuvable* (Paris: Fayard, 1968); Alain Touraine, *Le Mouvement de Mai ou Le Communisme Utopique* (Paris: Seuil, 1968); Bernard Brown, *Protest in Paris: Anatomy of a Revolt* (Morristown, N.J.: General Learning Press, 1974); Stanley Hoffmann, *Decline or Renewal? France since the 1930s* (New York: Viking Press, 1974), pp. 145–184; and Laurence Wylie, Franklin D. Chu and Mary Terrall, *France: The Events of May–June 1968, A Critical Bibliography* (Pittsburgh: Council for European Studies, 1973).

55. Fourastié and Bazil, pp. 258, 342–343, suggest that the "secular trend" toward income equality continues. S. Kusnets argues the trend weakens greatly in highly developed countries, while recent evidence points to an eventual increase in inequality. Kusnets, "Economic Growth and Income

Inequality," *American Economic Review,* 45 (1955), pp. 1–28; and J. Corina, M. Van Arnhem and Guert J. Schotsman, "Do Parties Affect the Distribution of Incomes?" in F. G. Castles, ed., *The Impact of Parties* (Beverly Hills, Cal.: Sage, 1982), p. 297.

56.   Jack Hayward, *The One and Indivisible French Republic* (New York: Norton, 1973), p. 215.

57.   *Le Dossier des Nationalisations, Le Monde, Dossiers et Documents,* November 1977, pp. 56–57.

58.   On the early postwar experience, see David H. Pinkney, "The French Experiment in Nationalization, 1944–1950," in Edward Mead Earle, ed., *Modern France: Problems of the Third and Fourth Republics* (Princeton, N.J.: Princeton University Press, 1951), pp. 354–367. For a more recent account, see *Le Dossier des Nationalisations.*

59.   On the common recruitment patterns and close relationship of the public and private sectors, see Ezra Suleiman, *Elites in French Society* (Princeton, N.J.: Princeton University Press, 1978), Chapters 8 and 9.

60.   *Le Dossier des Nationalisations,* p. 84, citing, among others an IFOP poll of November 1976 and a Louis Harris poll of June 1977.

61.   Jean-Pierre Cot, "Autogestion and Modernity in France," in B. E. Brown, ed., *Eurocommunism and Eurosocialism* (New York: Cyrco, 1979), pp. 67–103.

62.   Belassa, "The First Year of the Socialist Government in France," p. 339.

63.   This is the argument of Charles E. Lindblom in *Politics and Markets* (New York: Basic Books, 1977); see especially Chapter 13.

64.   Schonfield, *Modern Capitalism,* p. 139. Michael Watson argues that planning tended to "rationalize" the existing society, rather than reform it, in Britain and Italy, as well as in France. See the concluding chapter in Hayward and Watson, *Planning, Politics and Public Policy.*

65.   Hayward, p. 184.

66.   Michael Crozier, *The Stalled Society* (New York: Viking, 1973).

2

Political Pluralism and Economic Policy

GEORGE ROSS and JANE JENSON

Economic crises have always been critical moments for modern industrial societies, crucibles for new relationships between state and society, new arrangements between social classes and new paradigms of economic policymaking. One has only to remember the upheavals which followed the Great Depression. Such moments have invariably been prolific creators of new ideas as well as devastating critics of conventional wisdoms, whether of Right or Left. Moreover, they have been switchpoints of great political volatility—long accepted policy expectations, patterns of party politics, voting and party identification undergo strain and change.

The economic crisis of the 1970s and 1980s has, for France at least, supported these claims. When crisis hit France was governed by a regime of the Right. As the magnitude of new difficulties became clear after 1975, this regime slid away from its earlier Keynesian approaches toward a Gallic version of what later was labeled "neoconservatism," involving the conscious pursuit of policies to transfer resources from popular strata to profit. The main result of these policies turned out to be political rather than economic. They played a central role in precipitating the electoral shift which brought the French Left to power—for the first time in a quarter century—in 1981.

The Mitterrand presidency, and the Socialist-Communist coalition government which it brought, promised to resolve these economic difficulties with a combination of innovative macroeconomic policies and major structural reforms, which, it was claimed, would allow France to achieve new growth, prosperity and greater social justice without compressing the living standards or increasing the insecurity of the majority of the French people. This chapter is an assessment of the French Left's achievements to date. Since new ideas and strategies rarely come either from textbooks for correct action or from the heads of prescient individuals, but rather are most often the products of complicated interactions between social movements, political organizations and politicians, we will first review the complex history which determined the programs and goals of the French Left experiment. We will then examine the first year of the Left's performance in power in the light of the complex determinations of program and policy peculiar to the new French regime. What did the French Left do after May–June 1981? What were the central problems and contradictions which emerged, and how can they be explained? We will also analyze the government's rapid shift to the Center in 1982–83, present tentative conclusions and speculate about the near future.

Roads to Success: Political Pluralism and Program

One cannot comprehend the French Left until one understands the fact that it is, and always has been, pluralist in composition, a complex of political "families" or currents united in general sensibility but divided over much else. What makes the French Left different from other Lefts is that is has never been able to find a way to federate into one organization. Historically, moments of compromise between different parts of the Left have occurred less often than moments of struggle. Over time the French Left has been characterized by competition among theories, programs and organizations in which, even if some political families were stronger than others, none has had enough resources to become dominant.

This pluralist pattern of Left political development has had both advantages and disadvantages. On the positive side it has been possible for new political families created by social change to join an ongoing Left without sacrificing the sharp edge of demands most important to their constituencies. It has also meant that the French Left has consistently been highly ideological in its tone, a hotbed of ideas in which creativity and originality have not been squeezed out in a quest for catch-all consensus. More often, however, pluralism has been a source of weakness. Different Left families have tended to spend much of their time and the bulk of their energies debunking and attempting to undermine their Left rivals.

For the Left to succeed in France, then, it has had first to overcome this pluralism sufficiently to come to power. As we will see, unity, although created in a very complex way and broken at different points, was one source of victory in 1981. Perhaps more important, given such pluralism, it has been virtually inevitable that the program of any Left coalition powerful and convincing enough to approach victory would be an amalgamation of positions of its different components. Later in this chapter we will review the implications of this method of constructing a program for the Left in power after May 1981. At present, however, we must review the very complicated processes which endowed the Left with the program which it carried to victory in 1981.

SOCIAL MOVEMENT IMPULSES

Political programs and coalitions are the work of politicians. When politicians attempt such difficult work, they usually act as the translators of impulses or raw demands from broader movements of society around them. The interests and grievances of constituencies do not become the stuff of policy proposals until they have been translated into the vocabularies and currencies of politics—of organizations, parties and institutions. Nonetheless, at the beginning of the French Left's long march to power in 1981 lay a universe of different impulses from French society. The success of 1981 was in large part a success in translating these impulses into programs and practices which could win at the polls.

The French Left, in its different guises, traditionally represented a number of ongoing social movements based on continuously aggrieved constituencies, labor being perhaps the most important. Labor had been weak and divided throughout most of the Fourth Republic.[1] Gaullism, willing to devote an impressive energy to economic modernization and endowed with anti-labor Center-Right political perspectives, changed this. In the Fifth Republic, while labor benefited from economic change, it was also the object of it.[2] France's exaggerated workplace authoritarianism persisted, while Gaullist governments were quite willing to exclude labor from policymaking; there was no move to neo-corporatism in France. Unions and workers were thus left to themselves to respond to their new environment. By the mid-1960s the CFDT *(Confédération Française Démocratique du Travail)*, a newly militant ex-Catholic union, had emerged to act in common with the larger Communist-oriented CGT *(Confédération*

Générale du Travail). Militancy in the workplace was generalized and the number of strikes shot up. The huge movement of May–June 1968 symbolized this "resurgence of class conflict in France," but industrial strife, often raising new demands about authority in the workplace and working conditions, persisted well into the 1970s.[3]

The Left, the Socialists in particular, had also been the traditional political translators of grievances from parts of the middle class, those of educationally credentialed, publicly employed groups such as teachers and civil servants.[4] The truly massive social changes of the postwar period, intensified and accelerated in the 1960s, expanded such groups. Simultaneously, there was a burgeoning of urban intermediary social categories associated with advanced capitalism. The radicalism of May–June 1968 attested spectacularly to the energies of such groups.[5] The rightist political bias of the regime meant here, as with labor, that Gaullist governments were relatively insensitive to the grievances and energies of these groups. Older middle-class impulses directed traditionally to the political Left were thereby supplemented by new, quite stridently radical, demands coming from new middle strata. Moreover, like the labor mobilization of the 1960s, this radicalism persisted into the 1970s, often in new "single-issue movement" form.

FROM IMPULSE TO PROGRAM: THE SOCIALISTS

If the setting which emerged in the mid-1960s was propitious for the Left, nothing was guaranteed. In order to derive resources from the new context, the Left had to incorporate these energies into politics. To do so it had to overcome many of its fratricidal tendencies and translate social movement impulses into political programs plausible enough to propel the Left toward majority status. All major Left families played critical roles in such tasks. Two processes were central: the first was the reconstruction of French Socialism; the second was strategic jockeying for precedence between the *Parti Socialiste* (PS) and the *Parti Communiste Français* (PCF).

The Socialist Party formed in 1971 was forged from several different currents of Left political opinion coalescing out of the first decade of the Fifth Republic. "Third Forcism" had been the major Fourth Republic strategic legacy of the SFIO *(Section Française de l'Internationale Ouvrière)*, involving an alliance strategy directed toward the Center rather than the Left, so as to isolate both Gaullists and Communists. Third Forcism, which had followed Socialist majority-mongering in Fourth Republic parliaments plus Cold War ghettoization of the PCF, lost much of its attractiveness after 1958. One reason was that the strategy contributed to the loss of large numbers of Socialist Party militants to new parties and groups on the non-communist Left, such as the PSU *(Parti Socialiste Unifié)*, and to clubs of various sorts. In addition the replacement of Cold War tensions by "peaceful coexistence" reopened the prospects for Socialist-Communist alliances. In this context the PCF began to dust off its united front alliance strategy which had been in storage since 1947. Finally, the consolidation of a Right-Center majority around a strong Gaullist party created Left-Right polarization and thereby dashed any hopes that the SFIO might have had of being necessary to General de Gaulle's governments. International changes, then, allowed the Socialists to look Left. Domestic circumstances meant that if they did not look leftward, they had few other directions in which to face.

The political maneuvering which preceded the 1965 presidential election, as well as the results of that election, underlined the importance of these factors. The presidential hopes of Gaston Defferre were destroyed when the Christian Democrats (MRP) rejected the SFIO-MRP coalition which he proposed. The failure of this old-style Third Forcism plus the success of François Mitterrand, who subsequently ran with the backing of the Communists, left little hope for those who clung to the centrist opinions. The way was therefore clear for those who advocated more leftward-looking strategies, with the final push to change coming in May–June 1968 and the presidential election which followed in 1969. The radical mobilization of the intermediary strata in the 1968 events exposed reserves of energy for the Left; new groups had entered the lists, bearing innovative demands and ideas. In the 1969 election the ignominious score of Gaston Defferre (5 percent) was the final blow for Socialists with lingering dreams of a centrist strategy. The other major non-communist Left candidate, Michel Rocard of the PSU, did no better. Moreover, the support for the Communist candidate, Jacques Duclos (21 percent), indicated that none of the events of the 1960s, not even May–June or Czechoslovakia, had shaken the PCF's electoral support.

Such events encouraged Socialists struggling to create a new and more successful party and gave a very strong push toward François Mitterrand's *Union de la Gauche* strategy. To Mitterrand and others the collapse of the SFIO plus the blossoming of new, and often tiny, formations—clubs, parties and study groups—made the unification of the non-communist Left around modernized socialist ideas highly desirable. In addition Left-Right political polarization under Gaullism made some form of long-term relationship between Socialists and

Communists absolutely essential. Cold-War anti-communism and militant Atlanticism were luxuries which a new Socialist party could not afford; in essence Third Force politics no longer made sense.

The PS which was created in 1971 adopted the *Union de la Gauche* strategy of its new First Secretary, François Mitterrand. Agreement to accept the strategy did not mean that the proponents of other views were silenced, however. Right up through 1981, politics within the PS continued to reflect competition among the party's many political currents. The political skill of Mitterrand and the increasing electoral success of the PS were important in keeping this cantankerous coalition together. Lack of governmental power meant that contradictory policy positions could coexist within the party in an untested equilibrium held in place by astute maneuvering. The PS' internal pluralism of *tendances* was, in fact, officially enshrined in the party's formal procedures. In all of this the PS emerged as a party in which each of its major internal families could contribute to the program.

The first of the four major currents in the new PS—traditional French social democracy—was heir to the Guesdist side of SFIO tradition.[6] Regionally concentrated, with a stronger base in the working class than other Socialist families, it bore some resemblance to the social democracy of Northern Europe.[7] Economically, social democrats advocated Keynesian methods for managing capitalism, along with an expanded welfare state. Beyond this Left social democrats maintained traditional commitments to major statist structural reforms like nationalizations, pointing with enthusiasm to the social reforms in the Popular Front and Liberation years. Right social democrats were more hesitant about major structural reforms and more confident that Keynesianism by itself would be sufficient. The regional concentration of these traditional social democrats (in the North and in Marseilles) and their base in municipal power also gave them another major goal, that of breaking the *tutelle* relationship between the prefects and elected officials to give local government real power.

The "republicans" also came out of the SFIO tradition.[8] Much of the political place held by the Radicals in the Third Republic had come to be filled by republican socialists in the Fourth and Fifth. Within this family the influence of Pierre Mendès-France's neo-radicalism was immense. Institutional protection and individual rights were the republicans' major focus, which explained why Gaullist presidentialism, seen as a basic threat to representative democracy, galvanized them after 1958. Criticisms of Gaullist attitudes toward civil rights, military justice and the controversial Article 16 of the constitution united this current. Indeed, before 1971, François

Mitterrand could best be described as a republican. As leader of the *Convention des Institutions Républicaines* (CIR), created in 1964, his initial political strength was based with them. Thus the republican current was guaranteed great influence in the new PS. Radical in their civil libertarian positions, the republicans were much more moderate in economics. While Mitterrand and the CIR did commit themselves to a program for economic reform, couched in a language of "socialism," the proposals made were little more than mild reformism, a non-Marxist *socialisme du possible*. Moreover, economic policy in general was much less important to the republicans than were radical constitutional concerns and civil liberties.

The third current of the new PS was also composed of exiles from the old SFIO. In the late 1950s, criticizing both the SFIO's position on Algeria and its understanding of advanced industrial society, a group of disgruntled Socialists formed the *Parti Socialiste Autonome* (PSA), which eventually became the PSU.[9] As the 1960s went on PSU positions sharpened into a distinctive expression of several "modernist" themes of the French New Left. The current acquired the "Rocardian" label because its formal connection with the PS in 1974 was made under the leadership of Michel Rocard. The PSU itself amalgamated a number of political traditions—disgruntled Socialists, Left Catholics, ex-Communists disillusioned with Stalinism, even for a time Pierre Mendès-France. By the mid-1970s, however, the hallmarks of the Rocardians had become technocracy and *autogestion*. The theme of expanded *autogestionnaire* democracy in all relationships—workplace, social, political—made the current profoundly anti-statist and therefore lukewarm about structural reforms in the ownership of capital. At the same time, the social location of the current in the new middle class conferred upon it a heavy aura of technocratic superiority. Perhaps because of this, however, its lively theoretical debate was remarkable. Reflections on neo-capitalism, changes in class structure, new ways of planning, the Third World and neo-colonialism were all enriched by its work, testing the limits of traditional Marxist, social-democratic and liberal analyses. Finally, both its theoretical reflections and its social base among Catholics and the new middle class shaped its centrist alliance goals, based on profound antagonism to the workerism and organizational heavy-handedness of the PCF.

The final major current in the new PS grew out of a study group organized within the old SFIO, the *Centre d'études, de recherches et d'éducation socialiste* (CERES).[10] Founded by Left intellectuals determined "to bore from within" the declining SFIO, CERES was, like the Rocardians, based in the new middle class, with numerous graduates of the *grandes écoles* (especially ENA) among its members. In contrast to the Rocardians, however, CERES remained quite close to Communist formulations of economic policies, making commitments to nationalizations, planning, and to state-directed transformation more generally. The influence of CERES on the PS program was considerable in the early years of the new party, given the play of factions within the party. CERES promoted economic goals and notions of outreach to the working class, and both were enshrined in PS platforms. At the same time CERES was a strong advocate of *Union de la Gauche* within the PS, as it had been in the SFIO. Thus François Mitterrand could rely on CERES support to solidify a base within the PS for his own strategy.

FROM IMPULSE TO PROGRAM II: UNION DE LA GAUCHE

The new PS was thus a very mixed bag of contending political families with contradictory strategies. The uneasy equilibrium which came to exist was held together by the skill of François Mitterrand at imposing his own preferred electoral strategy. Mitterrand's first goal was to bring the Left to majority status. To do this the much-divided noncommunist Left had to be federated into a coherent and convincing socialist party. The emphasis in the new PS on republican values and greater democracy as well as Keynesian spending and social programs was designed to draw the support of different middle-class groups, old and new. Mitterrand's second goal was to undermine Communist electoral bastions by reestablishing the Left credentials of the Socialists and appealing to working-class voters. The alliance with the PCF as well as the activities of CERES and the municipal Socialists were crucial to the achievement of this goal. Here the objective was to make the PS the largest party on the Left, while the Left as a whole became the majority.

The PCF also had a strategy which depended upon *Union de la Gauche* for its success. The re-establishment of united front politics in the 1960s recommitted the PCF to economic proposals which recapitulated much of the program of the French Left in the Resistance-Liberation years. The Common Program which the PCF proposed to the PS in the early 1970s was a crypto-Keynesian document emphasizing expanded nationalizations, increased popular consumption, full employment, centralized state planning and some increase in power for working-class organizations. In other words the thinking of the PCF about economic policy for elected Left governments had evolved very little between the 1940s and the 1970s.

Politically, however, the PCF did evolve in response to the new situation. After a series of doctrinal changes and outreach efforts in the 1960s, the Communists finally accepted the notion of political pluralism by committing themselves to alliances with other Left forces throughout the transition to socialism. To improve its cross-class appeal, the PCF promised to accept the decision of the electorate against an elected Left government *(alternance)*, took distance from the Soviet model and Soviet-style socialism, took a strong civil-libertarian position and, in a final burst of Eurocommunism in the mid-1970s, formally abandoned the dictatorship of the proletariat as a principle. The Communists hoped that such positions would attract new voters from the intermediary strata. With new middle-class voters added to the existing working-class support, the PCF would increase its percentage of the expanded Left electorate (which it was counting on *Union de la Gauche* to create). In this way Communist dominance over the policy decisions of any Left government would be assured. Thus the PCF's alliance strategy was the mirror image of that of the PS—to bring a united Left to power with the PCF dominant within that Left.

In 1972, when the Common Program was signed, the Left was growing and the PS was weak. Thus the PCF's strategy looked plausible. However, the Communists' hopes were quickly dashed. Almost immediately the Socialists began to gain new electoral support from both their Right and Left. The PCF's hopes for greater support from the intermediary strata evaporated, while the PS—with the new Left cachet conferred on it by *Union de la Gauche*—began to make inroads into the Communists' traditional working-class constituency. Such tendencies were first underlined in 1974 by the presidential campaign and later by election results. By the time of the municipal election of spring 1977 it had become abundantly clear that the PS was dramatically outstripping the PCF. The Communists could no longer be certain of enough influence to direct the program of a victorious Left government. Worse still the PCF leadership also began to fear that the party was being weakened in absolute terms. The consequence of this fear was rupture of *Union de la Gauche* in September 1977. In an attempt to stop the Socialists' advance and to re-establish their own credentials among the working class, the Communists then turned to isolationism and sectarianism.

Official *Union de la Gauche* around the 1972 Common Program thus ended in acrimony long before 1981. The episode was nonetheless of immense importance. With the Common Program— whose economic policy goals were substantially those of the PCF—the Communists became a powerful fifth "current" (beyond the four internal to the PS which we have already reviewed) in the formulation of the Left platform which eventually won in 1981. This was because prior to and during the Common Program period, it was essential for the PS to offer concessions on programs to the PCF in exchange for the *Union* needed to pursue Mitterrand's strategy. In consequence the PS committed itself to a program well to the Left of the party's actual political center of gravity. After 1977, political circumstances were such that this direction was maintained. Thus the PCF, even if it chose to play a new sectarian game after 1977, remained an important indirect influence in PS program thereafter.

TOWARD 1981

The collapse of *Union de la Gauche,* the PCF's turn toward anti-socialist sectarianism, and, most important, the Left's defeat in the 1978 legislative elections, changed the political trajectory of the Left. Inside the PS the delicate equilibrium between currents which had prevailed gave way to a major battle.[12] The Rocardians, in temporary alliance with parts of the social-democratic current around Pierre Mauroy, moved to displace François Mitterrand and to shift the party away from his leftward strategy. A new centrism, they claimed, was necessary for the party to stand any chance in the presidential elections of 1981. To the Mitterrandists, in contrast, the withdrawal of the PCF from *Union de la Gauche,* if it had cost the 1978 legislative elections, in fact demonstrated that Mitterrand's strategy had actually worked—the PS had become the predominant force on the Left and the "first party of France." To abandon this strategy in the face of PCF sectarianism might give the Communists credibility in their accusations of a Socialist "right turn" and risk undoing the successes of the 1971–78 period. Rather than shift toward an updated Third Forcism, persistence on the same path, being *unitaire pour deux* while maintaining the basic leftward-leaning programmatic pledges of the Common Program, was what was needed.

Even if aspects of this conflict continued into late 1980 (when Michel Rocard was finally forced to abandon his presidential ambitions), the Mitterrandists had won what counted—control of the party—by the Metz Congress of 1979. To make this happen Mitterrand made a new deal with CERES, which had been in a minority position since the Congress of Pau in 1975. This deal in turn undid the Rocard-Mauroy alliance and left Rocard isolated. The consequent shift in majorities within the party not only saved Mitterrand and his strategy; it also meant that CERES found itself in a central position in

1980–81 when the Socialist election manifesto was composed. Not only did the Mitterrandist strategy win out, but it did so in circumstances which ensured that the Socialists' 1981 program would stress the positions of CERES, the most leftward-leaning tendency within the party.

Between 1978 and early 1981 there seemed few reasons to think that such internal PS events would make much difference, however, since everyone had concluded that the reelection of President Giscard d'Estaing was a certainty. Not far below the surface there were a number of processes unfolding which would, taken together, ultimately make François Mitterrand President of France. Here the most important factor by far was the economic crisis which had opened up in the mid-1970s. After years of boom, growth rates declined, inflation rose, unemployment shot up and France experienced progressively more serious balance of payments difficulties. Beneath such symptoms, as many commentators pointed out, were basic structural problems. France's industry was not dynamic and innovative enough to keep up with its international competitors.[14] Moreover, the Right had been in power for 22 years and Giscard for six, making it obvious at whose door the blame would be laid. Giscard's popularity was not enhanced after 1976 by the neo-conservative course set out and rigorously enforced by Raymond Barre, his prime minister. By 1980, after four solid years of "we are all in this together, we must all tighten our belts" rhetoric, plus a great deal of effort and sacrifice disproportionately distributed, there were very few positive results to show. The Left's programs, on the other hand, promised much and had not been tried.

The effects of crisis and the Giscard-Barre policies might not have been enough, however, without two important political changes. The first was the dramatic collapse of Communist electoral support. The PCF's post-1977 turn to sectarianism, culminating in Georges Marchais' presidential campaign, was a disaster. Attacks on the PS completely backfired. Because the PCF behaved outrageously, and because the Socialists were astute enough to hew to the Mitterrandist line in ways which made the PCF's claims about a Socialist "right turn" sound hollow and demagogic, a substantial minority of PCF voters concluded that the party which they ordinarily supported now wanted to destroy the PS much more than it wanted to defeat Giscard.[15] From this it was easy to conclude that Mitterrand was the only candidate in favor of real change. Then, on the Right, Gaullist leader Jacques Chirac, whose future depended upon Giscard's defeat, proved willing to risk a Mitterrand presidency to achieve this end.

Behind this lay considerable anger in parts of the rightist electorate
about the Giscard-Barre policies. In the no-holds-barred presidential
primary campaign which followed, Giscard won, but only after a
significant group of Gaullist voters had decided to vote against Giscard in the second round.

All of the processes came together in the presidential elections
themselves. In the first round Mitterrand did well enough to set up a
repeat of his 1974 confrontation with Giscard. Marchais, however,
received only slightly over 15 percent of the vote, the worst Communist score since the early 1930s. This result meant that the Right lost
its electoral tactic of last resort—hysterical anti-communism—for the
second round. Change-oriented centrist voters, who had been deterred from voting Left by the prospect of a government within which
the PCF would pull important strings, would be deterred no longer.
Moreover, the hostility between Chirac and Giscard proved intract-
able and Chirac was unwilling to provide more than lukewarm support for Giscard in the run-off. Thus anti-Giscardian Gaullist voters
were confirmed in their intention either to abstain or to vote for
Mitterrand.[16] Finally, on May 10, 1981, François Mitterrand was
elected President of France. The surprise of Mitterrand's success
tended to obscure an important fact, however. Not only had a Socialist become President, but he had been elected as the bearer of an
unusually radical program. As we have demonstrated, the complex
history of the pluralistic French Left in the decade prior to 1981 had
conspired to endow Mitterrand and the PS with commitments which
were considerably further to the Left than many of the party's activists and supporters. At its origins the new PS had been constructed
out of a deal passed between the non-communist Left's most leftward-
leaning fractions, CERES and the Left social democrats, and François
Mitterrand, a deal which was the source of the party's original Left
leanings. Next the PS adopted the left-facing logic of the *Union de la
Gauche* strategy. The programmatic effects of this, visible for all to see
in the 1972 Common Program, incorporated basic PCF goals. After
the rupture of *Union de la Gauche,* Mitterrand's success in having the
party keep a *unitaire pour deux* strategy, coupled with the new deal
struck with CERES, meant that the PS' left-leaning posture was maintained. The end result was that basic changes in substance between
the propositions of the 1972 Common Program, the *Projet Socialiste* of
1980, and the milder PS *Manifeste de Créteil* of January 1981 (Mitterrand's election platform) were hard to find. Finally, because François
Mitterrand remained a republican, loyal to Mendès France's teaching,
he enunciated the principle that "politicians must keep their promises" as a fundamental theme in his election.

Pluralism, Policy and Crisis:
The First Year of the Left in Power

If, and when, a Left as pluralistic as the French Left comes to power, a number of new issues are bound to arise. How much of its "conglomerated" program will actually be implemented? Which parts will be enacted, which set aside, and for what reasons? Quite as significant, for a program with origins in pluralism, is the question of coherence. The program-building process which we have discussed implies a margin of programmatic incoherence. How will the Left in power work to moderate such problems? Most important, nothing guarantees in advance that the proposals of different currents finding their way into a general Left program will be appropriate responses to the circumstances of power themselves. Having been in opposition for 23 years, French Left politicians were quite unfamiliar with the actual constraints faced by government; thus there was a risk of unrealistic expectations.

The legislative elections of June 1981 did resolve one of the more complicated programmatic issues arising from Left pluralism. The Socialists won an unprecedented victory, controlling a majority of seats in the National Assembly. This meant, of course, that the Socialists themselves acquired overwhelming power in deciding priorities for program implementation. The PCF did very badly electorally and its parliamentary support was not necessary to governmental survival. Thus, if four Communists became ministers, they did not have the power to force issues of programmatic precedence. François Mitterrand's pledge that the government would enact "no more, but no less" than the PS manifesto was, as it turned out, much more than rhetoric. But which parts of the program came first and received the greatest weight were questions to be resolved by the Socialists themselves.

The government's first flurry of policymaking, before the June elections, was heterogeneous, but with a deeper logic nonetheless. In the noneconomic realm a number of measures of a "republican" type were taken, including suspension of the death penalty, promise of a reform of the penal code, an end to the expulsion of immigrants, abolition of La Cour de Sûreté (an exceptional jurisdiction military court), and limits on police and court harassment. Ecologists were given a partial halt of nuclear construction and the resolution in their favor of a long-standing conflict about military use of the Larzac plateau: The government's economic measures, by far the most important part of this wave of action, had a "constituency targeting" aura about them as well, since the legislative elections were at the center of concern at this point. The minimum wage was raised by 10

percent, family and housing allocations by 25 percent, and the basic
allowance for the elderly and the handicapped went up 20 percent.
Supplementary medical charges for Social Security, decreed by Giscard in 1980, were rescinded. In addition 55,000 new public-sector
jobs were created, and a modified youth employment program was
adopted.

Despite their specific electoral targeting, the government's initial
macroeconomic policy goals were clearly Keynesian, conceived of as
parts of a broader scheme to regenerate growth, reduce inequality
and enhance social justice. It was obvious that most of the government
firmly believed that the road to new justice and prosperity passed
through more aggressive demand stimulation, aimed particularly at
poorer groups in the population. The strongest support for
Keynesianism came from the bulk of the political families on the Left
of the coalition which supported the government. It was not only the
PCF and CERES who were convinced Keynesians, but also the traditional social democrats. Even the republicans were initially tolerant of
it. Only those PS political families facing Center disapproved of this
Keynesian thrust—the Rocardians and people close to Jacques Delors,
the Minister of Finance (who was a respected and classic "right-wing
social democrat").

This initial Keynesian *élan* was a reasoned initiative, not simply a
visceral outburst or a patchwork of rewards to constituents. The
Keynesian Left believed that it was possible, within the limits of
France's open position in the international market, to manage demand more aggressively, and that doing so would limit further dramatic rises in unemployment and push up growth by about 1.5
percent during the government's first year in office. Such projections
were made with the knowledge that the Giscard-Barre years had left
France with a comparatively small cumulative deficit, and thus there
were reserves to be tapped. They were also made in awareness that
the policies being pursued in most other countries were explicitly
anti-Keynesian, designed to cut inflation rather than promote growth.
Thus Keynesians in the government were making a conscious bet that
France would be able to row against the international tide until defla-
tion gave way to the recovery predicted for early 1982. The Ameri-
cans were the key to this scenario, of course, and government
projections were that such an upturn was very likely, given the
Reagan administration's economic views and its electoral needs. Row-
ing against the tide would work, for a while, then. When others later
changed their policies, the French economy would be carried along
with everyone else.[17]

The next major stage in program implementation in the early fall of 1981 brought legislation for governmental decentralization. The actual content of the legislation need not detain us, since it does not bear directly on the economic policy thread which we want to follow most closely. Suffice it to say that these reforms combined the desires of several political currents. Municipal social-democratic machines, of course, had suffered endlessly from the limitations on their autonomy of action created by centralization and prefectoral power. Decentralization also appealed to the *autogestionnaire* enthusiasms of the Rocardians. The PCF, with its own hopes of deepening local positions of power, supported the policies. One important point should be made here, however. The decentralization scheme, as originally announced, was grandiose. The first pieces of legislation to be enacted were presented as only a preliminary step, to be supplemented later. Thus prefectoral *tutelle* was abolished, regional institutions were proposed and regional elections set up. But essential matters such as the assignment of actual functions to new institutions and the definition of their powers, especially their financial powers, were not immediately decided.

Later in the autumn of 1981 came perhaps the most important part of the government's reform legislation—extensive nationalization. The proposed nationalizations were the real hallmark of the Left experiment. France, like other European countries, had lived through a period of reforms in the immediate postwar years which had brought a wave of nationalizations, after an earlier flurry under the Popular Front. The new French public sector had been rather quickly turned to the task of serving as a countercyclical instrument to help set up a reliable macroeconomic framework within which private sector firms, the designated locomotives of growth, were to maximize their profit. France, of course, was a bit more *dirigiste* and statist than some other countries in its use of the public sector as part of a mixed economy, but the general scope of public sectors almost everywhere was similar. In its 1981 changes, however, the French Left government moved far beyond the established boundaries set for European mixed economies, proposing to nationalize virtually all of the banks which still remained in private hands, the iron and steel industry (the only "lame duck" on the list), plus nine industrial groups. This was the first time in modern Europe that any government had moved to extend public ownership to the core of the profitable oligopoly sector.

The actual processes of nationalization took some time; indeed they lasted until well into 1982. Problems with the Constitutional Council developed at the last minute, which forced a very expensive series of changes in compensation provisions. Negotiations about foreign-owned groups took even longer to complete. When, by late spring 1982, the deed had been done, however, the state controlled virtually all of France's banking and financial sectors plus 34 to 36 percent of its industrial capacity, including much of its advanced technology.

Demands for nationalizations had a long and honorable history on the French Left. Both the PCF and the SFIO had advocated extensive nationalizations. Indeed the proposals for nationalization contained in the 1972 Common Program, which had been pushed energetically by the PCF and supported by the Left of the PS, were not far, in spirit and conception, from those of the Resistance-Liberation period. In this long tradition the goals of nationalization were to dispossess capital and to expand social justice. Rarely, if ever, had they been conceived of as instruments of any concrete economic policies. By 1981–82, however, this had changed.

The new Left government presented its nationalization plans as necessary to ensure that new investment would occur in France and be directed to maximize chances for new growth and international competitive success. Behind this change in emphasis lay, of course, the international economic crisis itself. The analysis brought forward to support this shift (which the French shared with the Left in other European settings) went as follows. During the Giscard years, private sector oligopolies had proven both unable and unwilling to promote the best economic interests of the country. Instead, in a context of rapidly changing international economic relationships, their actions had produced unemployment, deindustrialization and the loss of industrial activities essential to national economic integrity. Tempted by market and political forces toward a course of irresponsible multinationalization, big capital had abdicated its national duty and could no longer be trusted. If private capital and the market could no longer ensure France's economic integrity and success, then the state, through nationalizations, ought to step in to do so. Nationalizations would allow direct investment to "reconquer the domestic market" and rebuild France's international competitiveness. Indeed, with nationalizations, France might come out of the international crisis in a much better position than it had been in earlier, or so the analysis went.[18]

The next major block of reforms included the four "Auroux Laws" on the rights of workers and trade unions in the firm, which came in the spring of 1982. The system of industrial relations which had developed in France was substantially different from that of most other advanced capitalist societies. The elaborate collective bargaining patterns and quasi-corporatist arrangements which regulated labor-capital and labor-state relationships in other places did not emerge at all or did so only primitively in France. In most ways labor and capital remained strident class enemies. Both sides conceived of the labor market as a battlefield on which one side had to attack whenever the balance of forces seemed in its favor. Given such a level of hostility, it was inevitable that the state would play a large role, and there was constant resort to politics to obtain objectives which elsewhere would have been bargained in a decentralized way. Moreover, this resort to the state tended to politicize the labor market and labor movement in ways which transformed day-to-day questions into confrontations of ideological principle. Clearly, much needed to be reformed in this area.

Very early in "Year I" Jean Auroux, the Minister of Labor, published a report on the "rights of workers" which reviewed this situation and made general proposals.[19] The four legislative texts made public in April 1982 followed this report closely. The first law was designed to strengthen legal obligations to bargain collectively by, among other things, requiring annual negotiations on wages, working conditions and the duration of work at firm level (even if there was nothing to compel bargaining "in good faith"). The three other laws were aimed at strengthening the position of workers and unions in the firm. The first, dealing with "liberties of workers in the firm," established a charter of rights vis-à-vis the disciplinary power of employers and the system of internal rules of the workplace. The second, on the "development of representative institutions for personnel," strengthened and extended the scope of existing institutions like works' committees, giving them access to a broader range of economic information and more time off work to function. Works' committees, which already existed in middle- and large-sized factories, were extended to smaller firms. The last of these laws, "committees on hygiene, security and working conditions," proposed the amalgamation of two separate existing institutions dealing with these issues.

The Auroux Laws were obviously important. They moved France toward a system of industrial relations which more closely resembled those elsewhere, constituting a very limited French "Wagner Act" decades behind its time. In terms of their filiation with the programmatic goals of Left currents, they were, strangely enough, somewhat *sui generis*. Almost all of the new majority shared notions that change of this kind was needed, but none had many concrete suggestions to make in advance. Auroux and his staff were the main creators of the proposals. The new laws were closest to positions advocated by some French unions over the years, in particular the CFDT. The most striking thing about the Auroux Laws, however, was their moderation. Depending on how they were implemented—for

their implementation was not to start until 1983—the laws provided
for a pale imitation of West German *Mitbestimmung* at best. At worst
they might not make much difference at all. The Auroux Laws also
had to be seen in the context of more than a decade of enthusiasm in
several different Left currents about *autogestion*. For by the time the
new regime turned toward reforming the workplace, this notion
seemed to have completely disappeared.

Social democratic governments have traditionally been committed to income redistribution. Yet, quite remarkably, in "Year I"
little income redistribution was proposed (beyond the mild effects of
the government's initial Keynesianism), despite strong urging during
the 1970s by several political families, the PCF in particular, that
"soaking the rich" not only would be just, but would promote economic growth. Other currents in the PS, however, were much more
cautious. The strange story of the "wealth tax," played out in the fall
of 1981, was the outcome of such contradictory pressures. It was
generally known that despite some improvements in the 1970s the
distribution of both income and wealth in France is, comparatively
speaking, quite unequal. The government's initial proposal in this
area was a strong wealth tax which would appropriate each year a
small percentage of very large fortunes. Social justice was the principle advanced in support of this. The initial proposal for an across the
board tax caused panic inside the government, however, primarily
because of the alleged effects which such a tax might have on capital
exports and investment (at the time none of the latter was occurring
and a great deal of the former). As a result the proposal was gutted by
exceptions, leaving the government looking confused and rather fool-
ish.

Tentative as it was, however, the wealth tax represented the government's furthest advance toward income redistribution. This outcome was partly based on a judgment that basic structural reforms
should come first, when the government's political momentum was
greatest. In part it was because of the economic realism of centrist
elements in the government coalition who insisted that fiscal reform
would be likely to transfer resources away from those groups most
prone to invest in the private sector. In all probability it might also
hurt some of the groups whose swing leftward had elected the Left in
1981. Broad fiscal reform, mentioned in the electoral program, was
thus put off until later.[20] When a basic shift in economic policy occurred in June 1982, fiscal reform was permanently postponed.

Government efforts to promote work-sharing were more substantial. The 35-hour week was a central pledge in the Socialist mani-

festo, presented as a means to increase the number of available jobs. The government decided to proceed in increments of one hour, beginning with a drop to 39 hours in the fall of 1981. The method chosen was a combination of incentives. Collective negotiations were the preferred route, but legislation would enforce the reduction, if bargaining fell short of the goal. The move to 39 hours snagged, however, on a series of strikes over the basic issue of whether or not the work week would be reduced without reduction in pay. The government—the president, in fact—under heavy pressure from the CGT, resolved this in favor of "39 for 40." Whether for this reason or for more basic ones, it became clear rather rapidly that reducing the work week to 39 hours had no job-creating effects. Further reductions in the work week were also casualties of the economic policy shift of June 1982.

In general work-sharing ideas, like Keynesianism, followed from insistence by the Left of the new governing coalition, particularly those families rooted theoretically or practically in the working class (PCF, CERES, Left Social Democrats) that there was sufficient space in the French economy to allow such initiatives. Such work-sharing notions, along with "popular Keynesianism," had honorable antecedents in Left responses to the Great Depression five decades earlier. Honorable antecedents, however, did not guarantee success.

The last wave of government action in Year I was of a very different kind, involving the introduction of new economic policies—a French NEP. Quite serious problems had arisen in France's international economic position at different points after May–June 1981, beginning with an immediate run on the franc and continuing through a currency devaluation in the fall. By the late spring of 1982, however, the situation was qualitatively worse. It had become clear by this point that the Left gamble on Keynesian macroeconomic policies had totally failed. On one level the failure involved the inaccuracy of projections about the international market. The American "locomotive" of recovery which was supposed to be barreling forward had not yet left the station. By spring, then, not only had the government's mini-growth spurt lost its momentum, but it had also exacerbated structural problems. The policies had boosted France's already high inflation levels (12.5 percent per annum in March 1981, 14.1 percent in March 1982) at a moment when austerity policies elsewhere were cutting inflation rates to single digits. Thus prices went up on French goods relative to those of international competitors, rapidly wiping out any advantages gained by the devaluation. Moreover, increases in disposable income led to disproportionate increases in imports,

reflecting not only changing consumer preferences but also the flag-
ging competitiveness of parts of French industry. The general result
was that the small growth spurt promoted by the new government,
designed to create additional domestic economic activity, had instead
benefited France's international competitors.

Despite the Keynesian-inspired *relance*, net investment in the
economy went down dramatically (from 4.2 percent in 1980 to −3.5
percent in 1981, with early 1982 even worse). Industrial production
levels stagnated. Unemployment increased much more than had been
anticipated with 285,000 new unemployed on the rolls between April
1981 and April 1982. Perhaps most eloquent were the dismal results
in international accounts. France's commercial balance got steadily
worse the longer the Left was in power, while its current balance of
payments became disastrous.[21]

The franc would have had difficulty even without these developments, given the determined reformism of the government (one
has only to think about the nearly 10 billion francs in government
bonds issued to compensate shareholders for nationalization) and the
equally determined profit hunger of currency speculators. The rapid
expansion of the budget deficit did not help, either. Likewise, persistently high interest rates, necessary to keep capital in France, discouraged investment and encouraged the speculators.

By spring 1982, a French NEP was in the air. In March the
president hinted that a moment of truth was at hand when he announced that, no matter what, the public deficit was not to exceed 3
percent of GNP. Not long thereafter the government announced a
substantial package of economic concessions for the private-sector
patronat—a reduction in the "professional tax" and in social security
payments as well as a pledge that no new work-sharing legislation
would be forthcoming for the near future. By May, Jacques Delors,
Minister of Finance and the most prominent centrist in the government, had begun preaching the virtues of "solidarity" in which "we all
give up a little bit of what we are entitled to."[22] In June there was a
very significant reconstruction of the government. Nicole Questiaux,
Minister of National Solidarity, was fired and replaced by Pierre
Bérégovoy. Questiaux had among other things demanded, as a condition of any reform, a major parliamentary discussion of increasing
worker and union participation in the social security system, in other
words a return to something like pre-1967 social security, when the
Pompidou government had removed such participation by decree.
She had also been quoted in the press, when the issue of the huge
social security deficit and reform was posed in Cabinet, that "talking

about numbers on this question is talking the language of the Right," and that a "reform now, pay later" position was appropriate. Bérégovoy had no difficulty in "talking about numbers," and his appointment meant a definite shift toward the Center and away from the Left on important social issues.

The actual NEP came in June, after the failure of the Versailles international economic summit. A second devaluation of the franc was only the beginning. With it came wage and price controls, legislated because "social partners" were unwilling to accept them voluntarily. The controls, which lasted until October 31, 1982, also included limits on dividends and rent raises and on the operation of escalator clauses in contracts to furnish goods and services to the government.[23] The basic aim of these controls was to strike a once and for all blow against inflation, to reduce the level of inflation for 1982 down to 10 percent. The government also intended to use the control period to begin reorienting a number of different behaviors, including the ways in which most wage agreements were indexed. These had been tied to escalator clauses which automatically raised wages in accordance with inflation indices, but the government hoped to link wage raises to government projections for inflation prepared in advance. The threat of full or partial continuation of controls beyond October 31 was the weapon later used to convince social partners of the utility of this and other changes.

That the rhythms, goals and balance of the government had shifted was unquestionable. Delors, who had been beaten back consistently on policy throughout much of Year I by the Left, was the new linchpin, giving speeches and interviews about the need for new quasi-corporatist contractual arrangements (harking back to *Nouvelle Société* programs of 1969–72 which he had promoted under the Gaullists). He also expressed new admiration for the "West German model" of controlling inflation via "concerted action by social partners" (which the German unions themselves had abandoned), for *Mitbestimmung*-like contractual dealings inside the firm, and for rigorous monetary policies. Bérégovoy was the enunciator of austerity in the social service area. Fabius, Minister of the Budget, constructed a restrictive new budget. The only major Centrist in the government who failed to become more prominent was Michel Rocard, who was excluded from the preparation of NEP measures and raked over the coals by almost everyone for his draft Ninth Plan. Pierre Joxe, perhaps the strongest remaining Left figure in the Socialist firmament, promised everyone "two terrible years." Even the PCF began reluctantly to talk austerity.

Contradictions and Problems:
A Left for the Eighties?

The new Left government in France cannot be indicted either for its inactivity or for its failure to act on its promises. It has been one of the busiest and most energetic producers of reform legislation seen in Western politics for a very long time. Moreover, given a very difficult environment, it has been steadfast in implementing its electoral program, including a number of measures which would have been politically inconceivable anywhere else. In addition the policy review which we have just presented clearly demonstrates that this government's experience, at least until mid-1982, was strongly weighted to favor the desires of the Left, and not the Center and Center-Right, of the complex coalition of political families which comprised the new majority.

At the core of the new government's first efforts was a two-stage vision of economic policy. Stage I—the moderate program of Keynesian demand stimulation which we have discussed—was designed to stimulate a mini-burst of growth directed primarily toward containing any new rise in unemployment. While hopefully such growth would lead to a degree of new private-sector investment, it was also structured to be mildly redistributive toward poorer groups and to serve as a short-run source of material rewards to many of the electoral constituencies which supported the Left. Stage I was, of course, premised on a belief that France's margin of maneuver in the international economy was large enough to allow such careful Keynesianism while other countries deflated. The government also anticipated an American-led international recovery to commence in early 1982, just when the effects of French domestic stimulation began to wear out. This general international recovery would float the French economy for a sufficient amount of time to allow Stage II of the government's vision to unfold.

Stage II, the longer-run dimension of government strategy, was a complex package structured around nationalizations to allow new investment control. Economic reflection, aided and abetted by a substantial increase in government-funded research and development expenditures, would coalesce into innovative sectoral and national industrial policies, scientifically founded bets against the future development of the world economy. Capital from the nationalized banks would then be mobilized behind the investment plans which these bets would entail, plans which would be carried out, for the most part, by the new public sector. One indirect effect of this would be a snow-ball leading the private sector to greater and more judicious investments. If everything went well in this admittedly ambitious scenario, the domestic market would be "reconquered" and France would "leave the crisis from the Left" in a greatly enhanced international market position. And, as success began to appear from this investment control package, the government could initiate a much more aggressive and redistributive program of Keynesian demand stimulation and social reform.

Understood in these ways, the approach of the new government was consistent. To be sure it was not the "Storming of the Winter Palace," nor the beginning of any evident "transition to socialism." It was pathbreaking, nonetheless, to the degree that it demonstrated profound mistrust of the mixed economy formula relied upon in earlier postwar years to resolve France's problems. In effect the new French Left government after 1981 was a pioneer in enacting the "Keynes plus Investment Control" package which a number of other European Left parties had begun to contemplate (as with the Swedish Social Democrats' Meidner Plan, for example, which had found a strong echo in the Italian Communist Party, or the "Alternative Economic Strategy" of the British Labour Left). Given France's past and the historic roots of the French Left's program, the investment control "plus" of this package in French circumstances could hardly be anything but statist. Internal political developments on the Left in the 1970s, particularly the crushing defeats suffered by the Rocardians (the most anti-statist group in the PS as well as the most consistent propagandists for *autogestion*) conspired in the same direction.

Consistency does not automatically create success, of course.[24] However elegantly assembled this economic strategy may have seemed to its proponents, it did not work out in reality. Stage I proved to be premised on the dangerous illusion that "Keynesianism in One Country" was possible in an open and crisis-ridden world economy. The French Left had simply been wrong in believing that the main barriers to more socially generous growth-oriented policies in France were Giscard, Barre and Malthusian monopolists. The first part of this chapter explored the origins of such illusions in the long-standing pluralist politics of the French Left. Many of the ideas and attitudes which shaped the Left's program in 1981 had their roots in the 1930s and 1940s. The basic outlines of the program had, moreover, been set out prior to the clear enunciation of crisis in the mid-1970s. While a number of adjustments to new realities had been made programmatically in light of new crisis problems, in particular a shift in orientation in the planning/industrial policy/nationalizations package from an original "anticapitalist–social justice" emphasis toward an investment control focus. But pre-crisis enthusiasm for Keynesianism persisted, carried into the 1980s by political groups who remained convinced that greater popular consumption would inevitably lead to greater growth and investment.

THE FAILURE OF KEYNESIANISM AND ITS IMPLICATIONS

The collapse of Stage I of the French Left's two-stage economic scenario is a political event of immense importance, in France and elsewhere. It has been a left-wing cliché for much of the twentieth century that when Social Democrats come to power—which they do by using leftist rhetoric—they will invariably "sell out," betraying the hopes and dreams of supporters who truly want to transcend capitalism. Whatever the truth of this cliché in other settings, it does not work at all in the case of France after 1981. The program which the French Left carried to power in 1981 was one which embodied the major goals of those mass-based political families standing furthest left in the broader coalition of forces in the new majority. Moreover, the new government did not shy away from enacting these goals; indeed the opposite is true. It is clear, of course, that beginning with the NEP policies of 1982, the balance of power in this government began to shift toward the political center. But it would be quite wrong to see in this shift any confirmation of the "perfidious Social Democrat sellout" cliché. For what happened, in fact, was that one major dimension of the program of the Left was tried and found wanting. Failure followed, then, not from betrayal, but because certain of the policy goals of the genuine Left were derived from, and essentially suited for, pre-crisis economic conditions.

It is even more interesting to note that the Left families in the new French majority, when faced with this failure, could find few viable substitute policy proposals. The Communists, for example, at first could only come up with jingoistic "make it in France" campaigns. Subsequently they devised the notion of "new criteria" to be used for economic policy decisions. Instead of immediate profitability, some measure of broader social utility was to be applied. Extensive trade protectionism was quite clearly implied by both positions. Moreover, it was obvious that the Communists were more concerned with making short-run electoral and other gains out of particularistic protest against austerity than with proposing serious new economic approaches. Left-wing Social Democrats were hardly better, advocating mild corporatistic coordination as a counterpart to an austerity relabeled "solidarity," but little more. Left intellectuals, often of a Eurocommunist persuasion, proposed that vast reserves of productivity could be tapped if only the government took *autogestion* more seriously in the workplace, but such proposals were abstract and vague in the extreme.

The adaptive tactics of much of the CERES Left in the face of such new realities were perhaps the most significant, especially given the considerable power which CERES leaders like Jean-Pierre Chevènement held inside the government. Essentially what Chevènement and others did was to accept the need for short-run austerity, or "solidarity," as a consequence of the failure of Keynesianism, while turning toward powerful advocacy of Stage II of the Left's strategy. Voluntaristic economic nationalism became their line. Prospects for any immediate increase in living standards, social justice and welfare were essentially shelved in the interests of promoting a statist "neo-Japanese" industrial investment program. In this program the central problem to be resolved before all others was that of restoring the integrity of the French economy by rebuilding and modernizing French industry. The instrumentalities falling to hand for these very large tasks were, of course, increased research and development, planning and capital mobilization by nationalized banks to implement new industrial policies through nationalized firms.[25] This abandonment of Stage I and strong stress on Stage II of the Left's initial program proposed participation in a national crusade for the reindustrialization of France and the regeneration of its international competitive position as a substitute for immediate material gains.

With the collapse of the Keynesian experiment and the practical absence of alternative Left policies, the balance of political power within the government inevitably shifted toward the Center. Indeed the most visible figures in the government after the NEP of summer 1982 became Jacques Delors, Pierre Bérégovoy and Jean-Pierre Chevènement. Chevènement, as Minister of Research and Industry, put forward the voluntaristic economic nationalist line which we have outlined, which became the preponderant Left position in governmental debates. Delors stood strong for "balancing the accounts," in particular the external trade accounts, in ways which clearly implied that no more major reform would occur. Bérégovoy, at the Ministry of National Solidarity, became the minister for compressing Social Service budgets in "solidaristic" ways. All major voices inside the government accepted that a long period of austerity was in order. Differences existed only on the purposes of austerity. For Chevènement it was to allow the full implementation of Stage II of the government's original strategy, transformed into the crusade for national industrial regeneration which we have described. For centrist elements austerity, accompanied with appeals to corporatistic solidarity, was mainly to get France's accounts in order.

THE NEW SITUATION AND DAY-TO-DAY POLITICS

Failed Keynesianism had other important consequences. Here some knowledge of the 1981 elections is needed. The electoral victories which brought the French Left to power were great to be sure. But like the victory of Ronald Reagan in 1980, they were not unambiguous. To begin with, the actual electoral shift which occurred was relatively small—on the order of 2 percent. In addition the deeper meaning of the shift was not completely clear, since people voted for François Mitterrand and the Left for a variety of different reasons. More than anywhere else, in France there were substantial numbers of voters who wanted major changes and therefore wanted the Left to implement its program to the fullest. Still such committed Left voters were a minority, even if a large minority, and they themselves were divided up by affiliation with the different Left families. Some wanted "revolutionary change." Perhaps more wanted the Left in power because they believed that it could deliver shorter-term rewards to them in ways which the Right either could not or would not. There were also substantial numbers of electors who were interested mainly in rewards for their own specific groups or in satisfactory responses to the narrow demands of their "single-issue" movements. Moreover, support for the Left's general program softened as one moved toward swing voters, many of whom were not partial at all to major structural changes, especially insofar as they might involve a significant redistribution of resources or life chances. Finally, there was a small but electorally critical fringe of Gaullist voters who had voted for Mitterrand and who wanted no part in the Left's major reformism at all.

The challenge which faced the French Left in power involved creating political hegemony over this heterogeneous electoral coalition.[26] The longevity of the Left in government depended upon this, and, with it, the Left's success in consolidating its new reforms. The failure of the Left's Keynesianism set back this task considerably. Keynesianism, of course, had been the "meat and potatoes" of Social Democratic governments after 1945. Such governments pursued growth-oriented macroeconomic policies and redistributed a portion of the fruits of growth to electorally targeted social groups in an effort to ensure continuity in power. Crisis conditions had rendered this kind of politics very risky, however, and by 1982 the French Left government was in trouble. Unable to come across with the material payoffs which it had promised it was in considerable danger of failing to consolidate the bulk of its political support, if not actually losing important ground. The cantonal elections of March 1982 showed some slippage as did the more important municipal elections of March 1983.

Perhaps more significant, the inability of the new government to provide rewards for constituencies and groups in the traditional vocabulary and its incapacity to invent a new vocabulary cost it considerable political dignity. Rarely had a modern government done so much changing and reforming amidst so little enthusiasm. Groups critical to the political future of the government—organized labor, intellectuals and "single issue" movements—lapsed into "wait and see" postures of "critical support" for the regime, with the accent ever more on criticism. The potential existed, for example, of substantial working-class rejection of austerity in the form of industrial conflict which, were it to occur, might well completely upset government economic plans. The government stood a reasonable chance of avoiding this, but for reasons which were as much liabilities as they were strengths. The French union movement was terribly weak, perhaps weaker than at any point since the Cold War, because of internal disunity and the labor market effects of the crisis. But even if the government could avoid this trouble, its inability to consolidate support gave the Right-Center opposition, which had been shattered by its defeat in 1981, precious new space to reorganize.

Rushing to the Center

The political/coalitional product of the collapse of the Left's Keynesianism in mid-1982 was a new balance of tendencies in the government, as we have seen. The new "Left" in the coalition—represented in the government by Jean-Pierre Chevènement—proposed a statist national crusade for reindustrialization. If Keynesianism had failed, the moment of austerity which ensued might best be used to implement a package of research and development/industrial policy/investment programs centered in the new public sector to rebuild France's industrial strength. In contrast centrists in the government coalition, led by Jacques Delors, were primarily concerned with putting order into France's national accounts by lowering inflation levels, cutting the budget deficit, and reducing the balance of payments problem. Both leading tendencies agreed that the time for a "pause" in reforming had come.

The results of the initial period of "rigor"—the months of incomes policy and price freeze after June 1982—were difficult to assess. The proposed 1983 budget demonstrated new governmental seriousness about controlling the level of public spending and limiting the budget deficit, as well as obvious concern for distributing austerity with some equity.[27] This period of "rigor" had been designed essentially to work a one-shot reduction in France's inflation rate. The goal was indeed achieved: inflation dropped from over 14 percent per year to under 10 percent. Unfortunately, the inflation rate of France's industrial competitors also dropped during the same period in ways which nullified any competitive gains for the French. Instead France remained at more or less the same difficult level of comparative disadvantage where she had been prior to "rigor." Thus the cost of marching out of international deflationary order after 1981 proved greater than anticipated. On top of this, France's balance of payments situation continued to be dismal; the deficit for 1982 was a record 96 billion francs. The structure of this deficit was even more telling. It was worst vis-à-vis highly industrialized competitors in the EEC and the OECD and best in trade with the Third World, demonstrating yet again the underlying structural weaknesses of the French economy.

The theme of France's industrial weakness predominated in governmental discussion during the fall of 1982, as Chevènement and the "new" Left of the coalition pushed forward their line of voluntaristic economic nationalism. Not only had French capital failed to promote France's industrial success in recent times, went the analysis, it had never done so. This discovery was useful in making the case that the "French way" to industrial modernization and growth had always been statist, from Colbert through Jean Monnet, to François Mitterrand.[28] This case was made to justify the major investment effort which Chevènement proposed in the new public sector, involving the mobilization of capital by public sector firms, the state and nationalized banks. Such investment would be designed to promote concerted growth in high-tech areas (mainly electronics), the modernization of mid-range technologies and production, and an *effet d'entraînement* for the private sector, leading to new investment in flexible, mid-sized industry.

By the end of 1982, however, evidence indicated that Chevènement was having problems getting his way inside the government. The most immediate question raised by the Minister of Industry's ambitious scenario was where to find the necessary capital to invest. Given the general economic situation, the high and rapidly growing level of France's foreign indebtedness (France was the number two borrower in the world in 1982), the absolute limits on private savings and the serious risks of "crowding out" private sector investment, the question was serious. By January 1983, Chevènement was in political trouble. When he came to the Industry Ministry in mid-1982, he had found an organization designed mainly to deal with firms teetering on the edge of bankruptcy and liquidation. Attempting to turn such a limited organization into the dynamic vanguard of a national crusade for reindustrialization was therefore not easy. A whole series of new skills—developing industrial policy, negotiating "planning contracts" with the public sector, and projecting a major new investment program—had to be learned essentially through "on the job training," moreover, at a moment when the number of delicate decisions to be made about declining firms was rising dramatically. Such an institutional context, together with Chevènement's own trenchantly voluntaristic ways of doing things, placed the minister in an exposed position. Private and public sector decision-makers both began to complain about, and appeal, the ministry's actions above the Minister's head. Excessive interference and general meddling were the main messages. Finally, in early February, Jean-Pierre Chevènement was openly rebuked by the president. Chevènement subsequently submitted his resignation, but stayed on the job until late March.

It is hard to know how much these events were produced by the very real problems encountered and created by the Chevènement ministry and how much by more basic Left-Center differences in economic policy. Unquestionably these differences grew ever sharper in the winter of 1982–83 as the contradictory consequences of "rigor" became clearer. The persisting differential between France's inflation rate and the lower rate's of France's major EEC partners, West Germany in particular, meant that the positive effects of the June 1982 devaluation were progressively lost. Moreover, the franc remained vulnerable. In turn this situation meant that France's grim balance of payments situation threatened to become grimmer still. Indeed the January 1983 trade figures were worse than ever.

As the economic handwriting appeared once again on the wall, a clash between the two major economic strategies in contention within the governing coalition became inevitable. A new set of basic policy choices had to be made as of late winter 1983. The moment of decision was predetermined, however, by yet another consequence of the failure of the government's earlier Keynesianism, the Left's electoral vulnerability. The municipal elections of March 1983, the last major poll to be held before the legislative campaign of 1985–86, had to be held in the best circumstances possible for the government. The announcement of a new economic policy package, which, whatever else it proposed, was bound to involve new austerity, would amount to an admission of failure and be electorally costly. Therefore it, and the denouement of the situation of intracoalitional conflict over economic policy, could only occur in the aftermath of the municipal elections.

The results of the municipal elections (March 6 and 13, 1983) were difficult to decode. First-round results pointed to a landslide victory for the Right opposition. Sixteen city governments were lost by the majority and many more seemed about to be lost.[28] The worst never materialized for the Left, however. By dint of an extraordinary mobilization of Left electors for the second round, an anti-government landslide was averted. Thus the actual extent of the Left's defeat (the Right won 53 percent of the vote to the Left's 47 percent, a loss of 7.5 percent from the second round of the presidential election of 1981, translating into a Left-Right shift of 31 municipal governments) was somewhat masked by the fact that the second-round results were markedly less disastrous than had been predicted.

The results of the municipal elections, together with those of the nearly simultaneous West German elections (a CDU victory), created a new run on the franc. Thus the atmosphere in which new economic policy choices were made was a difficult one. Indeed Mitterrand was obliged to refrain from a promised governmental shakeup for ten days while political in-fighting went on about the desirable course to follow. The immediate issue was whether and how to deal with the West Germans about revaluing the mark vis-à-vis the franc in the European Monetary System. Debate on this issue brought deeper conflicts to a head. The Left, Chevènement and others advocated a line of "maintaining internal credibility" by withdrawing from the EMS and beginning to deploy selective import controls. Here the reasoning was that Chevènement's ambitious industrial investment plans and the living standards of the Left's popular base ought to be protected. The Jacques Delors/centrist position opted, in contrast, for "external credibility," staying in EMS, devaluing the franc again and accepting drastic new austerity measures to reduce inflation and balance of payments problems.

The Delors position eventually won out. The EMS negotiations with the West Germans led to an 8 percent devaluation of the franc versus the mark. Next President Mitterrand rather surprisingly reappointed Pierre Mauroy as Prime Minister, apparently as a trade-off to the Left for the new austerity policies to be proposed. Governmental personnel were not dramatically changed, excepting the departure of Chevènement. But changes in functional attributions within the Mauroy government were significant. Jacques Delors became number two and complete overseer of the economic realm, including control over the budget. Pierre Bérégovoy was number three, given an equally broad mandate over all domains of social policy. Laurent

Fabius, Mitterrand's protégé, became Minister of Industry and Research.

The new austerity package immediately followed the naming of the new government. Its major purpose was to reduce household consumption in France by approximately 2 percent through an additional 1 percent tax on 1982 taxable incomes and a forced savings plan. Severe exchange controls, whose purpose was to eliminate foreign travel by the French in 1983, were also introduced as a way of working on balance of payments difficulties. The projected effect of these policies was to cut growth to nearly zero, boost exports and reduce the living standards of the French. There was considerable controversy about what this package—which was carried out by decree—would do in an international context where a mild upturn was anticipated. Government spokesmen claimed that the policies were designed to "purify" the French situation so that France could profit fully from recovery. Critics wondered whether the "purification" operation might cause France to miss recovery altogether. Finally, and perhaps inevitably, Laurent Fabius announced a new "hands-off" Ministry of Industry policy vis-à-vis public sector firms and major cutbacks in public sector investment plans.

THE NEW CENTRIST EQUILIBRIUM: HOW STABLE IS IT?

In the short run it seemed as if the Left to Center shift of French economic policies had been completed by the spring of 1983. In the conflictual play of tendencies and families within the coalition which came to power in 1981, the different policy lines which had been proposed by the Left had either been tried and found wanting—Keynesianisn in 1981–82—or begun and politically defeated, as with Jean-Pierre Chevènement's voluntaristic economic nationalism in 1982–83.

Politics is not Newtonian physics, however. Conclusions are rarely completely prefigured in earlier events. The French Left still faces an extended period of guaranteed power. New circumstances, such as a partial international economic recovery, might intervene to change seemingly fixed trajectories. Moreover, the leaders of the French Left are talented and creative people who may respond innovatively to the current period of on-the-job training which they are living. François Mitterrand's capacities to navigate shrewdly through a sea of political contradictions can never be underestimated, even if his economic sensibilities seem much less developed. Moreover, if the French Left is not saved by circumstances, its own creativity or presidential miracles, it may still muddle through.

The policy equilibrium struck in spring 1983, dominated by economic programs with which the much maligned Raymond Barre would have felt quite at home, was not certain to provide the final word. François Mitterrand, as always, left himself with a number of exits. Pierre Mauroy was clearly a prime minister of limited tenure, to be dismissed when greater wisdom decided to begin the broad turn toward the 1985–86 legislative elections. The race for prime ministerial succession has been rigged by the president for his own political advantage. If Jacques Delors had emerged as the government's dominant figure and the victor in protracted political conflict as of 1983, his success placed him, alone, very far out on a political limb. Acknowledged paternity of a Barre-type austerity plan was not likely to enhance Delors' popularity. Should the policies succeed, the president could take his share of the credit. Should they fail, the blame will fall on Delors. In addition the internal situation in the Socialist Party which prevailed in the aftermath of the rapid shift of the regime's center of gravity to the Center was one which promised conflict. Finally, the possibility of social unrest (particularly industrial conflict) in response to the Delors austerity plan could not be excluded.

Further uncertainty was introduced in the late autumn of 1983. From the beginning of its tenure, the Left government had recognized one very large imperative. The level of French unemployment had to be kept from rising much above the "magic number" of two million. To do so it perpetuated a set of practices which had been used by the Right in power throughout the 1970s, and largely for the same kind of political calculations. Maintaining employment in industry was of essential importance in maintaining electoral support. Thus, despite the modernizing rhetoric of the new majority after 1981, it proved loath to allow inefficient and overstaffed industrial activities to suffer the free market employment consequences of their weaknesses. Pious rhetoric about introducing new technologies conflicted with hard employment realities. The new technologies in question eliminated rather than created jobs. Moreover, public investment resources were limited. Either they could be used to introduce these technologies, whatever the cost in jobs, or they could be used to keep jobs filled artificially in inefficient sectors.

This contradiction had its own dynamics. Maintaining employment artificially through government subsidies and regulation meant that inefficiencies tended to be perpetuated. In addition France's competitors were busily modernizing on their own. The price to be paid for not facing economic facts in a number of important industrial sectors—steel, shipbuilding, textiles, coal-mining and automobiles, among others—grew year by year after 1981. For a number of political reasons, 1984 was the year chosen by the government to try and face such facts. The 1983 municipal elections were behind, while the 1986 legislative elections approached, for which the government would need at least a year for pump-priming maneuvers before facing the electorate. Thus in the government's program for 1984, "modernizing industry" was married to "rigor."

Chopping jobs is never easy for any government. It is even less easy for a government of the Left. "Industrial modernizing" in 1984 promised therefore to be a watershed for French leftists. The risks were great. The unions which had supported the government—the CGT and the CFDT—were not certain to follow. The Communist minority had by 1984 become quite uneasy in its junior partner role and was likely to become all the more unwilling to assume the task of providing social peace, through its control of the CGT, in support of unpopular policies. In addition the Socialist core of the government had become quite tired by 1984, and had moreover become largely consumed by quarrels over succession to the premiership.

The Left experiment in France transcends the French situation in importance. Rarely, if ever, has there been a Left government in Western politics endowed with more institutional power than this one. Rarely has such a government been so solidly weighted toward the Left of the political spectrum. What lessons has it taught thus far? In a word, humility. There can be no mistake about the fact that the French Left has indeed tried to implement its program. And there can be no mistake about the fact that in so doing it has proven one of the major tenets of the Left in the West—the belief that deliberate efforts to increase popular consumption are both feasible and progressive—no longer works in new circumstances of economic crisis. The second "Left" program, voluntaristic economic nationalism, was not proven unworkable. Its pursuit, however, in the circumstances of 1982–83 France, circumstances which were shaped in part by the earlier failure of Keynesianism, led clearly to the choice of retreat from the open international market. This choice was defeated politically. Are the constraints on reformist government in the 1980s so stringent that, short of storming the Winter Palace or autarky, the only option is using popular support to work a transfer of resources from the people to profit?

Notes

1. For a discussion of the reasons for this weakness, see G. Lefranc, *Le mouvement syndical en France de la libération aux évènements de mai–juin 1968* (Paris: PUF, 1969); and George Ross, *Workers and Communists in France* (Berkeley: University of California Press, 1982).

2. The specific of Gaullist labor relations are discussed in George Ross, "Gaullism and Organized Labor: Two Decades of Failure," in S. Hoffmann and W. Andrews, eds., *The Fifth Republic at Twenty* (Albany: State University of New York Press, 1981).

3. See the cross-national comparisons which place France's experience in perspective in C. Crouch and A. Pizzorno, *The Resurgence of Class Conflict in Western Europe* (London, Macmillan, 1978).

4. For a review of the Socialist party politics through the 1970s, see H. Portelli, *Le socialisme français tel qu'il est* (Paris: PUF, 1980), Parts I and II; H. G. Simmons, *French Socialists in Search of a Role, 1956–1967* (Ithaca, N.Y.: Cornell University Press, 1970); F. L. Wilson, *The French Democratic Left: 1963–1969* (Stanford, Cal.: Stanford University Press, 1971). On the sociology and organization, see R. Cayrol et al "Sociologie du PS," *Revue Française de Science Politique*, 28, April 1978, especially P. Hardouin, "Les charactéristiques sociologiques du Parti Socialiste."

5. The literature on May–June is vast. Perhaps the most astute sociological treatment of these strata is A. Touraine, *The May Movement* (New York: Random House, 1971). See also C. Posner, ed., *Reflections on the Revolution in France* (Harmondsworth: Penguin, 1969).

6. The families, or currents, described here are identified for analytic purposes. They do not necessarily correspond to the formally organized *tendances* which make up the internal organization of the PS.

7. On the social democrats in general, see Portelli, *Le socialisme français;* Simmons, *French Socialists in Search of a Role;* and J. Touchard, *La gauche en France depuis 1900* (Paris: Seuil, 1977).

8. The republicanism of François Mitterrand is fully detailed in O. Duhamel, *La gauche et la vie république* (Paris: PUF, 1980), and François Mitterrand, *Ma part de vérité* (Paris: Poche, 1971).

9. On the PSU and Rocardians see, G. Nania, *Le PSU avant Rocard* (Paris: Roblot, 1973), and C. Hauss, *The New Left in France: The Unified Socialist Party* (Westport, Conn: Greenwood, 1978). See also M. Rocard, *Le PSU et l'avenir socialiste en France* (Paris: 1969), and H. Hamon and P. Rotman, *L'effet Rocard* (Paris: Stock, 1980). For an interesting "inside" account, see A. DuRoy and R. Schneider, *Le roman de la rose* (Paris: Seuil, 1982), chapter 5.

10. M. Charzat et al., *Le CERES: un combat pour le socialisme* (Paris: Calmann-Lévy, 1975); M. Charzat et al., *Le CERES par lui-même* (Paris: Christian Bourgeois, 1978).

11. On the evolution of the PCF in these years, see J. Jenson and G. Ross, "The Uncharted Waters of de-Stalinization," *Politics and Society,* Vol. 9, 1979.

12. Portelli, *Le socialisme français,* Part III.

13. DuRoy and Schneider, *Le roman de la rose,* chapter 7.

14. On the French crisis, see A. Cotta, *La France et l'impératif mondial* (Paris: PUF, 1978), C. Stoffaës, *La grande menace industrielle* (Paris: Calmann-Lévy, 1978), and B. Camus et al., *La crise du système productif* (Paris: INSEE, 1981).

15. On the sources of this new sectarianism and for further details of its effects, see G. Ross and J. Jenson, "The Rise and Fall of French Eurocommunism," in L. Graziano, ed., *Eurocomunismo e partidi di sinistra in Europa* (Milan: Feltrinelli, 1983); and G. Ross, "French Communism

with its Back to the Wall: the 24th Congress of the French Communist Party," *Socialist Review*, Vol. 12, No. 65, September–October 1982.

16. For details, see *Le Monde: Dossiers et Documents: l'élection présidential 26 avril–10 mai 1981*. This *dossier* contains both the election results and campaign documents, including the PS Election Manifesto.

17. See *Le Monde: Bilan économique et social 1981*, especially pp. 4–6, 27ff.

18. The excellent book *Les nationalisations 1982*, by A. G. Delion and M. Durupty (Paris: Economica, 1982), reviews all sides of the nationalization process and covers the issues involved in an exhaustive way.

19. J. Auroux *Les droits des travailleurs: rapport au Président de la République et au Premier ministre* (Paris: La Documentation Française, 1981).

20. A task force had been formed around Pierre Joxe, President of the National Assembly Group of Socialists, to outline a proposal for fiscal reform. For some idea of the point which had been reached in June 1982, see *Le Nouvel Observateur*, August 7–13, 1982, pp. 26ff.

21. The statistics used here come from INSEE via *La Vie Française*, May 17, 1982 p. 25.

22. *Le Monde*, May 22, 1982.

23. *Le Monde*, June 12, 1982.

24. The argument developed here about France is very eloquently put in more general terms in A. Przeworski and M. Wallerstein "Democratic Capitalism at the Crossroads" *Democracy*, Vol. 2, June 1982, pp. 52–68.

25. For discussion and documents on this approach, see *Une Politique industrielle pour la France*, the report from Chevènement's November 1982 "Industrial Policy Days" (Paris, Documentation Française, 1983), and *Parti Socialiste, Nationalisations: La Voie Française*, papers from the PS colloquium of December 1982 on the public sector. See also Bob Kuttner's excellent review, "France's Atari Socialism," in *The New Republic*, March 7, 1983.

26. This line of argument is the central point in the excellent analysis of C. Mouffe, "Which Way France?" *New Socialist*, July–August 1982, pp. 26–29.

27. For a brief review of the economic and budgetary situation in 1982, see the indispensable *Bilan Economique et Social 1982*, published by *Le Monde*, especially pages 36–65.

28. See Chevènement's speech in *Une Politique industrielle pour la France* for a good example of this argument.

3

Agricultural Reform in Mitterrand's France

JOHN T.S. KEELER

No crystal ball was required to predict, in the wake of the 1981 French elections, that the ambitious reform visions of François Mitterrand and his Socialist government would face an extremely stiff test— perhaps their stiffest test—in the agricultural sector. Here, as in other sectors, an effort to implement what the Socialists termed a "more equitable" policy seemed certain to entail some negative economic consequences, including a higher inflation rate and a problematic shift in the balance of trade, which could well prove politically damaging to the government and stall the drive for reform. In addition, the path to agricultural reform featured two obstacles virtually guaranteed to frustrate the Socialists. First, an attempt to *changer la vie* would be constrained by the necessity of adhering to the extensive regulations of the EEC's Common Agricultural Policy (CAP). Second, a Socialist reform campaign seemed destined to meet with formidable political resistance in the countryside. Unlike most of their compatriots, the French farmers had not given the Socialists even a slim mandate for reform in the 1981 elections. Indeed, they had provided

60

both Mitterrand and the Socialist Party with less electoral support than any other occupational group.[1] Many farmers, especially the leaders of the major agricultural interest groups, remembered well their last encounter with a socialist government. In 1956, Prime Minister Guy Mollet outraged agrarian leaders by abolishing the post of Minister of Agriculture and attempting to push through a host of reforms unpopular in the farm community. Most of these "anti-peasant" measures never reached the floor of parliament, largely because they triggered a massive wave of rural demonstrations.[2] With this experience of the 1950s in mind, the forces of organized agriculture would be both prepared for "trouble" and reasonably confident of their ability to cope with it.

Given these seemingly insuperable obstacles to reform, it appeared in mid-1981 that only two basic scenarios for the first two years of Socialist rule were plausible: (1) the Socialists might discreetly jettison their more controversial plans for agricultural reform at the outset, maintaining social peace and economic stability at the expense of broken promises while concentrating their energies on other sections; or (2) they might embark on a confrontational reform campaign which would provoke strong resistance and eventually give way, after a few important promises had been translated into policy, to a period of retrenchment and moderated change. As this chapter will illustrate, it is essentially the second of these scenarios which has unfolded during the first 22 months of Mitterrand's regime. The story of agricultural policymaking in the new regime may be summed up in three words: reform, revolt and retrenchment. The fervor of the reform campaign, led by the first female minister of agriculture in French history, and the spectacular nature of the peasant revolt, capped by an unprecedented demonstration which brought 100,000 farmers to the streets of Paris, have combined to make this sectoral story one of the most dramatic of the Mitterrand era.

Reform: Toward a "More Equitable" Agricultural Policy

The reform effort launched by the Socialist government in 1981 can be fully understood only if viewed as a conscious reaction to, and alleged correction of, the agricultural policy which had been pursued under successive governments of the Center-Right for more than two decades. The foundations of this policy were laid in the early 1960s when the Gaullist government, driven by a desire to encourage rapid economic growth and by the need to make French farmers competitive enough to withstand the international competition soon to be introduced by the EEC's Common Agricultural Policy, produced a package of reforms portrayed as a new "charter" for the agricultural sector. This Gaullist charter promised to ensure parity between agriculture and other sectors by improving efficiency and productivity through the implementation of a host of coordinated measures: regional agencies (the SAFERs) were established to exert some control over the market for land so as to induce structural reform; new subsidy programs were created to hasten the rural exodus and the transfer of land from old to young farmers; steps were taken to encourage the organization of producer groups and to improve cooperative marketing procedures; agricultural development agencies (SUADs) were established in each department so as to improve technical education and the flow of information necessary for efficient farm management.[3]

To assure the support of the farmers for this new policy orientation, which was recognized to be controversial and potentially disruptive in the countryside, the Gaullist governments of the 1960s developed an intimate corporatist relationship with the major farmers' union, the *Fédération Nationale des Syndicats d'Exploitants Agricoles* (FNSEA). From the time of Edgard Pisani's tenure in the Ministry of Agriculture (1961–66) until the ouster of the Center-Right government in 1981, agricultural policy was thus formulated and implemented with a degree of group-state *concertation* unparalleled in other socioeconomic sectors. The FNSEA, whose leaders purported to be "apolitical" but were generally sympathetic to (if not formally affiliated with) the parties of the Center-Right, was accorded privileged access to the decision-making centers of the state, while the leftist organizational rivals of the "official union" were virtually excluded from the policymaking process. Moreover, FNSEA officials were granted—directly through state decrees or indirectly through favorable electoral regulations—control over a network of semipublic agencies charged with the administration of numerous important agricultural programs. While critics of the FNSEA condemned its "collusion" with the state and even charged that it had become the modern counterpart of the Vichy Peasant Corporation, FNSEA leaders proudly proclaimed that their privileged role amounted to professional "co-management" *(cogestion)* of the agricultural sector. Affording this role to the FNSEA entailed some financial and political costs for the governments of the Center-Right era, but these costs were offset by the invaluable services which the FNSEA as corporatist client provided: the official union served as a fixed channel of communication, a bargaining agent which could aggregate and moderate sectoral demands as well as mobilize support for the policies which it helped to formulate, and a supplemental bureaucracy capable of assisting in the policy implementation process.[4]

During the three years preceding the pivotal 1981 elections, the Giscard-Barre government worked to develop an updated agricultural charter and to consolidate its ties with the forces of organized agriculture led by the FNSEA. Giscard's orientation law for agriculture, drafted through an intense process of *concertation* stretching from early 1978 to the fall of 1979 and formally approved by parliament in the spring of 1980, reaffirmed the principles of the 1960–62 legislation and sought to reinvigorate the traditional policy of liberal *dirigisme* by introducing new programs designed to promote "investment, enlargement and specialization." While government spokesmen professed concern for "correcting the handicaps" of disadvantaged regions and stressed that their legislation represented an attempt "to reconcile employment and competitiveness," they acknowledged that "what we want is family farms of a very high technical level." The central concern of the orientation law was to improve productivity and thus enable agriculture to become, in Giscard's oft-quoted phrase of 1977, "the oil of France," that is, a source of export surpluses sufficient to offset the commercial imbalance imposed by oil imports. Agricultural productivity and export potential were to be enhanced through such means as an intensified commitment to research and development (focused on such objectives as reducing the costs of production and improving the efficiency of the food processing industry), new measures to encourage the organization of producers and the creation of a fund for the promotion of exports.[5]

The most celebrated institutional innovation of the 1980 orientation law, saluted by the FNSEA as a means through which the official union could "participate more actively in the elaboration and conduct of agricultural policy," was the *Conseil Supérieur d'Orientation de l'Economie Agricole et Alimentaire* (CSO). Composed of representatives of the state, the agricultural profession, the food processing industry and consumers, the new CSO was empowered to make recommendations in regard to "the general orientations of agricultural policy" and to help draft regional orientation programs for agricultural development.

The final years of the Center-Right era featured not only this tightening of the institutional links between the FNSEA and the state, but also an unprecedented enhancement of the personal/political links between the official union and the Center-Right government. In April 1979, FNSEA president Michel Debatisse—the man who had personified the official union's commitment to *concertation* or *cogestion* ever since the early 1960s—announced that he was resigning his post to become a candidate for election to the European parliament on the UDF (Giscardian) list. Debatisse was elected in June, but his tenure as a Euro-deputy was brief, for in October 1979 he was brought into the French government as *Secrétaire d'Etat aux Industries Agro-alimentaires*. In the cabinet which Debatisse formed were included two of his former associates from the FNSEA. According to some observers, it was only the Left's surprising victory in 1981 which precluded what would have been the apotheosis of *cogestion:* Debatisse's appointment as Minister of Agriculture.

As the Center-Right era drew to a close in 1981, it could not be denied that the balance sheet for Gaullist-Giscardian agricultural policy and *cogestion* was quite impressive in some respects. Over the past two decades, the volume of French agricultural production had increased by more than 70 percent. Throughout the 1970s, France's average annual rate of growth in agricultural productivity (measured by value added per farmer) had surpassed that of all other original EEC members; the French figure was 4.2 percent, compared to 4.0 percent for Italy, 1.0 percent for West Germany and 2.9 percent for the entire EEC. Furthermore, the modernization of French agriculture had also produced a dramatic change in the sector's commercial balance (the value of exports minus the value of imports). Whereas the value of agricultural imports had always exceeded that of exports until 1968, the balance became "structurally positive" during the 1970s, despite the negative impact of the oil crisis. With grain, wine and milk products leading the way, agricultural exports increased dramatically during the last few years of Giscard's *septennat* and the positive commercial balance for the sector rose accordingly: 1.12 billion francs in 1978, 6.75 in 1979, 11.7 in 1980 and 25.4 in 1981. The record figure for 1981 surpassed what many had considered to be an unrealistic goal (20 billion francs) set by Giscard in 1977. Ironically, of course, recognition that the goal had been achieved came only after Giscard had been replaced by Mitterrand at the Elysée Palace.

For the Socialists the fundamental flaw of what they termed the Center-Right's "*schéma productiviste*" was that it manifested insufficient concern for the human traumas entailed in the relentless process of agricultural modernization. As Socialist spokesmen stressed in the 1979–80 debates over Giscard's agricultural charter and again during the 1981 electoral campaigns, the survival of small and medium-sized farmers had long been jeopardized by a policy which perpetuated sectoral inequalities and produced a decline in real income. It was estimated that the poorest two-thirds of the farmers together received only about one-fourth of total farm income and that the per capita farm income of the poorest region was only one-fifth as high as that of the richest region.[6] Moreover, most French farmers had experienced a decline in income since the onset of the oil crisis. From 1974 onward, the annual increases in agricultural production costs (higher than the EEC average due to France's relatively high inflation rate, largely the result of heavy dependence on imported oil) had consistently outstripped the annual increases in prices for farm produce set in Brussels. Despite the sector's gains in productivity, therefore, gross income per farmer had declined significantly from 1974 to 1980 and net income per farmer (gross income minus debt liquidation) had declined even more. While other French socioeconomic sectors had also been affected by the oil crisis and the Giscard-Barre austerity program, the average French citizen had not suffered as much as the typical farmer. From 1975 to 1980 the purchasing power of the former had increased by an average of 0.4 percent per year, while that of the latter had fallen by 1.2 percent annually.[7] If this decline in income was troublesome for most farmers, it was—as the Socialists pointed out—often catastrophic for relatively small farmers working on slim financial margins. The rural exodus, which had reduced the percentage of the active population engaged in agriculture from 20 percent in 1962 to 8 percent in 1978, thus continued to claim about 3 percent of the farm population annually during the final years of Giscard's tenure, despite increasing unemployment in the industrial sector.[8]

It was bleak statistics such as these which motivated the Socialist Party (PS) to organize, in late February 1981, a National Convention on Agriculture devoted to condemnation of Center-Right policy and the presentation—by presidential candidate François Mitterrand—of a comprehensive reform program intended to assure agricultural "recovery" and the promotion of "family farming." Pierre Joxe, a PS expert on agriculture, argued that the problems—income decline, inequality and the consequent rural exodus—created by the current majority were "so enormous that even the most rapidly applied measures will take time to reverse the tendency." However, he pledged, the PS would go so far as to commit itself to a policy of "no longer losing a single active farmer."[9]

Achieving the Socialists' goals, Mitterrand acknowledged, would require a wide-ranging reform effort at home in combination with a reorientation of EEC policy in Brussels. Among the dozen measures which he proposed for internal reform, none stood out as departures from the party line presented during the 1979–80 debates over Giscard's agricultural orientation law (and many could be traced back to the 1972 *programme commun*).[10] Mitterrand's restatement of these ideas was viewed as politically important, however, for it seemed to signal a

serious commitment to agricultural reform on the part of both the PS
and its presidential candidate, neither of which was commonly perceived as placing a high priority on the affairs of this sector.

The most important and controversial planks of the reform program promised by Mitterrand were those calling for the creation of
offices par produits and *offices fonciers,* agencies inspired by the *office du
blé* which had been established by Léon Blum's Popular Front government in the 1930s.[11] The *offices par produits* (produce offices), which
would replace the privately managed *interprofessions* developed over
the years with state support by the FNSEA and other agricultural
organizations, were to be charged with organizing the produce markets (and possibly controlling imports) so as to guarantee a minimum
income for small farmers. The precise mode in which these offices
would operate was not stipulated, but Mitterrand stated that the modest minimum income was to be guaranteed by providing farmers with
"assured" (and relatively high) prices for a *quantum* (fixed proportion)
of their produce; beyond the *quantum,* prices would continue to be
determined by the free play of the market within limits imposed by
the EEC. To those who argued that the *offices par produits* would
contravene EEC regulations, Mitterrand and the Socialists offered a
dual response. On the one hand, they argued, the offices would be
tolerated as representing a national adjustment of European policy
no more problematic than others which had been approved in the
past. On the other, they pledged to fight for the institution of a
European offices system modeled after that to be created at the national level.

The *offices fonciers* (land offices), which would replace or possibly
supplement the SAFERs, were to be granted new powers to control
land speculation (and hence prices) and maximize the ability of marginal farmers to acquire the increments of land desperately needed to
render their operations viable. The specific powers to be accorded
these new *offices fonciers* were not enumerated by Mitterrand, but he
did highlight a structural difference between them and the traditional
SAFERs. While the SAFERs operated at the regional level under the
control of farmers delegated by the FNSEA and the other officially
recognized organizations of the profession, the offices were to function at the departmental and cantonal levels and were to be controlled
by farmers chosen through direct (sectoral) elections. Critics had long
charged that such offices would be far more subject to local pressure
than the SAFERs had been and would only serve to distribute land in
a politicized and inefficient manner. For the Socialists, however, the
offices fonciers seemed to represent progress toward a rural form of

autogestion. "We are not afraid," proclaimed PS spokesman Bernard Thareau at the 1981 Convention, "of a real local democracy."[12]

At the European level, aside from promising to push for adoption of the *offices par produits* scheme, Mitterrand pledged to abandon what he characterized as Giscard's policy of "submission . . . to the pretentions of Madame Thatcher" and pursue a hard line in Common Agricultural Policy negotiations. This would involve, first of all, "mobilizing opinion so that the French government could hold out against its European partners" and obtain a general price increase of 15 percent, "without which our agriculture would be drained of its substance." Second, it would mean demanding that "the Treaty of Rome be strictly applied." Efforts by Britain and others to scuttle the CAP would thus not be tolerated, argued Mitterrand, and the "play of influences . . . outside the Community"—that is, the United States, which had pressured Brussels to decrease its protectionism—would be combated.[13] No effort was made by Mitterrand or other participants at the 1981 Convention to explain precisely how such results were to be sought or to assess how a Socialist government could realistically be expected to bring home better deals from Brussels than the Giscardians had delivered.

While the Socialists thus challenged the fundamental principles of Center-Right agricultural policy at the convention of February 1981, they refrained from issuing an explicit call for dismantlement of the symbiotic FNSEA-state relationship upon which that policy had in large part been predicated. Nevertheless, a curtailment of the FNSEA's privileged status was implicit in the plans for both the *offices par produits* and the *offices fonciers.* Moreover, a number of Socialist spokesmen at the convention manifested sufficient animosity toward the FNSEA to leave little doubt that the Federation would fare poorly under a government of the Left. Bernard Thareau denounced FNSEA President François Guillaume for presenting his rank and file with a distorted view of the Socialists' program, especially the *offices par produits;* Guillaume favored retention of the present price-setting system, proclaimed Thareau, "because it perpetuates inequalities." Pierre Joxe went so far as to level personal attacks at the FNSEA's leaders, using words such as "braggart," "liar" and "trickster" to describe Guillaume and his predecessor, Michel Debatisse. It was curious, Joxe argued, that the FNSEA could presume to portray itself as an "apolitical" organization while its immediate past president was enjoying a post in the government and its current president was scarcely concealing his support for Jacques Chirac's presidential campaign. As will be shown below, this vitriolic verbal sparring of February 1981 was but a foreshadowing of the hostility which would characterize relations between the Socialists and the FNSEA after the elections of May–June.

Despite the Socialists' rhetorical commitment to reform, it seemed plausible to assume, even as François Mitterrand was moving into the Elysée Palace in May 1981, that the new president and his government might well opt for a policy of continuity in the agricultural sector. After all, the Socialists' highest priorities focused on other areas such as nationalization, industrial relations and decentralization. The financial and political costs of pushing ahead with reform projects in those key spheres would surely be considerable, one could reason, so perhaps discretion would prove to be the better part of ideological valor in the agricultural sphere. Such logic seemed all the more seductive when one added the fact that only a third of the farmers had cast their ballots for Mitterrand. To obviate a potentially disruptive political confrontation, what was needed at the Ministry of Agriculture was an experienced and politically deft administrator familiar with the agricultural dossier.

Once Mitterrand unveiled his cabinet it became clear that he had rejected the logic of caution in favor of an effort to fulfill his principal reform promises, even at the expense of confrontaton: his choice for Minister of Agriculture was Edith Cresson, in many ways the antithesis of the sort of politically "safe" minister described above. Cresson was not only the first woman in French history to be appointed Minister of Agriculture, reason enough for eyebrows to be raised in the countryside, but was also the kind of woman guaranteed to generate a negative response from the traditionalistic agricultural community: a very attractive feminist with a taste for brightly colored clothes and jewelry which one magazine described as "extravagant."[14] Throughout her 22 months in the agricultural post she would consistently ignore her associates' advice to tone down her flashy Parisian image, dismissing her critics—many of whom referred to her with such sobriquets as "the *parfumée*"—as "prehistoric animals." When a *Paris-Match* survey of January 1983 showed that Cresson was one of the 20 women (and the only politician) with whom French men would most like to have an affair, one could only wonder how many disgruntled farmers had cited her as a barbed political statement.[15] Setting aside the issue of her sex, other more important characteristics of Cresson made probable the development of tense relations with the leaders of the FNSEA and other established interlocutors. As one observer noted, her air of assurance and her "brutal candor" sometimes gave "her initiatives the appearance of a provocation."[16] And most significant of all, she was among the least experienced of the ministers appointed by Mitterrand. Whereas virtually all of her colleagues had served for years in the National Assembly, the only elected posts which Cresson had held by the time of her appointment (at age 47) were those of mayor in a small town and deputy in the powerless European parliament.[17] Her experience in agricultural affairs consisted of having written a doctoral thesis on the problems of women in rural France and having often "visited farms and stables" while a mayor in rural Vienne.[18]

Cresson's rise to power was based primarily, as farmers' union leaders noted with some trepidation, on her work within the Socialist Party organization. Since 1975 she had been a member of PS *comité directeur,* and she had earned a reputation as "one of the species of militants always ready to relaunch the debate when the smoke and fatigue" had begun to wear on others.[19] Cresson took party doctrine seriously and as minister she could thus be expected to strive for the implementation of the party's ambitious reform proposals. In reflecting on why Mitterrand had selected Cresson for the agricultural ministry, the *Nouvel Observateur* (a journal close to the PS) speculated that he deemed it "necessary to have at this post a militant, pugnacious minister rather than an expert technician" because he calculated that "faced with the Socialists, the FNSEA would be certain to adopt an oppositional and political stance."[20] To help prepare her reform legislation and to assist in coping with expected FNSEA resistance, Cresson surrounded herself with a cabinet which was also strongly politicized. As one would expect, Cresson's chief associates in the National Assembly also shared her conviction that the reform effort was vital and her perception of the FNSEA as an obstacle. One of the Socialist deputies who would serve—after the June election—as a major ally of Cresson and a key player in the agricultural policymaking process (as *rapporteur* for the agricultural budget) was Yves Tavernier, a professor from the prestigious Institut d'Etudes Politiques de Paris, who had published numerous articles criticizing the agricultural policies of the Center-Right and debunking the FNSEA's claim to be the legitimate spokesman for the entire French agricultural community.

If the leaders of the FNSEA viewed the appointment of Cresson as a portent of trouble, they soon learned that their fears had been justified. In her first speech as Minister of Agriculture, Cresson alluded to the system of agricultural group-state relations which had developed over the past two decades and then issued what might be termed an anti-corporatist manifesto: "It is necessary," she proclaimed, "to end the confusion between the role of professional organizations and that of the state. The former must negotiate and

contest if they feel it necessary; the state must make the decisions."[21]
Within a few days it became clear that the FNSEA was not only to be
stripped of its "right" to co-manage the sector, but was also to lose its
status as the only officially recognized union representative for agriculture—a status which had reinforced FNSEA hegemony by providing "*le syndicalisme officiel*" with tangible benefits, including millions
of francs in subsidies and exclusive seats on scores of commissions, as
well as an aura of authority. Announcing that she was merely ac-
knowledging "the union pluralism which exists in reality," Cresson
terminated the FNSEA's traditional "monopoly" by according official
recognition to three additional unions: the Communist-dominated
Mouvement de Défense des Exploitants Familiaux (MODEF), which polls
had long shown to have the support of 15 to 20 percent of the
farmers; the *Fédération Française de l'Agriculture* (FFA), an extremely
conservative union (it had branded many of the *Center-Right's* reforms
as "socialist") which could claim to represent only about 5 percent of
the farm community; and the *Confédération Nationale Syndicale des
Travailleurs-Paysans* (CNSTP), an amalgamation of six socialist-
leaning movements which was created on June 4, 1981, the day after
Cresson's inaugural speech.

Understandably, the imposition of this "new pluralist order" was
viewed as an affront and a threat by the FNSEA. As will be discussed
later, Cresson's decision to launch this revolution in group-state relations was definitely one of the major factors which provoked the
FNSEA to instigate a wave of peasant protest some months afterward.
For this reason many analysts would retrospectively view Cresson's
termination of the FNSEA's *monopole* as an enormous political gaffe.
To interviewers who queried her on this point Cresson insisted that it
was no gaffe, but rather an important and carefully calculated step in
the Socialist effort to democratize French politics and enhance equity
in the agricultural sector. "It was necessary," she argued, "to open the
process of *concertation* to other professional organizations" which
could claim a following in the countryside.[22] The FNSEA's union rivals had a "right to live," and the Socialist government—unlike the old
regime of the Center-Right—could not be expected to "destroy union
rights, since it was we who invented them!"[23]

Within limits the logic of Cresson's argument was incontestable.
Surveys and professional elections had repeatedly shown that the
FFA and especially MODEF could claim to represent significant segments of the farm community. Governments of the Center-Right had
accorded official recognition to industrial trade unions of lesser importance, and their stubborn refusal to incorporate the FFA and
MODEF into the policymaking process had obviously been a political

gesture in favor of the FNSEA. In righting these wrongs through creation of her new pluralist order, however, Cresson took at least two steps which severely weakened her claim to be acting simply in the name of democratization. First, the granting of recognition to the CNSTP was a move as blatantly political as the Gaullists' and Giscardians' support of the FNSEA had been. The article of the *Code du Travail* which spells out criteria according to which an organization's claim to official recognition is to be evaluated by the state specifically cites "experience and length of service" as a factor to be considered— and yet the CNSTP, the socialist-oriented union, was recognized within hours of its creation. Second, soon after assuming her office, Cresson met with leaders of a dissident faction of the FNSEA— *Interpaysanne*—at the ministry, apparently to discuss the possibility of their splitting from the Federation to join the new CNSTP. This move was most certainly a gaffe for it enabled the FNSEA to score political points by portraying Cresson as less a devout democrat than a clumsy machiavellian. "A government should not attempt to encourage division within a union organization," fumed FNSEA President Guillaume at a press conference, ". . . that is not democracy."[24] *Le Monde,* which generally manifests much more sympathy for the Socialist government than for the FNSEA, tartly criticized Cresson's action as an infringement on the union rights which she had pledged to protect and expand:

> Imagine how M. Seguy would react if the Minister of Labor were to receive a group representing a minority within the CGT. One would instantly hear something like "an intolerable intervention into the affairs of a democratic organization." Why should something which would be unthinkable for an industrial trade union not be for a farmers' union?[25]

What the *Interpaysanne* affair and the premature recognition of the CNSTP made patent was that Cresson and her associates were eager to use the levers at their command to alter the balance of syndical power in the agricultural sector and thereby create conditions conducive to the achievement of their policy goals. During the Gaullist-Giscardian era, efforts to create a farmers' union allied with the PS had failed repeatedly in the face of sectarian divisions within the socialist movement and predictable hostility on the part of the FNSEA (and its governmental patrons) as well as MODEF, which claimed to represent all leftist farmers.[26] With the PS ensconced in power, however, it now seemed feasible and politically expedient to foster development of a socialist "transmission belt" in the countryside. To assure the success of this venture and to maximize the prospects for

reform, it appeared vital to abrogate the *droits acquis* of the FNSEA.
Maintaining the traditional co-management system would probably
be counterproductive in policy terms, for the FNSEA could be expected to oppose the Socialists' initiatives at the legislative stage and to
distort them at the implementation stage. Furthermore, allowing the
FNSEA to retain its traditional status and privileges would be counterproductive in political terms, as the Federation could exploit these
resources to rally agricultural opponents of the Socialist government.
From the perspective of Cresson, therefore, imposition of the new
pluralist order thus seemed to be an indispensable first step toward
launching the drive for agricultural reform.

During the first six months of socialist government, while Mitterrand enjoyed what he termed his "*état de grâce*," Cresson and other
government spokesmen worked to appease the FNSEA and its allies
by stressing that their effort to fashion a "more equitable" agricultural
policy would not exclude measures intended to benefit all farmers,
large as well as small. In regard to Brussels negotiations, for example,
Cresson emphasized that the government "intends to pursue a policy
of greater firmness in regard to its partners and the commission when
the fundamental interests of the producers appear to be threatened
. . . the era of bad compromises in Brussels has ended."[27] Mitterrand
played on this theme as well; a hard line was not difficult to sustain
during these months, as no major decisions were scheduled to be
made at the European level until 1982. Cresson and Mitterrand also
tried to convince the farm community that their campaign to reduce
sectoral inequalities would be accompanied by a continued effort to
improve agricultural productivity and that they were no less concerned than Giscard with furthering the *vocation exportatrice* of French
agriculture. In a speech redolent of the former president, Mitterrand
proclaimed that agriculture was "a determinant force for the assurance of national independence" and that France must be "a great
agricultural nation." To underscore the seriousness of his commitment to the "international vocation" of the sector, Mitterrand delivered this address at his political base in Nevers before an assemblage
of ambassadors, including those from the United States and the
Soviet Union.

Against this reassuring backdrop, however, the government
steadily if slowly began to implement the more controversial aspects
of what Mitterrand termed simply the "new agricultural policy." In
June, Cresson announced that the government would depart from
the tradition of providing "undifferentiated assistance" to farmers;
henceforth "selective assistance" would be the guiding principle of
special state credit programs, with aid reserved for those most in

need. The first program tailored in this fashion was unveiled in August, as Cresson instituted a plan to aid "farmers in difficulty." Credits were to be distributed selectively, on a case by case basis, with state bureaucrats at the department level making the final allocation decisions. In line with the government's policy of pluralism, moreover, the FNSEA was not allotted an official role in the administration of the program.

More important initiatives were introduced, in accord with custom, at the sessions of the Annual Conference on agricultural policy held in October and December.[28] It was at these meetings that the FNSEA was forced most painfully to come to grips with its newly downgraded status. Policy departures were not prepared in *groupes de travail* composed of FNSEA and state officials, as in the past, but instead were drafted solely by bureaucrats of the ministry after brief consultations with all of the competing farmers' unions. At the formal meetings with the Prime Minister and the Minister of Agriculture, moreover, the FNSEA's input was limited in an unprecedented manner by the participation of representatives from the CNSTP, MODEF, FFA as well as the unions of agricultural employees. Whereas the government portrayed this new policymaking process as an enlargement of *concertation,* Guillaume dismissed the October meeting as "a succession of monologues" and announced to the press after the December session that *"concertation* no longer exists at all."[29]

While the new policymaking process generated discontent on the part of the FNSEA, the reforms discussed at the Annual Conference meetings provoked even more tension. At the October session Cresson announced that the government fully intended to go forward with its plan to create *offices par produits* and *offices fonciers.* The ministry was currently in the process of preparing bills for each of these agencies, said the minister, and they would be ready for delivery to the National Assembly by the spring of 1982. However much it may have been anticipated, this news was a blow for the FNSEA. The Federation had staunchly opposed both reform schemes and had fought especially hard to convince the government that the produce offices would be bureaucratically unwieldy in their operation and economically deleterious in their impact.

The *coup de grâce* was delivered at the final session on December 8, when Prime Minister Pierre Mauroy presented the government's plan to compensate the farmers for the estimated 3.1 percent (9 billion franc) fall in income which the agricultural sector had suffered in 1981, the eighth consecutive year (by most measures) of income decline. Mauroy's compensation package totaled 5.5 billion francs, 4 billion of which would aid the farmers indirectly in the form of increased budgets for various "economic" and "structural" programs administered by the Ministry of Agriculture. The other 1.5 billion francs were to be paid out directly to the farmers according to a formula which, in reflecting the government's commitment to "selective assistance," departed dramatically from traditional practice. Unlike the Giscardians, who in 1980 had distributed income support checks to all farmers in amounts proportionate to their turnover (*chiffres d'affaires,* or c.a.), the Socialists proposed to provide "national solidarity" assistance only to those most in need and to allocate the money in inverse relation to turnover: 3000 francs for each farm with a c.a. below 50,000 francs; 2500 for each farm with a c.a. of 50,000 to 100,000; 2000 for each farm with a c.a. of 100,000 to 250,000; nothing for those with a c.a. higher than 250,000. "I am not saying that [those who are to receive no direct support] are privileged," said Mauroy, "but we must reserve our credits for the most modest, those who are struggling on their farms, [so as to avoid] the continuation of the rural exodus and the concentration of enterprises."[30]

For the FNSEA, already profoundly disturbed by the processes and policies of the Socialist government, this income support plan seemed to provide proof positive that "social justice" as conceived by the new regime "rapidly finds its limits in the world of the peasantry."[31] The Federation condemned every aspect of the Mauroy plan: the amount of funds allocated for the total package, which represented compensation for only a little more than half of the 9 billion franc decline in income; the mode of financing the package, which entailed—in an unprecedented move—employment of 2.7 billion francs drawn from the capital surpluses of the farmers' cooperative bank, the *Crédit Agricole* (only slightly more than half of the total package was thus to be funded by the state budget); and the mode of distribution, which left more than one-third of the full-time farmers without any direct income support assistance.

To the government's consternation, even the farmers' unions of the Left—whose participation in the Annual Conference had been expected to counterbalance the ineluctable opposition of the FNSEA—reacted in an essentially negative fashion. "The orientations are good," proclaimed Bernard Lambert of the CNSTP, "but the volume of social assistance is insufficient. Before, one had either a scooter or a Rolls; today, one [who receives aid] is starting off again on a scooter." As Lambert and other critics noted, the fact that checks were to be allocated on a per farm rather than per capita basis meant that the actual amount received by the typical farmer in the poorest category would only be 1500 francs, for generally husbands and wives both worked on most farms. Even with the government's assistance check, therefore, most family farmers would still suffer a decline in income for 1981. This appeared to be a grave injustice in light of the fact that the government had recently announced a 21.3 percent increase in the minimum wage. Moreover, as the FNSEA's rivals on the Left noted dolefully, it seemed to substantiate the FNSEA's claim that the socialist government was interested only in "*ouvriérisme*" and simply did not care much about the plight of the farmers. The Socialists' *état de grâce* was now about to end in the agricultural sphere: the stage had been set for a full-fledged peasant revolt.

Revolt: The FNSEA and the "Hot Winter" of 1981–82

As a spokesman for MODEF lamented at the conclusion of the Annual Conference, the government's provision of only meager assistance to the small and medium-sized farmers was a "political and psychological mistake," for it seemed certain to "push them to rejoin *les gros*"—the relatively prosperous farmers controlling the FNSEA. This mistake was compounded when, to the embarrassment of the CNSTP and MODEF, Mauroy and Cresson sought to portray the FNSEA as the only farmers' union truly opposed to their initiative. What the government's spokesmen did not seem to realize, commented a reporter for *Le Monde,* was that their castigation of the Federation for its hostility toward an unpopular program would merely "reinforce the power of the FNSEA" and "facilitate the unity of action against [the government] *sur le terrain* . . . the government is going to propel the farmers out onto the streets and into the courtyards of the prefectures."[32]

"*L'hiver sera chaud!*"—this was the warning shouted out by a mob of 3,000 angry farmers who engaged in a bloody confrontation with riot police backed by armored vehicles outside the regional prefecture of Strasbourg on December 11, three days after the conclusion of the Annual Conference. The winter did indeed prove to be hot, as a wave of demonstrations rocked the French countryside from Alsace to Brittany and from the Ardennes to the Spanish border. Not since 1961 had such an extensive and violent outpouring of anger been witnessed in the agricultural sector.[33] With encouragement from François Guillaume and other national leaders, virtually all of the FNSEA's departmental branches organized local protest actions at some point from December to February, with other farmers' unions often joining in the fray. Groups of farmers ranging from a few hundred to several thousand paraded through the provincial capitals waving placards and shouting anti-government slogans. Everything from rocks to manure was hurled at the prefectures, which mobs sometimes attempted to occupy, only to be repulsed by the tear-gas and clubs of the police. Windows were broken, official cars were overturned and countless highways were blocked by tractors. In a widely publicized incident near Perpignan, farmers ripped up 800 meters of railroad track—causing damage estimated at a million francs—and deposited several dozen meters of track at the main entrance to the prefecture. Although no deaths were reported, scores of protesters and police were injured in violent encounters all across the country.

Faced with what the press was beginning to term "*la révolte des paysans*," Edith Cresson felt compelled to proclaim that "the government does not want war." The demonstrations had been provoked not by the government, she argued, but rather by "the policy of disinformation now being used for political purposes by a handful of FNSEA militants."[34] As the Socialists' weekly paper later reported, some of Cresson's advisors actually feared that the FNSEA was striving to emulate the truckers' union which had succeeded in destabilizing Allende's socialist regime in Chile during the early 1970s. Meanwhile the administrative council of the FNSEA issued a communique which restated the union's grievances against the government, voiced approval of the manifestations organized "to express [the] profound disappointment" of the farmers, and denounced "police provocations . . . which constitute a regrettable incitation to a chain of violence."[35]

As the "*manifs*" continued, week after week, it became clear to the government that steps would have to be taken to defuse the crisis and move toward a rapprochement with the FNSEA. The seemingly interminable rural disturbances, which received a great deal of media coverage, were beginning to tarnish the image of the regime and to embolden its opponents at a time when debates over other issues—including nationalization and implementation of the 39-hour week—were reaching a very sensitive stage. On January 20, Cresson announced a shuffling of her ministerial cabinet, a move widely viewed as a gesture of appeasement. At the same time she reiterated the government's hard line on EEC negotiations and appealed to the FNSEA to "work hand in hand" with her in preparing for the Brussels price talks due to begin near the end of the month. When the response to these overtures proved to be disappointing, President Mitterrand decided to intervene personally. In late January it was announced that the President would meet privately with the FNSEA's Guillaume on February 2 in an effort to "dissipate the peasant malaise" and establish the bases for group-state dialogue.

Only hours before Mitterrand was scheduled to receive Guillaume on February 2, the peasant revolt reached a symbolic climax.

On a visit to a farm in Calvados, Edith Cresson found herself surrounded by 1,200 protesters, many of them women, who pelted her
with eggs and insults. As the mob became ever more frenzied and
made it impossible for her to leave by limousine, she was forced to
escape by running across a meadow with her outnumbered guards
and leaping into a helicopter summoned by the anxious *gendarmes
mobiles.* Since television cameras were present, dramatic scenes of the
disheveled and mud-splattered minister fleeing from "her" farmers
were broadcast into millions of homes, providing what to many
seemed a vivid illustration of the Socialists' fading popularity and
faltering capacity to govern.[36] No one could remember when a Minister of Agriculture had been treated more rudely, although Cresson
tried to downplay the incident by insisting that her reception had
actually been worse a few days before in Poitiers (the major city of her
political base, Vienne), where she had suffered "an extremely violent
blow to the back and another behind the head."[37] Cresson and her
supporters charged that the assault in Calvados had been carefully
planned by the FNSEA to strengthen Guillaume's hand in his discussions with Mitterrand and, more pointedly, to demonstrate the need
for Cresson's dismissal. The FNSEA denied the charge, but it did
seem to be plausible. One thing at least was clear. As *Le Monde* commented, the helicopter incident served as a "spectacular symbol [of]
the divorce consummated between the government and the most
powerful of agricultural organizations."

While Guillaume and Mitterrand met on the afternoon of February 2, this "divorce" was at the top of the agenda. Two-thirds of their
hour-long discussion was reportedly devoted to the FNSEA's grievances over Cresson's policies, especially what Guillaume termed "systematic efforts to destabilize" his organization. Guillaume received no
promises of change from the president. Indeed he received the unwelcome news that Cresson would remain as Minister of Agriculture
and that a menacing reform of the Chamber of Agriculture's electoral
laws which she had proposed would be supported by Mitterrand.
Nevertheless, the tête-à-tête at the presidential palace did provide
Guillaume with some solace, and in retrospect it stands as a major
turning point in relations between the government and the FNSEA.
The FNSEA leader confided in an interview a few days later that
Mitterrand, unlike Cresson and other Socialists, seemed to have "a
real rural sensibility which could permit him to understand the problems of the peasant world. . . . He recognizes the importance of the
FNSEA. I think he understood that one cannot seek to weaken and
humiliate this union without consequences."[38] The wave of rural violence began to abate, and at the end of February a somewhat chas-

tened Cresson appeared—to the surprise of many—at the FNSEA's annual congress in Touquet to express the government's desire for renewed *concertation*. "The government is extending you its hand," she proclaimed, and "hopes to go beyond impassiond debate to employ the language of reason in dealing with the farmers."[39]

The drama of the 1981–82 peasant revolt was nearly over, but a denouement remained to be enacted. Despite the soothing words of Mitterrand and Cresson, the FNSEA continued to perceive the government as a threat to its organizational interests and its policy concerns. At the Touquet congress, therefore, the leaders of the Federation announced plans for what they hoped would be an eye-catching display of the FNSEA's power: 100,000 farmers were to be mobilized for a demonstration in Paris on March 23. Calling for such a manifestation entailed considerable risk on the part of Guillaume and his associates. Not since 1973 had as many as 40,000 farmers been assembled by the FNSEA, and never had such a massive peasant rally been staged in Paris. The logistical problems and the cost would be staggering. Moreover, there was always the possibility, especially given the experiences of the past few months, that the demonstration might lead to violent actions which would turn public opinion against the farm community. As *Le Monde* concluded, the FNSEA was making an "enormous bet."

In the eyes of virtually all observers the bet was won. Thousands of FNSEA activists began to pour into Paris by car and train beginning a few days before the "historic event" was to take place. On the morning of the 23rd, FNSEA members stationed at all of the major subway stops distributed 200,000 copies of an eight-page pamphlet entitled *Paris, The Peasants are Coming to Meet You* to startled Parisians on their way to work. A few hours later the demonstrators—whose numbers were estimated at between 60,000 and 100,000—brought traffic to a halt as they marched behind 30 tractors along the three-mile route from the Place de la Nation to the Porte de Pantin, where they gathered to hear speeches by FNSEA spokesmen. Throughout the day a special FNSEA security service composed of 5,000 union members managed to prevent any violent disturbances of note. All in all the events were remarkable enough not only to make front-page news all across France, but even to receive extensive coverage in the *New York Times* and a mention in the evening news programs on American television. As the FNSEA's leaders proclaimed, they had succeeded in delivering a "solemn warning" to the government of what could be expected if the Federation's demands were ignored and if the "governmental projects marked more by the stamp of doctrine than by realism" were not reconsidered.[40]

Retrenchment: Moderating the Reform Campaign

Not long after the FNSEA's stunning show of force, Edith Cresson felt compelled to pledge that reforms "will not be imposed against the will of the farmers."[41] The winter of peasant discontent thus served as a powerful brake on the government's drive for agricultural reform. It should be noted, however, that political resistence from within the agricultural sector was not the only factor which forced the government to opt for "realism" over "doctrine" at this juncture. By April 1982 the general "economic indicators were no longer at orange— they were scarlet." The inflation rate was rising rapidly, pressure was building for a second devaluation of the franc, the budget deficit for 1982 was projected to be almost a third higher than it had been in 1981, and the trade deficit was edging toward record levels. On April 16, the government thus initiated a "second phase of change" in the industrial sector, and two months later it was forced to go even further, imposing a general austerity program.[42] In this context the Socialists' enthusiasm for potentially costly agricultural reforms waned significantly. From the spring of 1982 through the end of Cresson's tenure in March 1983, economic as well as political constraints thus combined to produce an era of retrenchment. The difficulties faced by the government during this period can perhaps best be illustrated through an examination of the fate of what were to have been the twin pillars of the new Socialist agricultural policy: the *offices fonciers* and the *offices par produits*.

THE OFFICES FONCIERS

When the Socialists assumed power in 1981, it was expected that they would make reform of the traditional farmland management system one of their highest priorities within the agricultural sphere. Party spokesman had long argued that the land management agencies—the SAFERs—established by the Gaullists in the early 1960s were seriously flawed and should be replaced by the *offices fonciers*, agencies which would transform land from an "object of speculation" into an "instrument of labor" available to those "producers who have the most need of it."[43] The *offices* were to be governed in a more "democratic" and decentralized manner than the SAFERs had been. Moreover, the *offices* were to be accorded far greater control of the land market than the SAFERs had been allowed to exercise. While a narrowly defined "right of preemption" and a limited budget had prevented the SAFERs from purchasing more than 15 to 17 percent of the land placed on the market each year, the *offices* were to be armed with sufficient rights and funds to purchase much more of the available land. Furthermore, in allocating this land to needy farmers, the *offices* were to be empowered not only to sell parcels—as the SAFERs had done—but also to rent them, thus making it possible for young farmers without much capital to acquire viable farms.

It did not take the Socialist government long to realize that translating the abstract conception of *offices fonciers* into acceptable legislation would be a formidable task. Opposition to the scheme emerged on two fronts. Within the agricultural profession, the FNSEA and other organizations staunchly objected to both the mode of governance and the extended powers planned for the *offices*. Placing control of the *offices* in the hands of directly elected farmers would, they argued, not only politicize the land management process, but also generate tremendous personal conflicts. More importantly, granting the *offices* all of the powers desired by Socialist militants would undermine property rights and represent an intolerable step toward nationalization of France's farmland. "If you want to have an effective land policy," cautioned one FNSEA official, "be sure to consider what the farmers will accept and support."[44] Along with these objections from the farm community, proponents of the *offices fonciers* scheme also found themselves confronted by increasing skepticism within the government. Some officials were reluctant to risk conflict over the sensitive property rights issue and were also wary of the expense which the *offices* venture might entail.

Faced with these political and economic complications, the Ministry of Agriculture produced a draft bill for the *offices fonciers* in February 1982—one week after Cresson's helicopter incident—which was, in the words of *Le Monde,* "more moderate than anticipated." The bill called for the creation of *offices* at the departmental and cantonal levels, but it accorded them powers which were far more limited than originally planned: the cantonal *offices* were to play only an advisory role, and their departmental counterparts were to be given control only over the allocation of land. The crucial functions of land acquisition and management were to be left in the hands of the SAFERs, whose boards of directors would be only moderately "democratized." Several crucial questions, including the degree to which the SAFERs' "right of preemption" was to be extended, were left to be dealt with at a later date.

Since the spring of 1982, the handling of the *offices fonciers* bill has amounted to a veritable comedy of indecision. Buffeted by contradictory protests from the Left and the Right, and confronted with a worsening economic crisis, the government has repeatedly proven incapable of deciding how to formulate the bill's many controversial and complex elements. A polished version of the bill was initially scheduled to be deposited with the National Assembly by April 1982, but in May farm leaders were complaining that "no one knows where, in which ministry, the bill can be found."[45] Edith Cresson announced publicly in June that the bill was "practically ready." Six months later, in November, Cresson assured the legislators that the bill would be in their hands "before the end of December." In the middle of that month, however, Cresson was forced to confess to impatient militants that the bill continued to be "stuck" somewhere in the governmental machinery. By March 1983, when Mitterrand's cabinet shakeup removed Cresson from the Ministry of Agriculture, the bill had still not materialized. As *Le Monde* commented on that occasion, the *offices fonciers* were *"les grands absents* of these 22 months."[46] It remains to be seen when, and in what form, this crucial pillar of the Socialists' agricultural policy will be put in place.

THE OFFICES PAR PRODUITS

The government did manage to establish the other pillar of Socialist agricultural policy during Cresson's tenure, but it was a rather wobbly pillar bearing little resemblance to that which had been promised by the PS during the 1981 election campaign. As Cresson herself acknowledged, the *offices par produits* legislation sponsored by the government failed to incorporate many of the most important propositions of the *project socialiste*. What it represented, she argued, was an effort to go "the farthest possible" given the political opposition of the farm community and the constraints posed by the EEC's Common Agricultural Policy.

Seventeen different versions of the *offices* bill were considered by the government from the fall of 1981 through June 1982, when a *project de loi* was finally presented to the National Assembly. At each crucial step along the way, with the clamor of demonstrating farmers and the concern of EEC partners increasing, the successive drafts of the *offices* bill diverged further from the model conceived by Socialist militants. The most ardent proponents of the produce agencies were gravely disappointed as early as March 1982, for the text of the initial draft bill then made public included no references to the *quantum* or the possibility of controlling imports and proposed no mechanism for assuring a guaranteed minimum income. Only the preamble of the bill retained a semblance of the radical tone prevalent a few months before, and the vague promises therein presented were accompanied by an extremely important caveat: "To the extent that European regulations will permit it, [the *offices*] will guarantee to agricultural producers the prices paid for their produce within the limits of a certain volume of production and they will participate in the implementation of a modulation of subsidies . . . and taxes."[47] With this clause the government made clear, to the dismay of the extreme Left, that it did not intend to push forward with a national reform which might jeopardize the status of the Common Agricultural Policy. However objectionable the "liberal-capitalist" CAP might be, with its restrictions on national pricing policy and its requirement that imports from other EEC countries not be obstructed, it was impossible for the goverment to ignore the fact that the CAP continued to provide France with a net budgetary gain of millions of francs per year—indeed, a larger gain than that received by any other EEC member.[48] In the absence of a sweeping reform of the CAP, which the government promised to fight for but which no one could reasonably expect, the *offices* would thus not be allowed to pursue the most ambitious goals which had once been envisioned for them.

Before the draft *offices* bill was presented for approval by the Council of Ministers on June 2, the government retreated still further from its original reform scheme. Under pressure from the conservative farm organizations, President Mitterrand personally intervened to edit some of the bill's more controversial passage. "I have looked over this text," he confided to a group of farm leaders, "and I have crossed out everything that could be considered as statist." In the process Mitterrand produced what the FNSEA termed "some definite improvements"—modifications which a spokesman for the leftist farmers condemned as having "expurgated [the bill] of all of its content."[49] What the *toilletage* of Mitterrand accomplished, for the most part, was to assure that the private *interprofessions* (organizations controlled and financed by the farmers which strive to organize producers, regulate deliveries of produce to the market and promote consumption) developed over the years would continue to play an important role rather than being supplanted by the *offices*. Whereas the March draft had stipulated that the *offices* (whose boards were to include only a minority of farmers, with a president and director appointed by state decree) were "to organize the producers" and "to organize relations among the diverse professions" concerned with the various types of produce, the June draft reduced the role of the *offices* to "encouraging" such activities. Where the *interprofessions* were deemed to be playing an effective role, it was implied, the intervention of the *offices* would be minimal. Most importantly, the June draft explicitly downgraded the degree to which the *offices* could exercise administrative supervision over the *interprofessions*. While the March draft had said that the *interprofessions* would be required to submit their annual budgets and programs to the *offices* for approval, the draft edited by Mitterrand stated that the *offices* were simply to be "consulted each year" on such matters. As it had done in the case of the abortive *offices fonciers* bill, the government thus opted for a significant measure of continuity in formulating the *offices par produits* legislation; like the SAFERs, the *interprofessions*—which some viewed as being "undemocratically" controlled by the forces of the FNSEA— were to retain a good deal of their traditional influence.

The *offices par produits* bill which the government pushed through the National Assembly from June 29 to July 1 was thus a disappointment (an "empty shell") to many on the Left and, in most respects, a relief to the Right. As Edith Cresson acknowledged to the deputies, the government had sought to "make a tabula rasa neither of the past, nor of international commitments, nor of the organizations created by the farmers themselves."[50] When promulgated on October 6, the *offices* law created not a mechanism to assure a guaranteed minimum income for the farmers, but merely a set of agencies which would enable the state to play a somewhat increased role in organizing agricultural produce markets, especially those (such as the one for low-grade wine) which had not been effectively regulated by an *interprofession* committee. The FNSEA, which only months before had been gravely concerned that the government might impose a system of *"offices à la mode de 1936,"* could find little in the bill that was threateneing except for the mildly radical wording of the preamble and numerous ambiguities regarding the way in which the *"couple interprofessions-offices"* was to function once all of the implementing decrees had been issued.

OTHER REFORMS

If retreat and retrenchment characterized the government's handling of the two crucial *offices* initiatives during 1982, a similarly cautious style was manifested in regard to other programs as well. A reform of the complex agricultural taxation system, which assumed greater significance as a means of reducing sectoral inequalities once the *offices par produits* bill had been watered down, was originally scheduled to be sent to parliament in 1982, but was eventually shoved onto the back burner. Reports indicated that Cresson wished to move quickly on tax reform, but encountered resistance (as did many other ambitious ministers) from the Ministry of Economy and Finance. The budget managers, who were already experiencing enough difficulty in trying to cope with the economic crisis, argued that it was "urgent" to delay the tax reform after their computer simulations revealed that it would produce less revenue than the old system.

The government also moved more slowly and moderately than expected in implementing the reform of interest group-state relations which Cresson had initially promised. The FNSEA repeatedly complained about the government's unwillingness to respect its traditional status; officials at the Ministry of Agriculture did work much less intimately with the Federation than had their counterparts of the Center-Right era, and the government did institute an important reform of the electoral laws for the Chambers of Agriculture (replacing the old plurality system with a proportional system) designed to reduce the FNSEA's influence.[51] However, impatient rival unions such as the MODEF and the CNSTP protested that not enough was being done to further the new pluralist order, and they charged that—in the wake of the "hot winter"—the government seemed to be increasingly reluctant to alienate the FNSEA. As evidence they noted that the government had (1) granted the FNSEA a disproportionate (if reduced) percentage of state subsidies intended to further union activities; (2) accorded the FNSEA privileged access to top government officials (unlike the FNSEA, no rival union was treated to an audience with President Mitterrand or to the presence of the Minister of Agriculture at annual conventions); and (3) instituted a last-minute change favorable to the FNSEA in the reform of electoral regulations for the Chambers of Agriculture. Most of the critics' venom was directed not at Cresson, who was viewed as sincerely committed to weakening the FNSEA, but rather at Mitterrand, who was alleged to have blocked her initiatives on several occasions.

The critics' perception may indeed have been accurate, but it is probable that even Cresson gradually lost some of her enthusiasm for the new pluralist order venture, for two reasons. First, the FNSEA proved to be far more resilient than expected and showed that it possessed the means to plague a government intent on abrogating its *droits acquis.* Second, the effort to create a socialist "transmission belt" within the agricultural sector produced very discouraging results. From June 1981 through the spring of 1982, the CNSTP managed to enlist only a few thousand supporters, suffered from sectarian divisions and grew increasingly hostile to the government as more and more Socialist campaign promises were broken. By April 1982 it had become impossible for many farmers loyal to the PS to work effectively with the CNSTP majority. As a result some CNSTP dissidents joined with what had been the *Interpaysanne* faction of the FNSEA to launch a new leftist union: the FNSP *(Fédération Nationale des Syndicats Paysans)*.

When the first Chamber of Agriculture elections employing the new electoral law were held in January 1983, the failure of Cresson's campaign to weaken the FNSEA and bolster Socialist forces in the countryside was vividly illustrated. Although the number of Chamber seats held by the FNSEA declined from roughly 90 percent to 70 percent, the Federation retained a majority of seats in all but a handful of departments. Moreover, with a new-found popularity predicated on its staunch opposition to the Socialists' policies, the FNSEA actually increased its percentage of the vote (from about 65 percent to 70 percent) despite the fact that its rivals—backed for the first time by state subsidies and a sympathetic government—had been able to mount more extensive electoral campaigns than ever before. All of the Left-oriented unions combined received only 23 percent of the vote, with the CNSTP claiming a mere 6.0 percent, the FNSP 5.4 percent, and the MODEF 8.8 percent (a decline over previous years attributable mainly to competition from the new unions of the Left); the ultra-conservative FFA received 6.0 percent. With its hegemony clearly confirmed, the FNSEA—playing on Mitterrand's campaign slogan, "*la force tranquille*"—declared itself to be "*la force vive*" of the agricultural sector.[52]

INCOME AND THE EEC

It is probable that the 1983 Chamber elections would have produced even worse results for the Socialists had the farmers not benefited during 1982 from a reversal of the downward trend in income which had plagued the agricultural sector since 1974.[53] According to preliminary estimates released by the Ministry of Agriculture in November, gross agricultural income for 1982 rose by 2.9 percent; the average farmer's purchasing power, which had fallen by 14 percent in 1980 and another 5 percent in 1981, increased by 2.5 percent. Moreover, the inequality of income distribution within the sector was reduced somewhat during 1982, for the gross income of farmers with less than 20 hectares of land increased by an average of 4 to 6 percent, while that of farmers with more than 50 hectares declined by 1 percent.[54]

Edith Cresson reacted with understandable exultation to the publication of these statistics, citing them as evidence that "socialism is working in agriculture."[55] Given the meager progress which the government's reform effort had made even by the end of 1982, this assessment must be dismissed as ministerial hyperbole. Virtually all analysts agree that—as the farmers recognized—the single most important factor which generated the income upturn for 1982 was one over which the government had no control: the weather. Excellent weather produced abundant harvests for most crops (the volume of production, which had decreased for two consecutive years, increased by 2.7 percent in 1982), leading one farm official to quip that "the Good Lord has been with François Mitterrand."[56] Without the happy accident of bumper crops, no income improvement could have been achieved, for the average increase in produce prices for 1982 (11.2 percent) once again failed to keep pace with the increase in production costs (11.5 percent).[57]

It should be acknoweldged, however, that the government did deserve some credit for the positive income figures of 1982, for three reasons. First, the partial price freeze instituted in June 1982 helped (along with a decline in world oil prices) to limit the increase in production costs. Second the controversial income assistance program—intended to compensate for the income decline of 1981—which was implemented in 1982 contributed to the reduction of sectoral inequalities. Third, and most important, the EEC price hike which the government negotiated in May 1982 did represent an improvement over that of the previous year (11.2 percent compared with 10.3 percent), although it fell below the 15 percent figure which Mitterrand had once claimed to be necessary. As the Socialists had promised, the French government refused to yield to Margaret Thatcher's pressure. Indeed the French and six of their EEC partners used an unprecedented tactic to overcome British opposition: they pushed the 11.2 percent price increase through the Countil of Ministers with a "qualified majority" vote, thus departing from the EEC tradition (which, ironically, had been imposed by de Gaulle) of acting only by unanimous consent on important matters. This French-led coup left the British government in a state of "stunned disbelief" and, for once, earned Cresson at least some muffled applause from the farm community.[58]

Conclusion

This study of French agricultural policymaking since May 1981 has demonstrated what a difficult task it is to implement an ambitious reform program within a democratic political system, even one with a powerful executive backed by a large single-party majority in parliament. Unlike Guy Mollet's government of the 1950s or Léon Blum's government of the 1930s, the Mitterrand-Mauroy government of the

1980s has been able to embark on the path of agricultural reform unencumbered by fear of obstruction in either the National Assembly or the Senate. The lower house, which ousted Mollet and his reformist minister of agriculture only 16 months after they assumed power, has strongly supported the reform effort of the 1980s.[59] The upper house, which was a formidable obstacle for agricultural minister Georges Monnet during the Popular Front era, has posed no problem in the Mitterrand era, despite the fact that it is controlled by a Center-Right majority; when the Senate has attempted to block initiatives, as in the case of the *offices par produits* law, the government has simply bypassed it by invoking Article 45 of the Fifth Republic's constitution.[60]

Yet despite the absence of traditional legislative obstacles to reform, the government's achievements to date in the agricultural sector have been far from impressive. One of the two would-be "pillars" of the Socialist program, the *offices fonciers* network, has not yet been established; the other, the *offices par produits* system, has been implemented in such a watered-down fashion that it has been denounced by militants as an "empty shell." Some progress has been made toward reversing the decline of agricultural income and reducing sectoral inequalities, but this has been achieved largely through the conjunctural accident of an unusually abundant harvest. And as the 1983 Chamber of Agriculture elections showed, Edith Cresson's effort to alter the balance of union power within the sector has fallen far short of its goals. The influence of the FNSEA over the agricultural policy-making process has been somewhat reduced, and its privileges have been restricted in a way which might weaken it over time, but the Federation has gained popularity so far through its confrontations with the government. Meanwhile, the government's effort to exploit its power for the development of a socialist "transmission belt" in the countryside has met with problems reminiscent of those which frustrated a similar venture undertaken by Pierre Tanguy-Prigent, the Socialist minister of agriculture of the Liberation epoch.

As expected the agricultural reform effort of the Mitterrand era has floundered primarily because of the sort of constraints discussed in the introduction. Like socialist governments of the past, that of the 1980s has been forced to retreat from its original reform visions due to the political resistance of the farm community and the economic costs involved with translating campaign promises into actual programs. Unlike previous socialist governments, moreover, that of the 1980s has been forced to deal with a new constraint as well: the EEC's Common Agricultural Policy. During their years in opposition, the Socialists were able to condemn the Center-Right for its use of the

"Brussels alibi" and to pledge that, once in power, they would force the EEC partners to accept higher prices and agree to major reforms in France's favor. Since May 1981, however, the Socialists have learned just how perplexing the management of EEC relations can be. Some success has been achieved on the price front, but even the 1982 "victory" yielded lower prices than the government had promised to demand, and it was achieved through anti-British strong-arm tactics which could well prove politically impossible to use again. More importantly, no progress has been made toward convincing the EEC partners to accept the kind of reforms called for in the preamble to the *offices par produits* law.

After a brief flirtation with the path of disruptive change, the government has thus opted—or been forced to opt—for the path of problematic continuity. Even with a "pugnacious and militant" minister of agriculture, retreat and retrenchment could not be avoided. Now that Edith Cresson has been replaced by the more pragmatic Michel Rocard, it is probable that the next few years of the Mitterrand era will feature but a continuation of the era of retrenchment.

Notes

1. For statistics concerning the voting behavior of the various occupational groups during the 1981 elections, see Henry W. Ehrmann, *Politics in France* (Boston: Little, Brown, 1982), pp. 253 and 255.
2. Gordon Wright, *Rural Revolution in France* (Stanford, Cal.: Stanford University Press, 1964), pp. 136–140.
3. For descriptions and analyses of the Gaullist "charter" of the early 1960s, see John T. S. Keeler, "The Corporatist Dynamic of Agricultural Modernization in the Fifth Republic," in William G. Andrews and Stanley Hoffman, eds., *The Fifth Republic at Twenty* (Albany: State University of New York Press, 1981); Gaston Rimareix and Yves Tavernier, "L'Elaboration et le vote de la loi complémentaire à la loi d'orientation agricole," *Revue française de science politique* 13:2 (June 1963); Pierre Muller, *Grandeur et décadence du professeur d'agriculture: les transformations du système d'intervention de l'état en agriculture 1955–1965* (Grenoble: Institut d'études politiques de Grenobles, 1980); Wright, Chapter 8. SAFER is the acronym for *société d'aménagement foncier et d'établissement rural*, and SUAD for *service d'utilité agricole et de développement*.
4. John T. S. Keeler, "Corporatism and Official Union Hegemony: The Case of French Agricultural Syndicalism," in Suzanne Berger, ed., *Organizing Interests in Western Europe* (Cambridge: Cambridge University Press, 1981).
5. John T. S. Keeler, "Dreams of Green Oil, Nightmares of Inequality: French Agricultural Policy and the External Challenges of the 1980s," in Stephen S. Cohen and Peter A. Gourevitch, eds., *France in the Troubled World Economy* (Boston: Butterworths, 1982).
6. See *Le Monde*, September 18, 1981; *Graph-agri 80* (Paris: Ministère de

l'Agriculture, 1980), p. 41.

7. *L'Information agricole,* October 1982.
8. *Graph-agri-80,* pp. 25–27.
9. *Le Monde,* March 3, 1981.
10. Keeler, "Dreams of Green Oil," p. 106; *Programme commun de govrnement* (Paris: Flammarion, 1973), pp. 55–57; *Projet Socialiste* (Paris: Club Socialiste du Livre, 1980), pp. 204–208.
11. For a discussion of the *office du blé,* see Wright, pp. 60–65.
12. *Le Monde,* March 3, 1981.
13. For a discussion of tensions between the United States and the EEC over agricultural policy, see *L'Information agricole,* October 1982.
14. *Le Point,* April 12, 1982.
15. *Paris-Match,* January 28, 1983.
16. *Le Point,* April 12, 1982.
17. "Biographical Sketches: Second Cabinet of Pierre Mauroy, June 23, 1981" (Documents from France—Press and Information Service of the French Embassy); *Le Point,* April 12, 1982. Cresson was the mayor of Thuré (population 2500) from 1977 through 1983; in the 1983 municipal elections, she was elected mayor of Châtellerault (population 40,000). For an account of her victory in the 1983 election, see *Le Nouvel Observateur,* March 11, 1983.
18. *Paris-Match,* February 19, 1982.
19. *Le Point,* April 12, 1982.
20. *Le Nouvel Observateur,* January 30, 1982. Cresson's original cabinet is described in Monigue Dagnaud and Dominigue Mehl, *L'Elite rose* (Paris: Editions Ramsay, 1982), pp. 306–307.
21. *Le Monde,* June 5, 1981.
22. *Le Point,* April 12, 1982.
23. *Paris-Match,* February 19, 1982.
24. *Le Monde,* June 20, 1981.
25. *Le Monde,* February 2, 1982.
26. See Yves Tavernier, "Le Mouvement de défense des exploitants familiaux," in Tavernier et al., eds., *L'Univers politique des paysans dans la France contemporaine* (Paris: Colin, 1972).
27. *Le Monde,* June 5, and September 18, 1981.
28. For a description of the way in which the Annual Conference functioned during the Center-Right era, see Keeler, "Corporatism and Official Union Hegemony," p. 189.
29. *Le Monde,* November 1–2 and December 9, 1981; *L'Information agricole,* November 1981.
30. *Le Monde,* December 10, 1981.
31. *L'Information agricole,* December 1981.
32. *Le Monde,* December 10, 1981.
33. See Wright, pp. 167–169; Henri Mendras and Yves Tavernier, "Les Manifestations de juin 1961," *Revue française de science politique* 12:3 (September 1962).
34. *Le Monde,* December 17, 1981.
35. *Le Monde,* December 20–21, 1981.
36. *Le Point,* February 1982; *Le Monde,* February 4, 1982. Many newspapers unsympathetic to the government printed political cartoons mocking Cresson after the helicopter incident. One depicted her leaving the

Ministry of Agriculture in a suit of armor with an official in the background saying "have a nice trip in the countryside, Madame"; another blended sexism with sarcasm, showing a beaten and apparently raped Cresson explaining that "in fact it's my body which drives them crazy." *Le Crapouillot*, No. 67, 1982, p. 36.

37. *Paris-Match,* February 19, 1982.
38. *Le Monde,* February, 9, 1982.
39. *Le Monde,* February 27, 1982.
40. *Le Monde,* March 24, 1982; *L'Information agricole,* April 1982; *New York Times,* March 24, 1982; François Guillaume, *Le Pain de la liberté* (Paris: J.-C. Lattès, 1983), pp. 9–15.
41. *L'Information agricole,* June 1982.
42. Jean-Gabriel Fredet and Denis Pingaud, *Les Patrons face à la gauche* (Paris: Ramsay, 1982), pp. 61–66; *The Economist,* May 8, 1982.
43. *Programme commun,* p. 56.
44. *L'Information agricole,* March 1982; *Le Monde,* November 22–23, 1982.
45. *Le Monde,* May 20, 1982.
46. *Le Monde,* March 24, 1983.
47. *Le Monde,* June 29, 1982.
48. According to *The Economist* of March 6, 1982, France registered a gain of £259 million from the CAP budget system in 1981 and was thus—as it had long been—the CAP's principal beneficiary in absolute terms. For a brief description of the CAP, see *The Agricultural Policy of the European Community* (Brussels: European Documentation, 1979). See also Werner Feld, "Implementation of the European Community's Common Agricultural Policy: Expectations, Fears, Failures," *International Organization,* 33:4 (Summer 1979).
49. An extensive critique of the bill from the perspective of the FNSEA can be found in *L'Information agricole,* July–August 1982; for the views of disappointed Socialists, see *Le Monde,* June 29 and August 7, 1982.
50. *Le Monde,* July 1, 1982.
51. See *L'Information agricole* of November 1982 for a reprint of the decree (of August 3, 1982) which instituted this electoral reform and for an extensive critique of the reform by FNSEA officials; see also *Le Monde,* April 28, 1982.
52. The election results are discussed in *Le Monde,* January 30–31, 1983 and March 9, 1983; see also *L'Information agricole,* February 1983. As Jacques Grall's *Le Monde* article of January 30–31, 1983 explains, the "FNSEA" lists were presented in several different ways from department to department, thus manifesting the internal divisions of the Federation and complicating efforts to compute the exact percentage of the vote which should be attributed to it.
53. From 1974 to 1981, gross agricultural income increased only once (by a mere 0.3 percent in 1977) and net income declined every year. See *L'Information agricole,* December 1982.
54. *Le Monde,* November 26, 1982; *L'Information agricole,* December 1982.
55. *Le Monde,* November 16, 1982.
56. *Le Monde,* September 15, 1982.
57. *Le Monde,* November 26, 1982; *L'Information agricole,* December 1982.
58. *The Economist,* May 22, 1982.

59. For a discussion of agricultural reforms planned during the Mollet government, see Wright, pp. 136–139.
60. For a discussion of Monnet's battles with the Senate, see Wright, pp. 61–63; the Senate's futile attempt to water down the *offices* bill is discussed in *Le Monde,* September 24 and 25, 1982 and October 1, 2, 3 and 4, 1982.

4

Socialism and Social Security

GARY FREEMAN

After a hopeful beginning in which social benefits were sharply increased, the position of the least well-off was improved in the name of national solidarity, and structural reforms in social security finance and administration were promised, the socialist government of François Mitterrand adopted in June 1982 a policy of austerity painfully reminiscent of those of its conservative predecessors. The reasons for this mid-course correction seem evident enough: unemployment went up—not down—in the first year of the socialists' rule, investment stragnated, double-digit inflation persisted, the franc weakened, the balance of payments went alarmingly into the red, and the social insurance funds registered enormous short-term deficits. Critics of the government, and "realists" within the *Parti Socialiste* (PS) itself, drew the predictable conclusions: the government had erred in putting the cart of social reform before the horse of economic growth. Since the latter was not forthcoming, there was no alternative to sacrificing all but the most basic efforts toward increasing equality and solidarity.

This chapter reviews the social record of the Mitterrand government in its first 18 months. It will show that there have been real achievements, especially in increasing the generosity and equity of various social benefit programs and in opening up the policymaking

I would like to acknowledge a grant from the German Marshall Fund of the United States that allowed me to spend 1981–82 in France.

process. There has also been a serious attempt to fulfill campaign pledges that involved more fundamental or controversial modifications of existing policy. Many of the incremental improvements have now ground to a premature halt, however, and a number of substantive reforms have been significantly modified in the face of mounting economic and political problems. Moreover, promised structural changes in both the administrative apparatus and financial structure of social security have either been stymied or have never been launched.

A two-part explanation is offered here for the Socialists' very mixed social policy record. The first is that the social agenda of the new administration consisted of two relatively distinct and potentially contradictory parts. Many of the subsequent difficulties the government encountered can be traced to its failure to reconcile its initiatives to increase equality with its obligations to assure both that the system of social protection was financially sound and that its social policy reinforced rather than undermined its economic strategy. The *Parti Socialiste* did not deliberately seek social reform without regard to its economic consequences. On the contrary, its social policy goals, and especially its hopes of maintaining the solvency of the social insurance funds, were contingent on recovery. Everything was gambled on an early recovery *(relance)*. When it did not materialize, a good part of the Party's social program was left in a shambles.

Nevertheless, the deepening economic crisis was not the only problem. The second part of an explanation of the Socialists' difficulties relates to the unanticipated but profound lack of fit between the language of solidarity and *concertation* that animated the Party's thinking and the reality that much of its program would require reductions in the privileges of key components of its own constituency. The rhetoric of 1945 clashed with the reality of 1981. A large portion of the highly factionalized labor movement and important segments of the middle class would not readily accept "progressive" changes in social programs if these implied reductions in the benefits they already enjoyed. Nor had the government the stomach to impose such sacrifices. The stillbirth of the social *projet* was, therefore, as much the result of opposition from workers as from capitalists.

First to be examined is the nature of the social agenda in France in May 1981—to show the ambiguous position the Socialists occupied with respect to several of its major components, and to demonstrate how social policy proposals were linked to the government's more general strategy for ending the economic crisis. The origins of the social agenda are revealed by tracing the recent evolution of social policy in France and describing the financial disequilibrium of the social security system on the eve of the presidential election. This discussion will provide the historical and political context necessary to an evaluation of the socialist experience. After an analysis of the social program that formed the basis of the PS electoral campaign, the record of the government in its first year and a half will be assessed.

The Two Social Agendas and the Economic Crisis

There were essentially two social policy agendas confronting the new Socialist government in May 1981. The first, which will be referred to as the Type I agenda, included those issues that arose from the failures of France's vast system of social protection—its inadequacies, inequities and undemocratic features. These issues derived from defeats the advocates of a comprehensive and just social security system had suffered at several junctures since 1945. Promises to move swiftly to realize the unfulfilled ideals of the welfare state came easily to the Socialists both because they were consistent with the Left's legacy in the struggle for social security and because advances on this front were congenial to those least fortunate members of French society in whose behalf the PS claimed to be acting.

The second social policy agenda had less to do with equity and the rhetoric of national solidarity than with the more mundane but pressing issues of finances and deficits. Type II issues included the impact on employment and investment of rising payroll taxes, especially those on employers, the recurring threat of deficits in the various programs, and the escalating costs of the health care system. Type II issues had to do with the financial crisis of social policy and were the most salient and urgent problems from the point of view of business and government, at least those governments of the Fifth Republic that preceded the Socialists.

Obviously, the *Mitterrandistes* would have preferred to deal exclusively with Type I problems, as this was their natural turf. Indeed it seemed for a while as if the government would not only give priority to these matters but would try to ignore or deny the importance of Type II issues. Mme. Questiaux, the new Minister of National Solidarity, argued in the early days of the fledgling administration that the much-discussed deficits in the social security system were a figment of the Giscardian imagination. She persisted for a year in holding this view, a posture that eventually cost her her job.

The challenge for the government was to make headway on the Type I agenda while either ameliorating or at least not exacerbating Type II difficulties. Conversely, the government might have tried to tackle the financial and economic problems head-on in such a fashion as to advance toward Type I goals at the same time. Either strategy (and the government eventually explored both) had to be premised on the belief that the two sets of objectives—greater equity, solidarity and democracy on the one hand, and financial stability and reduced fiscal pressure on the other—were not necessarily incompatible.

Despite the hopes or fears of those who believed that Mitterrand would set French society on a radically new path of development, the economic policy his government adopted was little more than a species of retreaded social Keynesianism. This perspective sees expanded social benefits, modest income redistribution and policies designed to maintain full employment as means to increase the purchasing power of the working class and, therefore, enhance profitability and production. It holds out the hope, therefore, of allowing Left governments to avoid all manner of difficult structural issues. Social Keynesianism was a bold strategy only because it was so out of step with the thinking in other Western capitals at the time.[1]

Despite its obvious attractions to parties whose electoral appeal is based in the popular strata, social Keynesianism has a number of deficiencies as a social-economic doctrine for Left governments. For one thing, after more than 40 years of at least quasi-Keynesian economic policy in the West, many observers believe that the strategy has reached its limits. Such policies have created, or so the argument goes, a political economy of permanent inflation, systems of social entitlements that consume over a third of state budgets, deep and persistent deficits, and tax rates at or beyond the threshold of political acceptability. The latitude available for most governments to launch deficit-financed, Keynesian-style recovery policies is narrowing rapidly.

Secondly, in a highly interdependent world economy in deep recession, a single country has little chance of successfully pursuing an expansionary policy of reflation when all her principal trading partners are outdoing themselves with displays of fiscal austerity and restraint. To swim against the current in this way is to invite economic stagnation at best, disaster at worst. Expanded purchasing power may as easily result in a flood of imported goods (and a consequent balance of payments crisis) as in reinvigorated productive activity at home.

The Mitterrand government's economic policy was conceived in two stages: an initial period of old-fashioned expansionism in the traditional Keynesian mode, followed by sustained, non-inflationary growth founded on (1) a general international recovery, (2) state-directed investment through the nationalized industries and financial institutions, (3) state-sponsored research and development, and (4) other structural reforms such as decentralization and collective bargaining. The government's policy was not solely Keynesian in conception, but the effects of its reforms of French productive capacity would not be immediately evident.

The PS's social policy was consistent with its economic strategy. Early improvements in the living standards of the least well-off would help reflate the stagnant economy in phase one. Further improvements, however, would have to await the beneficial effects of phase two of the economic plan. The government could move forcefully ahead with those Type I reforms that entailed benefit increases because they would contribute to recovery. The recovery itself would help avert financial problems and allow the government to ignore, temporarily, the Type II agenda. Once recovery was underway, additional Type I reforms designed to enhance equity and democracy could be achieved and, having established its position, the government could begin to consider the fundamental changes in the financial structure of social security—changing the base of taxation, for example—that were its preferred approach to Type II issues.

ORIGINS OF THE TYPE I AGENDA

To appreciate fully the contradictory pressures the Socialists were under in 1981, it is necessary to understand both the achievements and the dashed hopes that the Left had experienced during the evolution of the postwar French welfare state. In 1945 the government tried to establish an integrated social security system (the *régime général*) covering the entire working population, but in the next three years this effort was decisively set back through the opposition of occupationally specific lobbies.

In the first place those occupational pension systems that were already in operation, those in the three *départements* of Alsace-Lorraine, and the family allowance system successfully fought to maintain their separate existence. In addition the self-employed managed to avoid being incorporated into the *régime général,* effectively limiting it to the industrial workforce.[2] The generosity of the basic plan was constrained by another series of defeats. In March 1947, supervisory and technical personnel *(cadres)* established a pension system for themselves that paid benefits in addition to those of the basic scheme. This plan, subsequently duplicated by a number of other occupational groups,[3] set implicit limits on the growth of the *régime général* because their beneficiaries resisted efforts to raise the ceiling on taxable wages *(déplafonnement)* under the basic plan, and the mere existence of the complementary schemes removed the most compelling argument for upgrading the former's benefits. The spread of complementary schemes meant that the majority of the population was covered by both a basic plan and at least one supplementary scheme, but the quality and cost of coverage varied greatly from sector to sector and across income groups.[4]

The financial arrangements of this mixed system reinforce its particularism and exacerbate its inequalities. The *régime général* is financed almost entirely from the proceeds of payroll taxes on employers and employees. Several of the special schemes, on the other hand, receive large susidies from the state treasury. Contribution rates are often lower and benefits higher in the *régimes speciaux* than in the basic plan. Moreover, the state has required the general regime to use its surplus revenues to bail out special funds from time to time. This procedure *(compensation)* was formalized in 1974.[5]

In addition the *régime général* pays for a host of activities that have little or nothing to do with the purposes for which it was created. The annual cost of these highly controversial "unjustified charges," which include such items as medical education and research, was estimated by the *Parti Socialiste* at between 20 and 32 billion francs in 1982.[6] The practice of raiding the *régime général* to pay tenuously related social programs serves to reinforce fiscal restraint because it accentuates the scheme's financial problems and is at least one of the reasons for the skepticism with which the Socialists greeted the Giscard government's estimates of the size of social security deficits.

The Left has always sought to control the vast administrative apparatus of the social security system. Neither wholly public nor private, the system has a highly decentralized administrative structure built around a large number of financially autonomous funds or *caisses*. Paris exercises a substantial *tutelle* over their activities and holds the pursestrings insofar as the government sets tax and benefit rates. The *caisses* are run by administrative councils, three quarters of whose members were selected by workers in special social elections until 1967. Since then members have been appointed by organizations of employers and the unions and seats have been evenly distributed between the two.[7] Reasserting working-class control over the *caisses* is one of the most cherished goals of the Left.

Apart from these substantive issues, a major point of contention has been the process by which social policy is made. Basic reforms of social policy have often bypassed parliament by means of the special powers provision of Article 38 of the Constitution of the Fifth Republic. Through this device the government may ask the legislature to grant it the right to deal with a specific issue or set of issues through ordinances adopted by the Council of Ministers rather than through parliamentary laws. This was the means by which the unpopular reforms of 1967 were achieved and on this and other occasions the procedure was severely criticized by the Left. In addition, in their normal policymaking activities, governments have failed to consult broadly and seriously with the social partners, especially labor.

In summary, by 1981 the evolution of the social security system had produced a number of Type I issues that dealt with the universality, adequacy and equity of coverage and benefits, the fairness of the system's financial structure, and the openness and flexibility of its decision-making arrangements. No socialist government could ignore these items without breaking faith with its working-class supporters and reneging on commitments repeatedly made during the long years of opposition.

THE CRISIS OF SOCIAL SECURITY FINANCES
AND THE TYPE II AGENDA

Whatever complaints the Left might have had about the content and structure of the system of social protection, its overall growth had scarcely been constrained by over two decades of conservative rule. Expenditures on all forms of social protection rose from 47 billion francs in 1960 to 752 billion in 1980. This constituted a jump from 15.9 to 27.3 percent of the gross domestic product (GDP) and an average annual increase of 15.75 percent. Social spending, which had accounted for 44.7 percent of total state spending in 1970, claimed 51.7 percent in 1980. Benefits from social protection made up 32.4 percent of disposable family income by 1980. The bulk of this aid (75 percent) took the form of social security payments. The largest shares of these expenditures in 1980 were absorbed by health insurance (36 percent) and the old age pension systems (43 percent).[8]

Taxes have gone up steadily to pay for these disbursements. Payroll contributions for social programs (*cotisations sociales*) went from 12.5 to 18.3 percent of the GDP in the decade of the seventies. France is not exceptional among her neighbors in overall spending for social purposes (she ranked only sixth in the European Community in 1979), nor in total taxation as a percent of GDP (the Netherlands, Belgium and Denmark taxed their citizens even more heavily in 1979), but she stands alone in the way in which the tax burden is distributed.

An unusually heavy reliance on indirect taxation (nearly 75 percent of total revenues) and social security payroll taxes in particular (42 percent of the total), sets France apart from the other European democracies.[9] Furthermore, a disproportionate share of the burden of these taxes falls on employers, especially those whose workers are covered by the *régime général:* 73.5 percent of all the revenues of this *régime* come from employer contributions. For all systems of social protection, the sources of revenues in 1980 were 54.4 percent from employers, 23.1 percent from the insured, 21.2 percent from the state, and 1.3 percent from other sources.[10] Altogether it is estimated that the social charges paid by employers were equal to between 45 and 65 percent of the direct salary a worker received.[11]

Recent debates over the proper mode of financing social programs have proceeded from concern over the impact of these "social charges" on employers. Two types of arguments are advanced: (1) that such taxation places France at a disadvantage vis-à-vis her principal trading partners since it raises the cost of labor and eventually the costs of export goods,[12] and (2) that such taxation falls unfairly on labor-intensive industries, driving marginal firms out of business and reducing the overall supply of employment.[13] The employers' association (CNPF) has lately grown increasingly insistent that payroll taxes must be at least stabilized if not reduced in real terms.[14] If this is to be done without reducing benefits, it will require the identification of new revenue sources. The traditional response of the Left to this dilemma is to demand a greater participation by the state in financing social benefits, which met only about one-fifth of the costs of all social protection schemes in 1980. There have been enquiries into the possibility of extending the base *(assiette)* of taxation for social purposes by taxing income other than wages or by instituting a form of value added tax for this purpose.[15] Giscard's Minister of Social Affairs, Mme. Veil, concluded that such a move would be unworkable and might destroy the contributory rationale which allows the "social partners" to manage the system through the administrative councils of the various *caisses*.

The taxation issue will not, however, go away. A combination of improving benefits, rising health care costs, a worsening demographic ratio and the prolonged economic crisis has recently generated chronic deficits in particular funds, if not in the social security system as a whole.[16] Forecasts indicate, moreover, that even without further improvements in benefits, the situation is likely to get worse. The general regime as a whole ran an annual surplus until 1974, at which time it went nearly 4 billion francs into the red. Large deficits were also incurred in 1975, 1976 and 1978. During the Giscard administration there were five separate rescue plans designed to resolve these financial problems.[17] Each involved a series of stop-gap measures to trim costs and raise revenues. That they had not dealt with the structural sources of the problem was evident from the fact that a further deficit of about 7 billion francs was anticipated for 1981. As the Socialists prepared to assume office, it was unclear whether they would in turn have to devote much of their energies to a breathless and seemingly fruitless effort to keep the social security system solvent.

In conclusion, for many people the most pressing problems of the social security system in 1981 were those having to do with re-equilibrating its finances. Chronic deficits required difficult and unpalatable choices if economic growth could not be achieved rapidly. As will be seen in the next section, the Socialists came to office with a social program heavily weighted toward social measures that either did not address these problems or would surely exacerbate them in the absence of a spectacular economic recovery.

The Socialist Projet

The pre-election social program of the PS contained two sorts of items tied to its economic policy: (1) those measures conducive to a *relance*, and (2) those related to a strategy of job-sharing. Both were politically popular and consistent with traditional socialist ideology. Neither really dealt with the financial problems of social security. The PS promised to boost social benefits and family allowances, to increase the minimum wage (SMIC), and to raise the minimum old age pension to 80 percent of SMIC.[18] This was part of a Keynesian strategy to stimulate the economy through enhanced consumption. Reinvigorated growth was expected to produce the revenues necessary to pay for the new benefits.

A second set of proposals was part of the Party's employment policy. Here the Socialists seemed to abandon their strongly expansionist posture and adopt a distinctly Malthusian strategy of sharing available employment more widely. The principal elements of this policy included a plan to give a fifth week of paid vacation to all French workers, to move gradually to a 35-hour work week, to institute voluntary retirement with full pension at age 60, and to create the framework for collectively bargained "solidarity contracts" that would provide for early retirement under programs heavily subsidized by the state. The job-sharing program was roundly criticized for potentially reducing productivity, raising labor costs, putting enormous new strains on the already teetering pension systems and ignoring the more important task of creating new employment. Although these observations carry a great deal of weight, they do not do justice to the reasoning that lay behind the PS strategy.

First of all such a policy was broadly consistent with thinking in the labor movement about the most effective means of raising the living standards of workers and increasing the share of national in-

come going to labor. French unions have for a long time been direct-
ing their efforts not so much toward higher hourly wages as toward
reducing the length of the standard work week, limiting overtime,
winning the right to early retirement and improving conditions at the
workplace. Their assumption is that the labor movement is too weak
to win a battle on the wage front. Labor is divided and the system of
collective bargaining is poorly developed and ineffective. Thus the
labor movement has sought to ameliorate working conditions primarily through winning supplements to wages through indirect payments
and benefits that can be acquired through the intervention of the state
rather than through one-to-one bargaining with the *Patronat*.[19]

From the PS point of view, the job-sharing strategy was more
than simply an act of national solidarity; it was also part of its plan for
restructuring the French economy. The Party's reasoning went something like this. The French tax system is sharply skewed in favor of
the indirect levies and particularly those that fall on wages. Of these
the heaviest overt burden is carried by employers. They in turn have
responded to this situation by trying to avoid putting on additional
workers for whom they would have to make social security contributions. Instead they ask their employees to work longer work weeks
with extensive overtime.[20] One long-term consequence of the fiscal
system, and the *Patronat's* response to it, is to create a structural im-
pediment to the expansion of the workforce, especially in labor-
intensive and low-skill industries and small and medium-sized
enterprises. In this context a determination to compel a reduction in
working hours through state-mandated reforms could be seen as a
plausible policy to create new jobs.[21]

Apart from its stimulative and job-sharing measures, the PS proposed to move toward the realization of the traditional socialist goals
of equality and democracy. One important means to this end was a
basic reform of the finances of the social security system: (1) the
assumption by the state budget of the "unjustified charges" being paid
by the general regime; (2) raising the ceiling on taxable wages for
social security; (3) equalizing contributions and benefits between the
various plans and between the classes; and (4) extending the tax base
for social security beyond wages and salaries. These changes would
generate more revenues, make the system more redistributive, and
mitigate its adverse economic consequences.

The rest of the Socialist *projet* dealt with services and benefits and
would have ambiguous effects on finances. In the area of health care
the PS proposed sweeping changes: the elimination of private beds in
public hospitals; the substitution of third-party payment (in effect by
the social security *caisses*) for medical and pharmaceutical services in

place of the traditional system of reimbursing patients; the creation of integrated health care centers (CSI) in local communities; the payment by social security of the costs of abortions and the rationalization of hospital budgets. This program was not internally consistent. The budget reforms (a plan to set upper limits on hospital spending and remove the incentive to provide as many services as possible) and the new emphasis on prevention through the CSI were intended to impose constraints on the costs of the medical sector and increase efficiency. The move to third-party payment was likely to ease those constraints.

Finally, the PS promised to re-establish working-class hegemony within the social protection system. The 1967 reforms would be undone—the *Patronat* would be stripped of its dominant position on the *conseils d'administrations,* elections would be reinstituted, the supervisory authority *(tutelle)* of the Paris ministry would be reduced and a serious policy of *concertation* would again bring workers as well as employers into the policymaking process.

The Record

The team that François Mitterrand put together in May–June 1981 included at least three contrasting elements relevant to social policy.[22] At the newly created Ministry of National Solidarity, the president placed the distinguished scholar, political activist and civil servant, Nicole Questiaux. She had written widely on social affairs, had played a leading role in a number of major governmental commissions and had worked at the *Conseil d'Etat.* Associated with the leftist *CERES* group within the *Parti Socialiste,* Questiaux's views were well-known.[23] Along with her colleague, Jacques Fournier, who became a presidential advisor at the Elysée, Questiaux saw the effort to create a more egalitarian and just society as the heart of the idea of socialism. Her primary concern was with Type I reforms enhancing fairness, democracy and equality. She believed that thoroughgoing social reforms would in the long run lead to a more productive society, but that was not her principal goal.

There were others in the Cabinet, Jacques Delors, the new Economics Minister; Michel Rocard at the Planning Commission; and Laurent Fabius, the Budget Director, who took a more limited view of the claims of social policy on government resources. Partly this was the outcome of their ministerial duties, but it was also a reflection of their ideological proclivities. Delors, who became the most influential member of the Cabinet, was an especially crucial appointment because he had articulate views on social policy that departed considerably from those of Questiaux.[24] All these men had strong incentives to focus on the Type II social agenda. After the early months when the expansion of public expenditure created a fortuitous coincidence of interests within all elements in the Cabinet, conflict began to surface between Questiaux, and to a lesser extent Labor Minister Auroux, on the one hand, and Delors, Rocard and Fabius, on the other. This jousting often took place in public. Questiaux played a determined game for some time, but the faltering economy and escalating social security deficits left her more and more defenseless against the arguments of the sound money men.

There was, of course, one other faction in the Cabinet—the Communists. One of their number, Jack Ralite, headed the Ministry of Health. The PCF and the PS agreed on specific social policy measures in many instances and, because the Communist ministers were careful to be more loyal than Caesar's wife in the first year of the new government, Ralite's presence did not create many headaches for Mitterrand. Describing himself in the press as being "infected with a virus for change," Ralite did anger doctors with his militant attacks on medicine for profit and his crusade against the *secteur privé* in public hospitals. Some of the PCF's official analysis of social security would have logically led them to the extreme position of demanding the highest benefits possible in order to lower the rate of capitalist exploitation.[25] In fact, however, they moderated their rhetoric considerably in order to stay in the government. Their major impact was to make the government more sensitive to the demands of the Communist-dominated labor federation, the *Confédération Générale du Travail* (CGT), than it might otherwise have been.

Two general conclusions can be drawn about the social policies of the Mitterrand government in its first 18 months. First, those aspects of the *plan social* that were predicated on a quick economic recovery went through three distinct phases: an initial period of bold increases in social benefits, a waiting period in which economic conditions worsened and a third phase in which a sharp reversal in policy was adopted. Secondly, a raft of more long-range and, in some cases structural, reforms was launched, but almost all of these ran into unexpected resistance, as much from organized labor as from more privileged strata.

SOCIAL BENEFITS AND FINANCES

In phase I of its social policy (May to November 1981) the government moved quickly to fulfill its campaign promises. Even before the legislative elections in June, the government raised minimum old age pensions and family allowances by 20 to 25 percent, made 6.5 billion francs available for the construction of low-cost "social" housing and annulled a scheduled 1 percent increase in social security taxes. By August, however, it was beginning to be clear that these enhanced expenditures, in conjunction with persisting unemployment and serious failures on the part of employers to pay their social security contributions in a timely manner, threatened to produce huge deficits in the various social insurance *caisses*. In the first official indication that the government's social policy had to be changed, Premier Mauroy instructed his Cabinet to draw up a plan for dealing with these financial problems. In early September Mme. Questiaux issued a dossier on social security that became the focus of an unprecedented round of consultations with the social partners. A highly detailed document, it proposed an overhaul of the family allowance system that would cost, in the near-term, 8 billion francs and in the long-term, as msuch as 7.7 billion more annually. Ameliorations of the retirement system would have a price tag of 13 billion. As for the medical insurance funds, Questiaux essentially threw up her hands. In the absence of "socially unacceptable" changes, medical costs would go up by 18 percent in 1982.[26]

None of these improvement costs was included in the troubling forecasts of social security finances the dossier presented. Using intermediate economic assumptions, Questiaux predicted a deficit for the system as a whole of 7.2 billion francs in 1981 and 24.6 billion in 1982. Only one quarter of this was the result of the expansions in benefits undertaken the preceding May. She laid out a range of revenue measures to meet the shortfall, the most significant of which were an increase by one point in medical insurance contributions (13 billion), lifting the ceiling for taxable wages for medical contributions (2.4 billion), and a one point increase in the value-added tax (14 billion). Shifting a number of "unjustified charges" onto the state budget would save several billion more. Significantly, none of Mme. Questiaux's trial balloons involved resorting to the Left's favorite source of revenue—the income tax.

The possibility that the government would push ahead with a structural reform of social security finances was dealt a definitive blow in October with the release of two official documents—the government's interim plan for 1982–83 and the *Rapport Maillet*. The *Plan Intérimaire* stated outright that no additional improvements in social benefits could be considered in the absence of corresponding savings in other areas. More specifically, the *Plan* called for the overall stabilization of fiscal pressures on employers and strict limits on any further taxation of salaries.[27]

The *Rapport Maillet* was yet another analysis of the feasibility of exploiting some source other than wages and salaries for funding social security. Ordered by Mme. Questiaux and written by the staff of the Ministry of National Solidarity, the report nonetheless drew sobering conclusions. It rejected a shift to income taxes because unless the tax fell only on very high incomes it would constrain recovery and the high-income class was not large enough to produce the revenues that were needed. The report gloomily concluded that equity was the only good argument for moving from payroll contributions to the income tax, and for this socialist government that argument was no longer persuasive: "Recourse to the Treasury does not appear, in present circumstances, to be an efficacious solution to the problem of financing social security."[28]

The *Rapport Maillet* was only an informal discussion paper. On November 10, however, the Council of Ministers adopted the *Plan Questiaux* for social security reform which went much of the way toward accepting the logic of the interim plan and the Maillet report and was much less ambitious than the dossier. A number of improvements in benefits were approved. Unemployed workers ineligible for jobless benefits were given back the right to claim sickness insurance that they had lost in 1979. The reimbursal of the costs of glasses, hearing aids and dental fees was improved, and the 80-franc-per-month charge that had been imposed on certain long-term illnesses in January 1980 was abrogated. In all the changes in sickness benefits would cost 1.8 billion francs. A few minor improvements in old age pensions were also adopted: the minimum pension would go up to 2000 francs a month in January, and certain individuals who had retired before 1973 had the base upon which their pensions were calculated adjusted upward. Altogether these and several other minor pension reforms would cost only 1.3 billion francs in 1982. Finally, housing allowances were to be raised by 25 percent in December, and a series of changes in the family allowance program were proposed that would cost 4 billion in 1982, 7 billion in a complete fiscal year.

To pay for these reforms (about 8 billion francs worth), to meet the deficit in 1981 (estimates of which had grown from 7 to 10 billion), and to head off the 22 to 23 billion franc shortfall in 1982, the government had to find nearly 40 billion francs. It did so in the following way:

1. Unspecified economies in the health care system (3.8 billion).
2. New taxes on workers: a one-point increase in the sickness insurance contributions of salaried workers (14 billion); lifting the wage ceiling on the widow's insurance contribution first

instituted in December 1980 (250 million); adjusting the wage ceiling of salaried workers in July rather than January (900 million); creating a 1 percent contribution to the sickness insurance fund by the unemployed if their benefits exceeded the SMIC (600 million); increases in family allowance contributions for small businessmen, artisans and the liberal professions (1 billion).

3. New taxes on employers: raising the wage ceiling for sickness contributions by 3.5 percent (9.10 billion); adjusting the wage ceiling in July rather than January (2.60 billion) and other changes (3.8 billion).

4. Other revenues: a doubling of the auto tax (1 billion) and a state contribution for 1982 (2.5 billion).

The *Plan Questiaux* opened phase II of the government's social policy (November 1981 to June 1982). Despite its important amelioration of benefits, the program constituted a frank admission by the social minister that the financial problems of the system of social protection were not an illusion created by conservative governments and that the continuing economic crisis imposed serious limits on the pace and direction of social reform. The plan differed only marginally from that of the preceding government. While it did stress lifting the ceiling on taxable wages rather than increasing the *rate* of taxation, it was nevertheless an ad hoc response to an immediate crisis, not a structural reform.[29]

Filled as it was with concessions to reality, the program was nonetheless insufficient. In March 1982, Mme. Questiaux issued the *Rapport Peskine* which outlined still another menu of responses to social security's financial nightmare, including a partial move to the state budget.[30] Before any action could be taken, however, huge new deficits in the system were forecast. Depending on the economic assumptions employed, the deficit in 1986 would be between 66 and 120 billion francs![31]

The continuing drama of the social security system was only one of a number of factors that converged in early June to bring about a major shift in the Socialist program. Stubbornly high rates of unemployment, rising inflation, stagnant investment, a falling franc and a deteriorating balance of trade led both Economics Minister Jacques Delors and Prime Minister Mauroy to call for a "pause" in further reforms. On June 12, the government moved decisively to implement an austerity policy: the franc was devalued a second time, wages and prices were frozen and certain planned increases in social benefits (the increase in family allowances scheduled for July 1 and the improvements in the housing allowances) were cancelled. A broad *concertation* with the social partners was launched to secure even further cutbacks. Two weeks later, Mme. Questiaux, who in any case could not endorse these decisions, was fired. Her replacement was Pierre Bérégovoy, formerly the chief of staff of the Elysée and an intimate of François Mitterrand. Unlike his predecessor, who saw the role of the social minister as that of advocate for solidarity against ministers who were guardians of the purse, Bérégovoy assured the press that his first responsibility was to "know how to count."

Thus a third phase of social policy was opened. On September 29, the Council of Ministers adopted the first *Plan Bérégovoy* to meet a social security deficit now estimated to be in the range of 30 billion francs in 1983. After a protracted and heated debate the National Assembly gave its approval on October 21, but with 12 PS deputies breaking ranks to vote with the opposition. On at least one issue reaction from the unions (especially the CGT) had been so strong that Bérégovoy "voluntarily" withdrew his proposal before a vote was taken. He had hoped to impose increased social security contributions on persons receiving "pre-retirement pensions" (a temporary system of benefits designed for the long-term unemployed between 60 and 65 years of age). For the rest the *Plan Bérégovoy* was a distinctly mixed bag. It imposed a tax on advertisements by pharmaceutical manufacturers, affirmed the principle of a set annual budget for hospitals, created new taxes on alcohol and tobacco, set a daily charge for hospital care except for the very poor, revised downward the method by which pensions are adjusted for inflation and brought the contributions of non-agricultural, non-salaried workers into line with those of the *régime général*.[32] It seems that further discussion of state participation or of structural reforms of social security finances has been indefinitely postponed.

OTHER REFORMS: THE MIXED BLESSINGS OF CONCERTATION

Not all problems the Socialists encountered in the social arena were related to money. The Party was strongly committed to an open decision-making process and, for the most part, it had one. The results of this policy of *concertation* must, however, have been disappointing to its architects. Consultation had the effect, in the first place, of providing a forum for the expression of opposition to those proposals of the government that would reduce the *droits acquis* of certain strata— professionals, *cadres* and employers—in the name of national solidarity.[33] Secondly, consultation brought to the surface unexpected criticism and hostility from the unions and served to publicize the deep jealousies and conflicts within the labor movement as a whole. Even those proposals that had been central planks of the Left program for years—reducing the age of retirement and the length of the work week, for example—sparked intense controversy among working-class organizations.

The Mauroy government pursued its social policy goals in two ways. Efforts to reform the administration of the social security system, to reinstitute the election of the administrative councils of the *caisses,* to reform the hospital system and, of course, the successive financial plans were undertaken through the normal legislative process,.modified by very extensive consultation prior to the submission to the parliament by the government of *projets de loi.* With respect to several other reforms the government decided to legislate by *ordonnances,* a move that provoked severe criticism from the Right and anxiety within the Left. The two legislative paths were contradictory, the one insisting that policy must be the outcome of the widest possible participation by the interested parties, the other implying that the government needed to move quickly and could be delegated powers that stripped even the legislature of its ordinary oversight role.

On November 18, 1981, the Council of Ministers announced that it was going to seek emergency powers under Article 38 of the constitution to deal with several social issues. Under this provision measures relating to the age of retirement, the duration of work, solidarity contracts and the right of individuals to accumulate multiple pensions would be taken through *ordonnances* rather than parliamentary laws. Mauroy assured the press that no actions would be taken without proper advance consultation, but he argued that the government had an unusually heavy workload and hoped to bring these matters to fruition no later than June 30, 1982. The irony of such a strategy was particularly rich. François Mitterrand had personally deposed a motion of censure against the Pompidou government when in 1967 it had used the same procedure to enact social security reforms. Article 38 had been a favorite target of leftist criticism since 1958. Now Mitterrand found his own government the object of a censure motion for the same offense. Moreover, he was subjected to the indignity of having his use of the authority defended in *Le Monde* by the chief author of the Gaullist constitution, Michel Debré.[34]

Fears that the government would use this procedural short-cut to run roughshod over opposing views was unfounded. Instead, even with the special powers which the government duly received on December 23, the road to reform was very rocky. On January 13, the Council of Ministers adopted *ordonnances* to take effect February 1, 1982, calling for a 39-hour week (to be gradually reduced to 35), and a fifth week of paid vacation for all French workers. It also passed an *ordonnance* facilitating solidarity contracts designed to create 50,000 to 100,000 news jobs. The potential impact of this package on the unemployment rate was severely diminished on February 10 when the president, responding to especially severe criticism from the CGT, announced that "not one worker should fear that his real income will decline as a result of the move to a 39-hour week."[35] This personal intervention by Mitterrand may have secured broad popular support, but it greatly angered the *Patronat,* which complained that as employers would have to pay the same wages for less work, their costs had been raised and their productivity reduced—just the opposite of the government's stated goals. Moreover, Planning Minister Rocard and Labor Minister Auroux let it be known that protecting the purchasing power of the employed threatened to jeopardize the hopes of those without jobs. Finally, Edmond Maire, the General Secretary of the *Confédération Française Démocratique du Travail* (CFDT) took the government to task, calling the President's comments a "serious faux-pas" and observing that "if one wishes to create jobs, it will be necessary to put the finger on those with high incomes."[36] On the whole the government paid for the acceptance of its long-run objective of reduced work time by sacrificing any short-term amelioration of the unemployment problem.

The effort to reduce the retirement age to 60 was impeded by several more or less unanticipated roadblocks. That lowering the age of retirement in a system where pension costs were already in excess of revenues could only exacerbate the financial pressures was evident, but this was an objection the government's electoral commitments forced it to ignore. A more serious problem resulted from the pre-retirement pension and the "guarantee of resources" that supported persons 60 or older who experienced long-term unemployment in the years before they were eligible for retirement. These temporary measures (the guarantee of resources was due to expire on December 31, 1982) were extremely generous, providing 80 percent of previous earnings.[37] No pension at 60 would thus be acceptable if it did not at least keep these individuals as well off as they were before the reduction in the retirement age. Finally, in the complex French retirement system, most workers depended upon the joint income from at least two pensions to achieve a comfortable standard of living in retirement. If the *régime général* reduced its age of eligibility to 60, while the complementary *régimes* preserved 65 as their starting date, no rational worker would quit work at the earlier date. Should that happen the lowering of the retirement age would be an empty reform and again the government would have failed to achieve its job-generating objectives. Hence, though the government's reform affected only the general plan directly, it was obvious that its effectiveness depended on the complementary systems following suit. This, however, could be done only through delicate private negotiations between employers, employees and the relevant *régimes* and would create heavy new financial burdens for the latter.

An interministerial committee met in Paris on January 21, 1981, to develop the broad outlines of the retirement age proposal. It decided that as of April 1, 1983, workers could choose to retire at age 60 with full pensions if they had accumulated 37½ years of contributions. The pension would be equal to 50 percent of previous salary, up to one-half the wage subject to social security taxes, or 3195 francs a month. Women would retain the right they already enjoyed to retire at 60, but they would need only 37½ rather than 40 years of contributions. The reform proposal, which would cost 17.5 billion francs (11 billion for the *régime général* and 6.5 for the complementary *régimes* if they followed the government's lead), was submitted to the social partners in early February. Plans were laid to discuss the proposal in the Council of Ministers on March 3. On March 1, however, the Prime Minister announced that he was postponing adoption of the *ordonnance* pending further consultation with the unions. Several events had transpired. The Social Affairs Committee of the National Assembly had insisted that Mme. Questiaux appear personally to testify on the matter, which she agreed to do. The *Conseil d'Etat* had issued an opinion challenging the legality of certain aspects of the proposal. Moreover, in over 45 separate meetings with the unions, the complementary *régimes* and various interested voluntary groups, a host of objections to the specifics of the proposal had arisen.

It looked for a while as if the idea of proceeding by *ordonnance* might have to be scuttled, but on March 26, just five days before the government's authority under Article 38 was due to expire, the Council of Ministers gave its approval to a plan roughly similar to the original proposal of January 21. It was not, however, until July 21 that a decree of application was issued and even then the new Social Minister, Bérégovoy, conceded that it might be necessary to create a new interim state scheme to assure the benefits of persons retiring at 60 if their complementary pensions were not available until age 65.[38]

The government appeared to stumble at several key points in its efforts at social reform through the regular legislative process as well. Attempts to abrogate the despised reforms of 1967 and reinstitute both union control of the social security funds and election of the councils ran into unexpected opposition from the unions as well as the predictable and vehement resistance of the *Patronat*. Originally determined to hold the first social elections in 1982, the Council of

Ministers decided, over the strong objections of Mme. Questiaux, to delay them until 1983. The *projet de loi* eventually adopted on June 9, 1982 fell considerably short of the government's election promises: only with respect to the administration of the funds of the sickness, old age and family allowance systems would the 50–50 division of seats between employers and employees be altered. For the important institutions that actually collected contributions and those that supervised personnel, *paritisme* remained the order of the day. Moreover, even on the *conseils d'administration* the *Patronat* would retain 25 percent of its seats. Finally, to ensure that all unions would have some representation, each organization officially designated by the government as "representative" would be able to name one administrator whatever the outcome of the elections—a provision hotly contested by the CGT and CFDT and eagerly sought by the smaller federations.

The issue of reimbursing the costs of abortions out of social security funds is another example of the difficulty the government had in speaking with one voice and following through with its campaign pledges. François Mitterrand had personally promised that abortions (which had been legalized under Giscard d'Estaing) would be paid by the sickness insurance *caisses*. An interministerial committee headed by Mauroy had decided in March 1982 that as of September 70 percent of the costs of abortions would be paid by social security. Mme. Roudy, Minister for Women's Rights, apparently leaked this to the press, effectively calling the government's hand. After the imposition of austerity in June, however, the plan was shelved as part of more general budget cuts of 10 billion francs. In August, Bérégovoy implied that money was not really the issue: "In matters of morality, when the issue is delicate and the solution controversial, it is desirable to seek the largest possible consensus among the various elements of the society."[39] What he did not report was that there was an intense battle going on behind the scenes between Finance Minister Delors and Budget Director Fabius, on the one hand, and Mme. Roudy and PS militants and deputies, on the other. Eventually the President came down in favor of reimbursal and ensured that his earlier commitment would be kept. On October 16, it was announced that a rider would be appended to the *loi de finances* for 1983 to provide for payment of abortions out of general revenues rather than social security funds.[40]

Conclusion

The government's social program was bedeviled by the contradictory demands of the social agenda, by the government's preference for egalitarian reforms in benefits rather than measures designed to improve the financial status of the system of social protection. Given the severe crisis of the social security trust funds, the government could hope to expand benefits only if a robust economic recovery replenished the funds or gave the state the surplus it needed to pick up part of the tab out of the general budget. The predictably huge deficits that appeared in the funds when the stagnant economy failed to improve derailed the government's reformist policies.

The social program also foundered because though its rhetoric tended to imply that its social reforms would enhance the lives of the great majority of the population who suffered from the indifference and exploitation of Giscard's "liberal society," the reality of the French welfare state in 1981 was different. Under the weak governments of the Fourth Republic, French social policy had developd along extremely particularistic lines—each occupational group or sector winning approval for its own system of benefits and seeking to push as much of the costs as possible off onto some other group. But the particularistic dynamic of welfare state development had not been incompatible with the rapid expansion of social spending, especially under the Fifth Republic. Indeed, after 1974, expenditures for social security grew faster than the economy or the state budget as a whole. Even the *régime général* shared in this enhanced social spending.

The combination of fragmented, sector-specific programs and overall high levels of spending means that the latitude for a reform-minded government is limited. A large part of the population is organized and willing to fight to maintain its privileges under the status quo. Even among the manual working class in the general scheme, proposals to direct more effort toward the least well off will meet resistance. There simply is not a majority constituency for structural or redistributionist reforms of the system. Too many people have too much to lose. The Party's pronouncements imply that it is leading the fight for social justice against a privileged few. In fact a large proportion of the Party's own electorate oppose its plans.

Despite the setbacks this chapter has described, the Mitterrand government accomplished a great deal in its first 18 months. If not every proposal was approved, that is in part because so much was attempted, and not only in the social arena. Indeed the government stood by most of its campaign pledges having to do with benefits and services, a remarkable record given the exceedingly unpropitious economic context. It is also true, as spokesmen for the government claim, that the austerity measures have been designed to protect the poorest segments of the society from their full force. The major defeats—the democratization of the social security funds, the reform of social security finances and the decision to give priority to the maintenance of purchasing power over the fight against unemployment—involved measures that threatened powerful entrenched interests. It may well be that these are only temporary retreats. The government, after all, has at least until the legislative elections in 1986 to carry out its program. Those who fear that the June 1982 "pause" will have the same disastrous consequences for Mitterrand that a similar policy had for Léon Blum during the Popular Front period ignore the vastly changed institutional framework within which the present government operates.

Finally, one ought not conclude that the rancorous and cumbersome process of bargaining and negotiation that was a part of all the government's initiatives—even those taken under Article 38—is necessarily a sign of weakness or failure. On the contrary, it is the most persuasive evidence we have that the *Mitterrandistes* mean business when they talk of the democratization of French policymaking.

Notes

1. On the theory and practice of social Keynesianism, see Anthony Crosland, *The Future of Socialism* (New York: Schocken, 1963), Part 3.
2. On this period, see Henry Galant, *Histoire Politique de la Sécurité Sociale Française, 1945–1952* (Paris: Armand Colin, 1955), especially pp. 65–69, 107–116; Pierre Laroque, "La Sécurité Sociale de 1944 à 1951," *Revue Française des Affaires Sociales* 25 (April–June 1971).
3. "France," in Thomas Wilson, ed., *Pensions, Inflation and Growth* (London: Heinemann Educational Books, 1974), Chapter 6.
4. For good overviews of the social security system, see Jean-Pierre Dumont, *La Sécurité Sociale: Toujours en Chantier* (Paris: Editions Ouvrières 1981); Maurice Rustant, *La Sécurité Sociale en Crise* (Lyon: Chronique Sociale, 1980); and the special number of the *Revue Française des Affaires Sociales* 34 (October–December 1980). The most recent official study of poverty in France is the Rapport Oheix, Contre la Précarité et la Pauvreté (Paris: 1981).
5. Jean-Francois Chadelet, "La Compensation," *Droit Social,* Special Number (September–October 1978), pp. 85–115, includes an analysis and the texts of the law and degree of application.
6. *Livre Blanc sur la Sécurité Sociale* (Paris: Parti Socialiste, 1982). Cf. Franz Masnago, "Les Charges Indues," *Droit Social,* Special Number (September–October 1978), pp. 116–127; *Rapport Gregoire* (Paris, 1975).
7. Antoine Ferry, "La Sécurité Sociale depuis les Ordonnances de 1967," *Revue d'Economie Politique* 82 (September–October 1972), pp. 983–997; Dumont, *La Sécurité Sociale,* p. 40.
8. *La France en Mai 1981* (Paris: Documentation Française, 1981), Vol. III, pp. 29–32.
9. *La France en Mai 1981,* Vol. III, p. 32; Association Nationale des Directeurs et Chefs de Personnel, "Salaires et Charges Sociales en Europe" *Revue Trimestrielle* 57 (November 1960) pp. 9–19.
10. *La France en Mai, 1981,* Vol. III, p. 40.

11. Dumont, *La Sécurité Sociale,* pp. 218, 238.
12. See, for example, Alain Euzeby, "Faut-il Fiscaliser la Sécurité Sociale?" *Droit Social,* (May 1978), pp. 181–190; Bertrand Larrera de Morel, "La Competitivité des Entreprises," *Projet* 161 (1982), pp. 62–71.
13. See Alain Euzeby, "Financement de la Sécurité Sociale et Emploi," *Droit Social,* (November 1979), pp. 384–395; *Rapport Ripert,* "Assiette des Charges Sociales et Industries de Main-d'Oeuvre," (Paris, 1977); *Rapport Boutbien,* "Problèmes Posés par le Mode de Calcul des Cotisations Sociales, Notamment au Regard des Industries de Main-d'Oeuvre," Conseil Economique et Social (Paris: Journal Officiel, 1974); *Rapport Calvez,* "L'Assiette des Charges Sociales et les Industries de Main'd'Oeuvre," Avis et Rapports du Conseil Economique et Social (Paris: Journal Officiel, February 9, 1979), pp. 225–255.
14. See the interview with Yvon Gattaz, President of the CNPF, in *Le Monde,* March 10, 1982.
15. *Rapport Boutbien* (1974), *Rapport Granger* (1975), *Rapport Ripert* (1977), *Rapport Calvez* (1979).
16. A good attempt to sort out the relative contribution of each of these factors is Dumont, *La Sécurité Sociale,* pp. 222–235.
17. For an analysis of the Giscardian policy on social security, see Gary Freeman, "Social Policy in France," paper presented at the 1981 Meeting of the American Political Science Association; and Dumont, *La Sécurité Sociale.*
18. The discussion of the Socialist electoral program is taken, unless otherwise indicated, from the Party's document, *Projet Socialiste* (Paris: Club Socialiste du Livre, 1980).
19. For good treatments of collective bargaining in France and its role in labor strategy, see Janice McCormick, "Gaullism and Collective Bargaining: The Effect of the Fifth Republic on French Industrial Relations," in William G. Andrews and Stanley Hoffmann, eds., *The Impact of the Fifth Republic on France* (Albany: SUNY Press, 1981), pp. 197–215; and Martin A. Schain, "Corporatism and Industrial Relations in France," in Philip G. Cerny and Martin A. Schain, eds., *French Politics and Public Policy* (New York: St. Martin's Press, 1980), pp 191–217. The PS plan to reinforce labor's rights in the collective bargaining process was designed to alter the structural conditions that had encouraged the unions to focus on indirect benefits rather than money wages. See Jean Auroux, *Les Droits des Travailleurs,* Rapport au President de la Republique et au Premier Ministre (Paris: Documentation Française, 1981).
20. The length of the work week has been falling steadily. In 1972 the average manual worker was at the job 43.8 hours per week and 20 percent worked 48 hours or more. By January 1981, the average work week was 40.8 hours and only 1.7 percent worked 48 hour weeks. See Catherine Blum-Girardeau, *Les Tableaux de la Solidarité* (Paris: Documentation Française, 1981), Annexe 26, p. 233.
21. The government argued that its measures to reduce the work week from 40 to 39 hours, to create an additional week of paid vacation, and to facilitate solidarity contracts would create between 50,000 and 100,000 new jobs. See *Le Monde,* January 14, 1982.
22. For a detailed discussion of the personalities in the new government, see "Les Elections Legislatives de juin 1981," *Le Monde, Dossiers et Documents* (Paris: 1981).
23. See, for example, J. Fournier and N. Questiaux, *Traité du Social* (Paris:

Dalloz, 1976); Questiaux, "Les Moyens Administratives," in Pierre Laroque, ed., *Succès et Faiblesse de l'Effort Social Francais* (Paris: Colin, 1961); Questiaux, "La Politique de la Vieillesse dans la VIᵉ Plan," *Droit Social* 4–5 (April–May 1972), pp. 192–197. On CERES (Centre d'Etudes et de Recherches Socialistes), see *Le C.E.R.E.S. par lui-même* (Paris: Christian Bourgois Editeur, 1978). Especially relevant is the discussion of the "Stratégie pour la rupture," pp. 245–254.

24. Delors had served as social policy advisor to Prime Minister Jacques Chaban-Delmas and was the architect of his "politique contracturelle." His social views are discussed extensively, if uncritically, in Eric de Bodman and Richard Bertrand, *Changer les Relations Sociales: La Politique de Jacques Delors* (Paris: Les Editions d'Organization, 1976). See also his "L'Adaptation des Prestations Sociales aux Mutations de la Société" (Paris: Fondation pour la Recherche Social, 1967).

25. See Albert Dupuit, "Défendre et Étendre le Droit à la Santé et la Protection Sociale," *Cahiers du Communisme* 57 (April 1981), pp. 36–43; Maurice Hartman, *Evolution du Régime Général de Sécurité Sociale et Capitalisme Monopoliste d'Etat* (Paris: Economie Politique, 1973).

26. Ministère de la Solidarité Nationale, *Dossier,* 1981.

27. *Plan Intérimaire: Stratégie pour Deux Ans, 1982–1983* (Paris: Documentation Française, 1981), pp. 235–256.

28. Ministère de la Solidarité Nationale, *Eléments de Réflexion sur la Réforme de l'Assiette des Cotisations Sociales* (Rapport Maillet), 1981, p. 54.

29. Nevertheless, Questiaux appeared on French television several days later and said that "From this time forward, no one will talk anymore about the social security deficit." She went on to promise that there would be a "greater recourse to the state budget to pay for social benefits." These comments indicate how far out of step the minister was with the rest of the Cabinet. See *Le Monde,* November 18, 1981.

30. For details, see *Le Monde,* March 6, 1981.

31. Mathieu Feroldi, Emmanuel Raoul and Henri Sterdyniak, "Sécurité Sociale et Evolution Macroéconomique," *Economie et Statistique* 143 (April 1982), pp. 59–77.

32. See *Le Monde,* September 30, 1982.

33. Social policy had always been the result of negotiations, but they were typically unplanned and after the fact—negotiations forced on a reluctant government unable to have its own way. The PS changed this pattern fundamentally by holding general consultations in the formulation stage of policymaking. For a discussion of the process under previous governments, see Gary Freeman, "Social Policy in France."

34. Michel Debré, "Ce Bon Article 38," *Le Monde,* November 20, 1981.

35. *Le Monde,* February 10, 1982.

36. *Le Monde,* February 13, 19, 1982.

37. Between 1972 and 1978, some 240,000 persons benefited from this program. Thierry Beranger, "La Garantie de Ressources aux Travailleurs sans Emploi Agés de 60 Ans et Plus: Pré-retraite ou Prestation de Chomage Améliorée?" *Droit Social* 9–10 (September–October 1978), pp. 67–77.

38. *Le Monde,* July 25, 1982.

39. *Le Monde,* August 6, 1982.

40. This account draws on an interview I conducted with François Mercereau, chef du cabinet to Bérégovoy, Paris, August 4, 1982.

5

Equality and the Politics of Education

JOHN S. AMBLER

A socialist government committed to the creation of a more egalitarian society could not long ignore those institutions of secondary and higher education which in this century have become the primary gatekeepers guarding entry into elite positions in France as in other industrialized societies. In his introduction to the 1972 Socialist Party program, François Mitterrand charged that "big capital . . . has measured out general education and oriented it to its fancy. . . . "[1] And yet French public education, with its tradition of leftist teachers and at least limited social mobility, could not be viewed as a totally dependent superstructure, exclusively serving the interests of the capitalist class. As the Socialist Party education plan of 1972 puts it,

> The nature of the school is thus contradictory, as is its function: instrument of domination by big capital, but also a vehicle for emancipation and contestation. As such, it finds itself at a point of natural convergence between the antagonistic revolutionary class and the ruling class. The educational system is neither above classes nor integrated into the governmental and sociocultural system of the dominant class. It is at the same time one of the sites and one of the stakes of the class struggle.[2]

This conception of the educational system as one with progressive elements and at least limited autonomy allows the Party to expect that under new leadership some democratization of the schools can be accomplished even before the basic structure of inequality in French society has been corrected. In his introduction to the Party's 1978 plan for education, Louis Mexandeau, then head of the Party's Delegation on National Education, defined the "general principle" of that plan to be "the search for a great equality and the means which that supposes. This choice is justified if one considers that for twenty years, for economic, social and finally political causes, inequality in the schools has been aggravated despite the inflation of words, promises, and appearances."[3]

The Educational Record of the Fifth Republic, 1958–81

In education the gap between social classes remains great; but here, as in the case of income distribution, there is a modest trend toward greater equality. With unprecedented economic growth spurring demand for education, the governments of the Fifth Republic responded with a program of rapid expansion. Pre-elementary programs grew rapidly, spurred on by the demands of working mothers, who were increasing in numbers, and by the hope that pre-elementary instruction would reduce later failure rates, especially for disadvantaged children. By 1976–77, almost all four-year-olds and over four-fifths of all 3-year-olds were in school. By 1981, with the proportion of 2-year-olds in school up to 35.7 percent, and the average size of all pre-elementary classes down from 40 children in 1970 to just over 30, France had become one of the leading nations in the world in the field of education for small children.[4]

At the secondary level, the proportion of 15-year-olds in school increased from 53 percent in 1958–59 to 62.2 percent in 1967–68 (as the 1959 Debré Law raising the school-leaving age to 16 began to take effect), to 92.2 percent in 1976–77. The proportion of 17-year-olds in school increased as rapidly, from 26.9 percent in 1958–59 to 38.6 percent in 1967–68 to 51.7 percent in 1976–77.[5] University enrollments increased by 420 percent from 1955 to 1975 and the proportion of the age group entering some form of higher education rose from 7 percent in 1955 to almost 25 percent in 1975. In the 1970s, higher education in France drew approximately as large a proportion of the age group as in most other industrial societies with the exception of the United States and Sweden.[6]

An educational system may be "inclusive" without being "progressive" as Fritz Ringer, among others, has argued.[7] Indeed numerous scholars have contended that the primary beneficiaries of this expansion of French enrollments were the children of the middle

TABLE 1. Comparative Evolution of the University Student Population by Occupational Category

Occupational Category	(A) Student Population			(B) Total Working Population			Ratios of A to B		
	1961-62	1967-68	1974-75	1962	1968	1975	1962	1968	1975
Farmers	5.7	6.0	6.0	15.7	12.0	7.6	0.36	0.50	0.79
Farm laborers	0.6	0.7	0.7	4.3	2.9	1.7	0.14	0.24	0.41
Business owners	18.2	14.6	11.7	10.4	9.6	7.9	1.75	1.52	1.48
Liberal professions and high managers	29.2	33.0	32.9	4.0	4.8	6.7	7.30	6.87	4.91
Middle level managers	18.4	16.6	16.4	7.8	9.9	12.7	2.36	1.68	1.29
White-collar workers	8.1	8.9	9.2	12.6	14.8	17.6	0.64	0.60	0.52
Industrial workers	6.6	10.6	12.6	36.7	37.7	37.7	0.18	0.28	0.33
Service personnel	0.9	0.8	0.8	5.4	5.7	5.7	0.17	0.14	0.14
Other	5.1	7.4	7.0	3.1	2.6	2.4	1.65	2.85	2.92
Without profession (incl. retired)	7.2	1.4	2.7						

The ratios are calculated by dividing the share of the occupational category in the student population (A) by its share in the total working population (B).

A ratio of greater than 1 indicates that the occupational group's representation in the student population is larger than its representation in the total working population.

A ratio of less than 1 indicates that the occupational group's representation in the student population is smaller than its representation in the total working population.

Source: Ministère de l'Education, Service des études informatiques et statistiques, Etudes et Documents, 80.2. "L'Enseignement Supérieur en France: Etude Statistique et Evolution de 1959-1960 à 1977-1978," p. 120.

class and that the schools simply reproduced existing elites.[8] This is generally true, but only with qualification. The ratios columns in Table 1 show that the child of a member of the liberal professions or of a high-level manager had 41 times as great a chance to be in the university as did a child of an industrial worker in 1962 and 15 times as great a chance in 1975. The percentage of university students from families headed by industrial workers increased substantially from 3.7 percent in 1959–60 to approximately 13 percent in the late 1970s; yet these students tended to take short, technical programs or to drop out early. In 1978–79 they represented 14.9 percent of all university students in the first two-year cycle. Their share dropped to 10 percent in the second, full-degree cycle, and to 7 percent in the third, or doctoral cycle, which included medicine, law and pharmacy, as well as science and letters.[9] Those who complete the full second cycle tend to select general programs in letters and science which, given the rapid increase in the number of degree-holders, offer limited prestige and career opportunities.

While the long jump from the working class into the liberal professions in one generation is still a difficult feat, it is more thinkable than 30 years ago. The evidence does not support Mexandeau's conclusion of 1978, cited above, that "inequality in the schools has been aggravated" over the first 20 years of the Fifth Republic. Whatever its motives, which no doubt included a desire to project a socially progressive image and an expectation of eventual economic rewards, the conservative majority attempted to delay and to moderate academic segregation, recognizing that definitive tracking at age eleven was a major reason why children from modest backgrounds were strongly underrepresented in higher education. Continuing a trend toward social integration begun in 1937, the governments of the Fifth Republic not only extended the school-leaving age, but created the common middle school, the College of Secondary Education (CES) in 1963, with a "common trunk" of liberal arts instruction for grades six and seven, but with three ability groups. Then in a dramatic assault upon elitist structures, the Giscard government set about formally abolishing the ability tracks in the Haby Reforms of 1975.

René Haby, a professional educator, Minister of Education and author of the Haby Law, enlisted the support of Giscard d'Estaing against his many conservative critics, inside and outside the government, to create a new form of *collège* that goes further toward social integration than the British comprehensive school, which maintains formal ability tracks.[10] The *école unique* and the "common trunk" were ideas promoted by socialists, with little success, from the Popular Front reform plan of Education Minister Jean Zay to the Langevin-

Wallon report of 1947 to the aborted 1957 reform proposals of René
Billères and the National Assembly's Education Committee.[11]

The Haby reforms were enacted against vehement opposition
from some conservative circles. Raymond Aron, among many others,
vigorously defended the traditional French *lycée* education. The National Union of *Lycées* and *Collèges* (SNALC) charged that the reforms
were inspired by Communist Party doctrines. The attack from the
Left was more vigorous and concerted. The Socialist Party, the Communist Party and the major teachers' associations, the Federation of
National Education (FEN) and its affiliates, the National Union of
Secondary Education (SNES) and the National Union of Elementary
and General College Teachers (SNI-PGC), joined in a universal rejection of the reforms. SNES, whose positions are close to those of the
Communist Party, rendered this verdict in its journal: "There again,
the democratic verbiage on 'equalization of opportunity' and 'the
middle school for all' is contradicted by the real content of the reform."[12] The Socialist Party's 1978 plan for education dismissed both
the Haby Law and the Royer Law, which allows part-time apprenticeships in certain cases beginning at age 14: "Articles 56 and 57 of the
Royer Law concerning compulsory education and apprenticeships,
the Haby reform in its general orientation, are the negation of what
the Socialist Party proposes. Measures suspending this conservative
ensemble thus will be taken without delay."[13]

In view of the fact that both the Haby Law and the Royer Law
were still largely intact two years after the establishment of a socialist
government, one might conclude that the Left's opposition to what
appeared to be originally one of its own ideas was motivated simply by
a virulent hostility to the government and to all that emanated from it.
Indeed education—higher education even more than secondary education—was an arena in which a mood of sharp confrontation prevailed in relations between the government and the opposition in the
1960s and 1970s, with the major teachers' unions supporting and
goading on the latter. As we shall see, opposition to change on
ideological grounds often meshed neatly with corporate interests and
traditional, elitist attitudes toward education. Yet political opportun-
ism, while clearly a factor, is too simple an explanation of the Left's
opposition to the Haby reforms.

The goal of these reforms, like that of the Giscardian program in
general, was a meritocratic rather than an egalitarian society. The
general tension between these two values is reflected in Wilensky's
study of 22 affluent countries, which shows a negative correlation
between social security spending and the percentage of 20- to 24-
year-olds who are in institutions of higher education.[14] A policy of

equality of opportunity, when announced by a conservative government, is often perceived by those on the Left as a device for legitimating the status of the ruling class and for co-opting a few ambitious young people out of the working class, leaving the mass to be exploited. The 1978 Socialist Party plan for education makes this point clearly:

> It is in no way a question of "equality of opportunity" understood as a kind of race where one tries to line up all candidates at the start and let the best one win. . . . The practice of class struggle teaches us that inequalities are primarily social in nature and that these are the ones which first must be remedied. To fight against inequalities is also to refuse an ideology which privileges the cadre of the nation, as opposed to other citizens.[15]

However one reacts to the Marxist language of this statement, its point has been well documented in many countries: social background has a predominant impact upon academic performance, even among children of apparently equal ability.[16]

Soon after the Haby Law went into effect in 1977, Socialist critics found new grounds for skepticism. Unauthorized ability groupings began emerging, sometimes through the choice of elective courses and sometimes through the policy of the school principal. For example, the word may spread among affluent and attentive parents that the better students are selecting German as their language. These students then are scheduled together for all classes. Such opportunities abound, beginning with the eighth grade, when students are offered options in addition to the common program. Moreover, *collèges* differ dramatically in quality, depending upon their clienteles and the type of institution (*lycée* or college of general education) out of which they emerged.[17] A survey conducted by the Inspectorate General of the Ministry of Education in 1979–80 concluded that only half of all *collèges* were applying the heterogeneity rule strictly, and only 38 percent were offering the required three supplementary hours per week of instruction to weaker students.[18] Despite such resistance to integration from teachers, principals and parents, one has only to listen to the chorus of anguished voices of *collège* teachers who are facing classes of mixed ability for the first time to realize that France has never had such academic and social heterogeneity at the middle school level. The complaints of unmotivated students, uninterested parents, violence in the school, immigrant children with limited language skills, declining standards and wildly diverse, unteachable classes are evidence that France is attempting to cope with both mass education and comprehensive schools. Now in power, the socialists are intent upon improving the *collège unique* rather than dismantling it.

The Socialist Program for Education

The proposals of the Socialist Party and of François Mitterrand relating to education may be grouped into three categories: those that essentially enhance existing policies, those that reverse prior policy and those that are essentially novel.[19] Proposed incremental changes—and these are the most numerous—include expansion of nursery schools to accommodate all children from the age of 2, reduction of class size in all schools to a maximum of 25, improvement of training and retraining of teachers, development of technical and vocational training, upgrading of the status and salaries of teachers and expansion of continuing education. Education was promised a higher priority in funding to accomplish these goals.

The Socialists promised a reversal of policies in three areas. They pledged a swift repeal of the Sauvage Law, which had restored some of the power to senior faculty in elected university councils by reducing representation of junior faculty and students. They vowed to expand the corps of secondary teachers, rather than to reduce it as the Giscard-Barre government intended. They pledged to create a "secular and unified" educational system, integrating subsidized private schools (which are predominantly Catholic) into the state system.

The first two of these proposed changes were significant, but hardly revolutionary. If the Socialists insisted on repulsing the counterattack of the university mandarins, as expressed in the Sauvage Law, they accepted the system of elected councils established by the Faure Law of 1968. The call for further expansion of educational personnel and resources came after the Fifth Republic had already increased expenditures for education from 10.3 percent of the total budget and 2.6 percent of the GDP in 1958 to 17.6 percent of the budget and 3.4 percent of a greatly expanded GDP in 1979.[20]

The Socialist position on private schools represents a more fundamental change, reversing a policy of state subsidies which dated from the Barangé Law of 1951 and the Debré Law of 1959. Yet Mitterrand pledged that unification would come through negotiation rather than through coercion. He pledged in his presidential campaign that "I intend to convince and not to coerce. . . . no establishment will be forced to integrate. . . ."[21] State contracts for support of private schools—themselves a limited form of integration providing for payment of teachers' salaries by the state—would be honored until new legislation was passed.

Five Socialist proposals contained important novel elements, although each built to some extent upon existing programs. The first would allow all workers a two-year "training credit" to be used for further education and retraining at any time during the worker's career, during which time he would continue to draw his salary. This major addition to France's underdeveloped system of continuing education was perceived as a means of encouraging technical retraining to keep up with the demands of the economy and as an opportunity for dropouts to get back on the educational ladder. A second innovation which appears in the Party's programs of 1972 and 1978, but not in the statements of Mitterrand in 1981, is the call for integration into the university system of the prestigious *grandes écoles,* along with their preparatory programs in certain *lycées.* The critical role of a few elite *grandes écoles* in producing high officials for both the public and the private sectors has been well documented.[22] Students from working-class families made up even a smaller proportion of those admitted to the *grandes écoles* than of those admitted to the universities.[23] As at the secondary level, the Socialists hoped that by integrating various types of institutions of higher education they might delay and open up recruitment into elite programs, increase exchanges of students and faculty among institutions, and infuse the demoralized universities with new ideas and higher status.

The Party further proposed to create what the 1978 program termed *l'école inégalitaire* as a condition for the creation of "a true equality."[24] In a veritable battle against scholastic failure, disadvantaged students would receive a disproportionate amount of available resources, not only in the form of enhanced scholarships, but also in the form of smaller classes and new teaching methods. The Party pledged to support this effort to democratize the schools by "opening the school to life," by expanding school programs in which students could express their artistic, manual and athletic as well as traditional academic aptitudes. Moreover, the Party, which repeatedly warned of a sellout to the capitalists when outside professionals were called upon for assistance in the universities and secondary schools in the 1970s, now called for participation of a wide variety of outsiders in school activities. The 1972 Party program explains this attitude: "In order to resist the pressures of capitalist society, the schools were forced to turn inward. In a socialist society, they no longer will be on the defensive."[25] Evidence of this new confidence is seen in a final socialist innovation which would tighten the links between the society and its schools by decentralizing school management and expanding the role therein of parents and local officials. The principle of self-management would be applied not only to the factory and to local government but, within limits, to the educational system as well.

This program of democratization could be accomplished, the

Party believed, with no decline in the high standards of French education. If the *grandes écoles* were to be integrated with the universities,
the intent was not to lower standards or to create uniform institutions,
but rather, at least in part, to make their multidisciplinary style of
instruction available to a broader range of students.

PLANNING AND PRIORITIES

Amidst the frantic activity which accompanied the implementation of
campaign promises in economic policy in the first year of the life of
the socialist government, education remained relatively calm. The
new minister was not the Socialist Party's primary spokesman on education, Louis Mexandeau (who became Minister of Post, Telegraph
and Telephone), but Alain Savary. Savary first entered the National
Assembly in 1951. Over the next three decades he became known as a
genuine man of the Left, a man with strong convictions, but with a
penchant for negotiation and conciliation. He briefly succeeded Guy
Mollet as head of the old socialist party, the SFIO, in 1969. As Minister of Education, he appointed a series of *chargés de mission* and study
commissions to survey problems and propose possible remedies in a
variety of areas: Laurent Schwartz and the *Commission du Bilan* on the
educational system as a whole, Jean-Louis Quermonne on the status
of teachers in higher education, André Peretti on training of elementary and secondary teachers, Bertrand Schwartz on the educational
and employment problems of 16- to 18-year-olds, the Legrand Commission on the *collèges,* the Prost Commission on the *lycées* and the
Jeantet Commission on higher education.

In order to prepare for policy changes, Savary oversaw a massive
movement of high civil servants. The Ministry of Education took
seriously the maxim, "for new policies, new men." The rectors, heads
of the 27 geographical academies which oversee French education at
all levels, were viewed by the Left as having played a partisan political
role in Saunier-Séïté's battles with the universities. Of the 27 rectors,
only eight were left in place. One was transferred to another academy
and 18 were replaced with new apppointees.[26] Within a year after the
socialist victory, almost all of the Ministry's directors, or heads of
departments, had been replaced, along with the majority of assistant
directors. The politicization of the high civil service, which Ezra
Suleiman noted in 1974, has continued under socialist leadership in
the field of education.[27]

The high priority which education was promised was not strik-
ingly evident in the 1982 budget. The education budget increased in
1982 by 17.3 percent, compared to an inflation rate of approximately

14 percent and a general budget increase of 27.6 percent. Education received higher priority in the next two austerity budgets, with increases of 15 percent in 1983, compared to 11.8 percent for the total budget, and 13 percent in 1984, compared to 6.3 percent for the total budget. All three budgets provided a real increment of approximately 4 to 6 percent after inflation. To those Socialist deputies and teachers' union officials who felt that the pace of change was too slow, Savary responded, "The task is long, therefore we must begin slowly."[28]

Pursuant to its campaign pledges, the government created 14,760 new permanent teaching posts at the elementary and secondary levels in June 1981, and provided for 16,800 more in the 1982 budget and an additional 8370 in the 1983 budget.[29] In March 1982, a major increase in the modest salaries of elementary school teachers was announced. Technical education at the secondary level was declared to be a priority area, with special attention in the form of additional teaching positions, more scholarship money and the commitment of 430 million francs per year for three years for the introduction of new technologies into the school program. These actions—particularly the creation of only 400 new technical teachers' positions in 1981, when enrollment rose by 11,000—were viewed as wholly inadequate by the National Union of Technical Education–Autonomous Apprenticeship (SNET-AA). In its March 1982 congress, this union, of which Prime Minister Pierre Mauroy once was secretary-general, declared that conditions were worse than before the socialist victory and threatened a strike unless the government provided additional funds. With many of the new permanent teaching posts going to auxiliary teachers already in the system in the fall of 1982, and with a decline of the dropout rate among secondary students at a time of rising unemployment, the Ministry struggled to place teachers in schools where enrollments surpassed expectations.[30] Given the high funding expectations of teachers' unions, it was not surprising that the government received more abuse than applause for its early efforts in education.

ELEMENTARY AND SECONDARY EDUCATION

One of the more promising programs designed to carry out the pledge to help the disadvantaged was a well-publicized "struggle against scholastic failure." Critics of French education have long deplored the high failure and dropout rates in French secondary schools and universities. The spread of pre-elementary education contributed to a decline in the failure rate of elementary pupils in the late 1970s. Yet in 1980–81, 44 percent of sixth graders were still a

year behind normal progress. The percentage of seventh graders who
moved up to the regular eighth grade rather than repeating, drop-
ping out or moving into special vocational programs, increased only
modestly from 62.2 percent in 1974–75 to 64.8 percent in 1980–81.
In the critical orientation after the ninth grade, the percentage continuing on to the second long cycle, preparatory to the *baccalauréat*,
was 53 percent in 1980–81, as it had been in 1974–75.[31] Over one-
third of all candidates still fail the state examinations. Of those who
pass and go on to the universities, only about 40 percent ever receive a
full university degree.[32]

In order to begin breaking this pattern of failure, in 1981–82 the
Ministry of Education subsidized projects designed to help weaker
students in 4500 of the nation's 7300 secondary schools. Although
these subsidies totaled only 30 million francs, the program encouraged secondary school administrators to pay attention to the
problem. Subsidies were heaviest in designated priority education
and action zones. These zones were selected, beginning in the summer of 1981, on the basis of high average rates of scholastic failure.
They often included large immigrant worker populations. For example, in Gabriel Havez College, in the Plateau de Creil priority zone
near Paris, 25 percent of the students are from foreign immigrant
families, 126 out of 231 sixth graders have failed at least one grade
and the dropout rate from the sixth to the ninth grades is 57 percent.[33] Subsidized programs in schools like this include tutoring, new
pedagogical approaches, extracurricular activities to arouse student
interest in school and the solicitation of parental participation.

An ordinance issued on March 26, 1982, implemented some of
the proposals made in the report of Bertrand Schwartz on the problem of salvaging school dropouts in the 16 to 18 age group. Some 50
local missions were to be created in areas of high youth unemployment for the purpose of offering special combined training and apprenticeship programs for unemployed youth. Municipalities were
expected to initiate the program and to supply 50 percent of the
funding, except in certain rural communes where the local contribution could drop to 25 percent. As in the case of the priority zones, the
Ministry was attempting to attract the attention of local officials and
solicit their help in resolving a growing social problem; yet the modest
sums which the central government was prepared to spend and, more
important, the paucity of apprenticeships and of jobs available in a
period of rising unemployment limit the potential success of this program in time of recession.

Among other significant innovations was the creation, in December 1981, of a general science program in the eleventh grade (*premier*)

to replace the mathematics program (the *"Bac C"*) which, after the fall from favor of Latin and Greek, has come to be known as the royal road into elitist schools and careers. In 1980–81, among tenth-grade students in the long cycle, only 21 percent of all working-class children were in the *"Bac C"* programs, compared to 58 percent of all children from families headed by a person in the liberal professions.[34] The *"Premier S"* program was another attempt to delay definitive scholastic and social segregation. It also was an attempt to reduce the importance of mathematical aptitude as the primary criterion for selection into elite schools, even those like the *Ecole Normale Supérieure,* for which mathematical skills may be less important than verbal skills. It will take continuing attention by the Ministry to deter ambitious students—and parents—from creating yet another informal, "royal road."

Initial steps also were taken toward decentralization of French education, to fit within the government's broader plans for self-management. The Ministry's circular of March 31, 1982 established tripartite councils within schools, composed of representatives of teachers, parents and local government officials. Sentiment for decentralization was strengthened by the Soubré report, which called for local control over teaching methods and materials, but not over the basic content of programs leading to national diplomas.

Some of these same themes—the "struggle against scholastic failure," new pedagogical approaches, delay of scholastic segregation and greater involvement of parents in the schools—were central to the thought of Louis Legrand and his commission on the *collège.* Their report, "For a Democratic *Collège,"* submitted in early January 1983, quickly became the focus of heated debate over the future of secondary education. Legrand, a Professor of Education at the University of Strasbourg, proposed a series of fundamental changes in the structure and style of the *collège.* He proposed that, with rare exceptions, the common practice of requiring pupils to repeat a grade at the middle school level be abandoned. In place of the rule against ability grouping, the Legrand Commission proposed dividing each class alphabetically at the beginning of the year into "ensembles" of not more than 104 pupils. These children would be grouped randomly into four classes. Beginning in the second month of instruction in French and mathematics, and in the second semester in modern languages, classes in these subjects would be regrouped by ability, but with movement among groups encouraged as indicated by rate of progress. Other classes, including an increased dosage of art, sports and technical subjects, would be heterogeneous. More shocking yet to the traditional and highly independent professor was the proposal that all teachers assigned to an *ensemble* constitute a "pedagogical team," responsible for planning, with the direct participation of teachers and pupils, for interdisciplinary team teaching and for tutoring small groups of children. Each child would be allowed to select his tutor. Moreover, all teachers, including the esteemed *agrégés* whose teaching load was 16 hours per week, henceforth would be expected to devote an additional six hours to tutoring, planning and coordination.

While most of the general teachers' unions were favorable to the Legrand report, the reaction of the National Union of Secondary Teachers (SNES) was rapid and predictable, parcticularly on the proposal of an increased and standardized teaching load. Gérard Alaphilippe, Secretary General of SNES, told a meeting of that association in Paris on January 22 and 23 that Legrand had not taken trouble to win the support of the "mass of teachers."

> In advancing, on his personal behalf, unacceptable proposals which would worsen the already difficult working conditions of the teaching corps, he has added to a profound discontent and created a movement of legitimate defense. . . .[35]

At the conclusion of the meeting, teachers poured out of Mutualité Hall and marched, 5000 strong, across the Seine to the Place de la Bourse, shouting "Revive the *collèges,* yes; on the backs of the teachers, no."[36]

Savary the peacemaker quieted much of the opposition by announcing on February 1, 1983 that while he agreed with the need for a drastic reduction in the compulsory repeating of grades, for more personalized teaching, for a more varied curriculum, for an assignment of teaching loads based on the grade being taught rather than on the original credentials of the teacher, and for the involvement of parents and local elected officials in policymaking at the school level, he would not at this time impose a 22-hour load, nor was he favorable to the idea of letting children choose their tutors. Moreover, the new organization would be tried, with volunteers, beginning in 1984. It was not, he stressed, "the new dogma of the Ministry."[37] Much further study and consultation would be necessary. Two "days of information and collective reflection" were scheduled in all *collèges* in the spring of 1983 to discuss the proposed reforms. Much retraining of teachers would be necessary to prepare for them.

When the government talks in general terms about education's responsibility for increasing social equality, it can count on the support of the principal teachers' unions, which are sympathetic to the Left—the Federation of National Education, its components, the SNI and the SNES, the *Syndicat Général de l'Education Nationale* (SGEN) and the teachers' branch of the General Confederation of Labor (CGT). The real challenge, as Savary was aware, is to persuade teachers to accept specific changes which disrupt established patterns of behavior and traditional privileges. In presenting his reflections on the Legrand report, he warned that "nothing will change in the schools without the teachers, even if they should not alone decide on the future of the educational system."[38]

The support in principle which the Left offered to Savary's revision of the Legrand proposals did not extend to the Right. SNALC, the conservative secondary teachers' union, announced that these proposals constitute "a triple threat to the quality of instruction, to the dignity of teachers" and "to the correct usage of the French language."[39] Savary's immediate predecessor as Minister of Education, Christian Beullac, was equally negative:

> For twenty years the same superspecialists of pedagogical research, insulated from the world, have, by ideology or unrealism, imposed their point of view on the mass of teachers and on the government. In the Legrand report one finds again, pushed to the absurd, instability, complexity and sophistry.[40]

Many of the local officials whom Savary would like to bring into school councils are conservatives. Consensus will be difficult to reach in support of such ideas as the involvement of children in decision-making, individualized and informal instruction, a ban on the failure of whole grades, and the introduction of more "nonacademic" subjects.

PRIVATE SCHOOLS

For an important segment of the government's clientele, particularly public school teachers' unions, no educational reform was more vital than the integration of subsidized private schools into the public sector. The secularist camp viewed the Debré Law of 1959, which allowed direct government subsidies to private schools under contract, as a reactionary attempt to reverse the trend toward secular education that began with the Revolution of 1789. The Debré Law allowed private schools three options: to remain completely independent; to enter into a "simple contract" with the state whereby most of the cost of teachers' salaries is paid by the government; or to make a "contract of association" providing that the state pay all teachers' salaries and the costs of operating the school in return for an agreement by the school to follow the "general rules of the public instruction program." In addition local governments were authorized to provide supplemental funding for contract schools. In 1981–82, 99 percent of all Catholic schools (which taught 95 percent of all pupils in private schools) were under either a "simple contract" (71 percent of Catholic elementary schools) or a "contract of association" (29 percent of Catholic elementary schools and 99 percent of secondary schools).[41] The private sector as a whole enrolled about 14 percent of preschool and elementary pupils and 21 percent of secondary students.[42]

As promised, the government honored existing contracts with private schools, with the anomalous result that in 1981–82 funding for the private sector increased by 22 percent, compared to 17.3 percent for the public sector.[43] The Socialists felt bound to implement the Guermeur Law of 1977, which required that within five years teachers' salaries in private schools be raised to public school levels. The government found, moreover, that under existing contracts it was required to pay for new programs offered by contract schools even if it believed them to be unnecessary or unwise. Such expansion was discouraged thereafter, and the 1983 budget provided only a 10.3 percent increase for private schools, compared to an overall education budget increase of 15 percent.

The forces of *laïcité* grew restless when action on unification was first studied, then delayed. The Federation of National Education (FEN), its elementary school component, SNI-PGC, and their allied parents' associations reacted impatiently to the government's cautious policy. In May 1982, the National Committee of Secular Action (CNAL) drew 200,000 people to a celebration of the 100 anniversary of the French public school. Pierre Mauroy was met with whistles from militants in the front row when he called for "concertation" and "unification" without "integration" or "uniformization." Savary spoke of the need for "tolerance" and "pluralism."[44] By 1982, tension was building on this issue between the Socialist leadership, both in the government and in the Party, and Socialist deputies, 48 percent of whom were teachers, most with a long-standing commitment to unification.[45] The leadership is aware that the private school issue is one of the last residues of religious conflict in France and could easily overshadow and jeopardize all other reform efforts.

In December 1982, with reports of four study commissions in hand, Savary was ready to begin negotiations with representatives of the private schools. As a basis for negotiation he made five proposals:

1. In all of those private schools which chose to accept public funding, lay teachers would be incorporated into the civil service, along with public school teachers. Clergy would continue to teach under contract.
2. Private schools henceforth would be included in the *carte scolaire*—the overall plan for the creation and location of schools.
3. Participating private schools, to be called *établissements d'intérêt public* (public interest establishments), would be run by administrative councils representing the state and the local government, as well as the sponsoring association, which would remain owner of the buildings.
4. Families would be allowed to choose freely among all schools in the area, subject to review by a committee of school principals, teachers and parents.
5. Each school (or set of schools) would be allowed to select a particular focus, be it spiritual, cultural or athletic.[46]

The reaction from defenders of *l'école libre* (the free school) was rapid and vigorous. Claude Labbé, the President of the Gaullist RPR group in the National Assembly, viewed the Savary proposals as an attack "on the fundamental liberties of the Fifth Republic, even of the Republic itself."[47] Michel Debré, De Gaulle's former prime minister and author of the Debré Law, regretted that at a time when national unity should be the highest priority, the government had chosen to "give ideological satisfaction to the militants" by "inventing a problem and reviving archaic quarrels which are incomprehensible to the young." For Debré, "The cancer of intolerance exists not only in the domain of education. One sees it everywhere, and it is one of the most bitter and agonizing signs of national decline."[48] The *Union Nationale des Associations de Parents d'élèves de l'enseignement libre* (UNAPEL) began to mobilize public defense of private schools, which eventually took the form of a petition with one million signatures sent to President Mitterrand.

In early January the Church itself responded: there would be no negotiations until the government offered "explicit guarantees" to Catholic education that the new structure would "safeguard the values which it defends."[49] The Church was content with the status quo and did not seek negotiations. To the dismay of militant secularists, Savary accepted another delay, preferring to talk informally with Catholic educators in search of a compromise settlement. Mitterrand apparently still believed, as he wrote in 1977, that "one does not nationalize minds."[50] No doubt he also was aware that with a majority of the population favorable to some form of state aid to private schools, he has few votes to win, and potentially many to lose, by coercive merger.

HIGHER EDUCATION

The Socialists arrived in office at a time when relations between universities and the government had become highly conflictual.[51] In the aftermath of the massive student demonstrations and riots of May 1968, which set off a general strike and shook the Fifth Republic, communist factions gained control of the largest student union, the National Union of the Students of France (UNEF-*Renouveau*, later known as UNEF-*Solidarité Etudiante*) and the largest faculty union, the National Union of Higher Education (SNE Sup). In France as elsewhere on the continent, the anarchist and utopian student movements of the 1960s tended to give way to better organized communist groups in the 1970s.[52] By the mid-1970s, a UNEF-SNE Sup coalition was powerful enough to control perhaps a dozen of France's 64 universities and to wield considerable influence in another 15 to 20. Still other universities, particularly those with large programs in medicine and law, were dominated by conservative or apolitical coalitions. The press took to categorizing universities, like the Michelin Guide, according to their political complexion.[53]

Alice Saunier-Séïté, the Minister of Universities under Giscard d'Estaing, set about to restore order in leftist universities. She told a group of conservative students in October 1980 that the recently passed Sauvage Law, which limited student representation on elected university councils to 15 percent and increased senior faculty representation to 50 percent, would reduce seats held by "communist officials of UNEF-*Renouveau* and *apparatchiks* of the Communist Party" who perpetuate "Marxist domination" and "ideological imperialism."[54]

It is not surprising that after more than two decades of conservative government, the Mitterrand administration was greeted with joy and high expectations by UNEF, SNE Sup and other unions of the Left, and with suspicion by rightist groups. The new government quickly met some of the expectations of the academic Left. The Sauvage Law was repealed by vote of the National Assembly on October 1, 1981, amid charges from conservatives like Senator Miroudot that "the government purely and simply was abandoning the university to certain groups of the extreme Left."[55] The linkage between student representation on elected councils and student turnout in university elections was eliminated. Authorization was restored for a number of advanced undergraduate and graduate programs which Saunier-Séïté had rejected on grounds of economy and "rationalization" of resources.

The outgoing government also was perceived to have harassed university assistants, the most junior faculty rank, by publicly questioning their qualifications, by increasing the teaching load of those who had not completed doctoral theses and by limiting prospects for promotion and tenure. In May 1982, after several unions and associations announced a strike of assistants to call attention to their unmet grievances, Alain Savary assured union leaders that all assistants who wished to continue a university career would be granted tenure. Promotion would be facilitated by the creation of a thousand new *maître-assistant* post per year for four years. In April 1982, after several strikes and demonstrations by the National Associations of Assistants (ANA), 2000 new tenured assistant positions were created. Under Saunier-Séïté, the High Council of University Corps (CSCU), the national body whose approval was necessary for recruitment and promotion of university faculty, was broadly viewed as overrepresenting conservative scholars. The CSCU was abolished in early 1982, but to the dismay of the unions representing junior faculty, it was replaced, in August 1982, by the High Provisional Council of Universities (CSPU), then, in April 1983, by the High Council of Universities (CSU), both of which were similar to their predecessor. The Ministry still appointed some of its members (one-fourth rather than one-third in the CSCU), and the principle of national control over promotions was retained.

Protest from university circles in the first year of socialist leadership related primarily to the government's slowness to effect changes. In "Year II," 1982–83, when the government began to lay out its plans, faculty and students reacted more with dismay and anger than with satisfaction. The academic year began with a circular to universities from Jean-Jacques Payan, Director General of Higher Education and Research, warning that funds for "complementary hours" of instruction, which accounted for over one-third of all classroom hours—were being cut by an average of 20 to 25 percent. Funds were being spent to create more regular, tenured positions, rather than for nontenured instructors and supplementary salary for regular staff. Payan had the temerity to suggest that the universities compensate by extending the academic year from 25 to 32 weeks, and by increasing teaching loads.[56] Many university councils assumed, incorrectly, that the ministry would bail them out when their funds were exhausted. By February several universities had expended most of their funds for *heures complémentaires.* Paris III (Censier) was canceling classes, and its students were in the streets in protest. Teachers' unions, like industrial trade unions, expected generosity, not austerity and a call for sacrifice, from a government of the Left.

The government's plan for a new higher education law, to replace the Faure Law of 1968, aroused further and broader discontent, although the proposal was widely acknowledged to contain progressive elements. The principal faculty unions of the Left—SNE Sup and SGEN—whose members predominantly are assistants and master assistants, urged the government to abolish all faculty ranks. When the Ministry decided instead to reduce the three existing ranks to two, SNE Sup and SGEN called a brief faculty strike on November 25 and a "week of action" in December 1982. One union leader announced bitterly, "Never has a government been as isolated in higher education."[57] The Federation of Independent Unions (the *autonomes*), as if to confirm the point, announced its own "week of action" to protest "the policy followed for 18 months by the government."[58]

In the summer of 1983, the government decided to settle by decree the questions of teaching loads and ranks in higher education. In June, Savary circulated a draft decree extending the normal teaching load for full professors from 3 hours of lecture per week for 25 weeks (75 hours per year) to 4 hours per week for 32 weeks (128 hours), with some adjustment permitted for research and administrative duties. The equivalent requirement for "directed study" rose from 150 hours to 192 hours annually. The two leftist unions, the SNE Sup and the SGEN, reacted angrily to these draft decrees. Jean-François Tournadre, Secretary-General of the SNE Sup, describes them as a "tentative de coup de force."[59] The SNE Sup's eight representatives resigned in protest from the national *Comité Technique Paritaire,* which must be consulted on decrees affecting personnel policy. The SGEN's seven representatives boycotted the July 11 meeting, leaving the remaining 15 members, all appointed by the ministry, without a quorum.[60] The rump committee met again on July 8 and, under the rules which reduce the quorum at a second meeting, unanimously accepted the decree on teaching loads and extension of the academic year, beginning in 1983–84, but delayed action on reorganization of faculty ranks and career development.

The remainder of the government's plan, based on a revision of the Jeantet report, did nothing to reassure faculty and set off an unanticipated wave of student protest that revived memories of May 1968. Savary stated, correctly, that the proposed law "prescribes little and permits a great deal."[61] As the law emerged from the Council of Ministers on March 30, 1983, it had six principal components.

1. The proposed law reaffirmed the grand principles which were stated in the Faure Law of 1968, but often not practiced: autonomy for the universities, a multidisciplinary approach to teaching and research, and participation of all members of the academic community in university governance.
2. Professional education and continuing education were to assume "a larger place" in higher education, as the Socialists promised in 1981.
3. All students with the *baccalauréat* would be admissible to the first two-year cycle at the university, except in a few unspecified cases. The governments' goal was to expand, not to reduce, the proportion of the age group entering the university. Yet admission to the second cycle would be based upon the student's capacity as well as an assessment of job opportunities in each field.
4. Universities and schools—including those *grandes écoles* controlled by ministries other than education—all were to be part of "the public service of higher education," each a "scientific, cultural and professional public establishment" with legal powers to contract with private firms and local governments.
5. The existing university councils would be replaced by three separate councils—for administration, research and university life—each elected but with different proportions of faculty, staff, students and "outside personalities." The latter were to be more numerous and to be named by their organizations.
6. Departmental and regional councils would be created to join the existing National Council of Higher Education and Research (CNESER) in the tasks of coordination and planning.

The thousands of students who went on strike, marched in protest and scuffled with police in Paris and in several other university cities, in the spring of 1982, all to force a withdrawal or postponement of consideration of the "Savary Law," were different in some respects from their predecessors of 1968 and 1976. In earlier years, demonstrators were predominantly from the less professionally oriented fields of literature, social sciences and natural science. The 1983 class of student demonstrators—better dressed and groomed than its predecessors—was composed of students in medicine, law, economics and pharmacy, with a scattering from other fields. The conservative student unions, which had largely opposed student protests before 1981, were now very much in the forefront, along with ad hoc "nonpolitical" groups. On the Left, UNEF-*Solidarité Etudiante* was sympathetic to the Savary proposal, but fearful of being bypassed by the mass of student protesters, as it was in 1968 and 1976.

What the 1983 student population had in common with those of 1968 and 1976 was a general anxiety about career prospects and a more specific fear that the government intended to restrict access to desirable fields. Medical students were the first to strike, in February 1983, in protest against the creation of a new examination at the end of the sixth year, which students feared would be used to exclude many of them from specialized training and the higher income it often brings. The strike among interns and heads of clinics in university hospitals, which erupted in March 1983, was occasioned by a similar anxiety that the government would fail to create adequate permanent positions in these institutions. Underlying both strikes was a growing surplus of doctors, despite strict quotas on entry into medical school from 1971 onward.

In fields other than medicine, conservative student unions posed a number of objections to the Savary Law. The emphasis on professionalization would lower the value of degrees, some argued, as did students in 1976. The increased number of "outside personalities" on university councils would reduce student representation and open the universities to greater external political pressure. The feature of the Savary Law which aroused the greatest indignation seems to have been the introduction of formal selection into the second cycle. In 1968 and 1976, the rumor that the government intended to institute formal selection helped to set off massive student protest movements. Now, ironically, a selection process was to be implemented by the Left, which repeatedly had criticized earlier governments for similar ideas. Savary concluded that the gross imbalance between supply and demand of trained manpower in some fields was wasteful and harmful to student morale:

> At the moment when the student, in the course of his studies, chooses a program of professional training, we must take into account his real prospects for employment and, if necessary, decide whether he should be admitted.[62]

The motives of student demonstrators, no doubt, were mixed, as they had been in earlier periods of protest. As two perceptive journalists put it, "Bravado, springtime games, the desire to show that they are as good as their elders, and real political conscience all join forces."[63] Yet beneath the playful and anti-leftist aspects of the protest lay a malaise from which the university has been suffering since the rapid expansion of enrollments in the 1950s and 1960s. That expansion increased the bureaucratic and impersonal nature of the larger urban universities, devalued the worth of university degrees and widened the prestige gap between the *grandes écoles* and the universities. Under these conditions, and often faced with job prospects well below their aspirations, French students, more than their American and British peers, are disposed to turn their anger and frustration to the government.

The "Savary Law" emerged from heated and lengthy debate in the National Assembly and the Senate, stretching from May to December 1983, with its central elements intact, but with several of its more controversial features weakened by concessions to critics of the bill both inside and outside parliament. The government made no major concessions on its plans for creation of three elected councils in each university, in place of two, and for a more professional orientation in undergraduate programs. On other points the required quota of "outside personalities" on university councils, which had been 30 to 40 percent, became 20 to 30 percent, and the government pledged that "orientation" after the first cycle normally would follow the student's desire. In keeping with a concession made in early May to end strikes by interns and medical students, medical schools were granted special autonomy, both in pedagogical and financial matters. The government abandoned its proposal to institute student evaluation of university teachers when many of its supporters found the idea to be outrageous.

The most hotly contested innovation was the election of faculty representatives to administrative councils by all faculty ranks voting as a single electoral college. The opposition was joined by several leading intellectuals of the Left in warning that the enhanced power of junior faculty, who outnumber full professors by more than two to one, would increase the trend in universities toward unionization, politicization and "mediocratization." The government strengthened the assigned role of professors in guiding research and instruction but, faithful to its union supporters, retained the single electoral college in the final law adopted in December 1983. The professors had their revenge a month later when the Constitutional Council struck down the faculty election provisions as unconstitutional on the grounds that full professors must be allowed to select their own representatives. In the end the changes produced by the Savary Law were much more modest than the government originally intended.

In his initial proposal for the higher education law, Savary called for the creation of an Interministerial Commission on National Titles and Diplomas to examine requests from universities and from *grandes écoles* to grant national degrees. The article was not included in the version approved by the Council of Ministers, suggesting that the defenders of the independence of the *grandes écoles* had won another round. Indeed, even though the *grandes écoles* were declared to be part of the general public service of higher education, little was done to carry out earlier pledges to integrate the two sectors. The National Assembly was assured that each *grande école* would retain its autonomy unless it chose integration. *Grandes écoles* graduates were well represented in the Socialist government, as they had been in its predecessors. They could argue quite sincerely that the socialists, even more than the conservatives, need first-rate administrators. Integration of the *grandes écoles* into the universities would risk diluting the high educational quality of the former without necessarily improving the quality of the latter.

Among the *grandes écoles* it was the National School of Administration (ENA) which received the greatest attention from the reformers, even before the debate on university reform. Since it is the exclusive entry to many high civil service positions, and since only 4 percent of its students are from the working class, the Minister of Public Service, Anicet Le Pors (then one of the four Communists in the government) proposed that an alternative access route be created. In October 1982, a "third route" was created (the first is direct from higher education, the second from within the civil service), open only to candidates who have had ten years of experience as leaders of local governments, unions and certain other associations. The proposal was adopted by the National Assembly among Gaullist warnings of "French nomenklatura" and "totalitarianism."[64]

Conclusion

Chided first for inaction, then for action of the wrong kind, Alain Savary must have felt, as did one of his predecessors, Alain Guichard, when he delayed introduction of Latin in the secondary schools from the sixth grade to the eighth, that any change proposed in educational structure or content seems to set off "a war of religion."[65] Savary hoped to limit conflict with a strategy of careful planning, broad consultation and gradual change. He is known to believe that French education needs reforms of content and method more than of structure. Through smaller classes, better trained teachers, new teaching methods and more support for disadvantaged children, the Ministry hopes to reduce failures, keep children in school longer and graduate them with professional skills as well as a general education.

Despite the minister's cautious treatment of the private school issue, the *collèges* and higher education, he was not able to prevent massive opposition, demonstrations, and violence. Why did a government which was welcomed so warmly by the majority of teachers in 1981 find itself as quickly caught up in heated controversy on several fronts? Among the many factors which no doubt contributed three merit consideration. First, limited financial resources made it impossible to satisfy the high expectations of teachers and students. Most of the government's plans could be implemented without massive increases in funding, but only if teachers were willing to accept change, and particularly to teach differently and sometimes more. Their cooperation has been difficult to obtain. A second possible explanation is politically motivated opposition. The strikes of students in law and medicine, often with the support of conservative faculty members, have been tinged with politics, as has the "free school" campaign. Yet in the public sector, the largest teachers' unions at all levels and the largest student associations are all sympathetic to the Left. The FEN, representing approximately 70 percent of all public school teachers, has access to ministry dossiers and is consulted regularly and in detail on policy decisions.[66]

Serious as they are, the financial and partisan political obstacles to change ultimately are less important than a third obstacle: the corporatist, conservative attitude which pervades much of the educational establishment. The long-standing quarrel between the major associations of secondary teachers (SNES) and elementary teachers (SNI-PEGC) over control of middle school education contributed significantly to the failure of a series of reform proposals from 1945 to 1975.[67] Elementary school teachers traditionally have been trained in normal schools, and secondary teachers in the universities. The two groups are in sharp conflict over the proper training for *collège* teachers. The SNI was incensed at the conclusion reached by Laurent Schwartz and the *Commission du Bilan* that many former elementary teachers now in the *collèges* are inadequately trained.[68] The SNES found unacceptable the recommendation of the Peretti Commission that for the present *collège* teachers should be required to have only four years of education beyond the *bac*, rather than the five years which the SNES believes to be minimal.[69] Even though the SNES presently is controlled by a faction close to the Communist Party and the SNI by a faction close to the Socialists, the conflict between the two is essentially corporatist rather than ideological and dates from a time when both unions were controlled by their socialist factions.

Among university faculty, the controversy between unions of the "Left" and "non-Left" tends to divide the liberal arts programs from professionally oriented programs; but it also reflects a conflict of interest between younger faculty, who more often prefer the elimination of ranks, and senior faculty, who fear a decline in status and the final abandonment of quality to equality. Even students behave as if the imposition of new examinations were a violation of inalienable rights.

Officials both in the Socialist Party and in the Ministry sometimes feel that the education system is partially "blocked," as Michel Crozier would put it, by the educational conservatism and corporatism of the teachers' associations.[70] They observe teachers who are highly critical of the educational system as a whole, but who resist change in their own sector, either on the grounds that the real problems are elsewhere or that no progress can be made in education until the whole society has been reformed. When teachers' unions do accept change, they typically demand a great infusion of funds for fewer teaching hours, smaller classes and higher salaries. Change also is inhibited by the enormity of the educational machinery which, as one specialist on education in the Socialist parliamentary delegation puts it, "is like a great ocean liner which has so much momentum that it takes a long time to turn or stop it."[71]

The Ministry is seeking to "deblock" the system by means of modest financial incentives for experimentation and change and by working with those teachers and administrators who want change. More importantly, it hopes to inspire change in teachers' attitudes through decentralization. Parents and local officials on school councils are expected to press for more attention to the needs of the community and of the students. If the powers delegated to local education councils are modest, as the Soubré report seems to portend, the extent of change will not be great. If control of funding, programs and personnel were delegated, the system clearly would be transformed, but perhaps not in the intended directions. In Brittany and Vendée, local control often would mean even greater public support for Catholic schools, whatever their formal status.

The experience of the universities under the Faure Law of 1968 suggests that decentralization may have the effect of intensifying corporatism and political conflict.[72] Michel Alliot, who was principal assistant to Edgar Faure in drafting the 1968 law and later president of the University of Paris VII, eventually concluded that "Democracy is incompatible with innovation."[73] Indeed such changes as were implemented in the 1970s were imposed upon reluctant universities from the top. In Crozierian fashion the universities continued to look at Paris for solutions to problems while denouncing overcentralization. To be sure Paris controlled funding and authorization to give national diplomas, as well as many personnel decisions, and was deeply suspicious of leftist elements in the universities.

The infusion of outsiders also had little impact upon the universities. A 1977 survey found that attendance at university council meetings averaged only 38 percent for "outside personalities," compared to 79 percent for nonteaching staff, 73 percent for faculty and 55 percent for students.[74] Although local officials and parents might well take a stronger interest in elementary and secondary schools, it is not at all clear that they would work for greater equality. Local officials might be expected to differ on the relative importance of equality versus quality as they vary in their political views.

Even if the full effort of the teaching corps could be enlisted to fight scholastic failure and greater funding were available to support that effort, one would still expect the children of the working class to be underrepresented in institutions of higher education so long as their aspirations remain modest. In his perceptive analysis of this question, Boudon concludes that it is not a difference in family values, but rather a difference in starting point on the social hierarchy which leads the child of a worker to feel himself a success when he finishes his education with a technical *bac*, while the son of a doctor must push on up the ladder or feel himself a failure.[75] The educational record of American immigrant groups suggests that family values also can be important. The Socialist government believes this to be the case and hopes to draw more immigrant and working-class parents into school activities.

In sum the socialists came to power with the intention of creating a more egalitarian society, in part through reform of the educational system. In principle they reject the notion that there is a trade-off between quality and equality. In practice their acceptance of ability grouping in the secondary schools and their reluctance to press for integration of the *grandes écoles* with the universities suggest a recognition of the costs of full equality. They are reluctant to jeopardize the capacity of the system to select young people of extraordinary ability and to hone their intelligence in a few schools of the first rank, of which many socialist leaders are graduates. They have started slowly to bring more young people up to higher levels of education. They face a multitude of obstacles, not the least of which are limited funds, a network of unions which ultimately are more corporatist than leftist, and the low aspirations of many working-class children. Savary's chosen strategy of careful preparation, persuasion and deliberate progress may ultimately succeed, but only if he and his successors prove to be master teachers in educating educators.

Notes

1. Parti Socialiste, *Changer la Vie: Programme de Gouvernement du Parti Socialiste* (Paris: Flammarion, 1972), p. 16.
2. Parti Socialiste, p. 150.

142 *The French Socialist Experiment*

3. Parti Socialiste, *Libérer l'Ecole: Plan Socialiste pour l'Education Nationale.* Presented by Louis Mexandeau and Roger Quillot, with a preface by François Mitterrand. (Paris: Flammarion, 1978), p. 12.
4. Commission du Bilan, *La France en mai 1981*, Vol. IV, *L'Enseignement et le Développement Scientifique* (Paris: La Documentation Française, 1981), and Ministère de l'Education Nationale, *Tableaux des Enseignements et de la Formation, Statistiques Rétrospectives, 1967–1968—1976–1977* (Paris, 1979), pp. 274–5.
5. Ministère de l'Education Nationale (hereinafter MEN), *Tableaux des Enseignements et de la Formation: Statistiques Rétrospectives 1967–1968—1976–1977.* (Paris: MEN, 1979), pp. 500 and 502.
6. Raymond Poignant, *Education in the Industrialized Countries*, Plan Europe 2000, Project 1, Vol. 5 (The Hague: Martinus Nijhoff, 1973), p. 288, and MEN, Service Central des Statistiques et Sondages, *Etudes et Documents,* 1975, No. 31, and UNESCO, *Statistical Yearbook,* 1981 (Paris: UNESCO, 1981), Table 3.2.
7. Fritz Ringer, *Education and Society in Modern Europe* (Bloomington: Indiana University Press, 1979).
8. P. Bourdieu and J. C. Passeron, *Les Héritiers* (Paris: Editions de Minuit, 1964); Bourdieu and Passeron, *La Reproduction* (Paris: Editions de Minuit, 1970); C. Grignon and J. C. Passeron, *Innovation in Higher Education: French Experience before 1968* (Paris: O.E.C.D., 1970), Chapter 4; A. Girard, J. Bastide, and G. Pourcher, "Enquête nationale sur l'entrée en sixième et la démocratisation de l'enseignement," *Population,* 18 (1963); and C. Baudelot and R. Establet, *L'Ecole Capitaliste en France* (Paris: Maspéro, 1971).
9. MEN, *Note d'Information,* No. 79:42 (1979), Table III.
10. Haby describes the history of the reforms and vents his annoyance with his critics in *Combat pour les Jeunes Français* (Paris: Julliard, 1981). Giscard defends the *collège unique* as part of his plan for a society based on liberalism blended with social solidarity and fraternity. See Valéry Giscard d'Estaing, *Démocratie Française* (Paris: Fayard, 1976), pp. 81–82.
11. John E. Talbot, *The Politics of Educational Reform in France, 1918–1940* (Princeton, N.J.: Princeton University Press, 1969); Antoine Prost, *L'Enseignement en France, 1800–1967* (Paris: A. Colin, 1968); and *Journal Officiel, Assemblée Nationale, Débats,* July 24, 1957.
12. *L'U.S.: L'Université Syndicaliste,* No. 11, September 4, 1975, p. 31.
13. Parti Socialiste, *Libérer l'Ecole,* p. 41.
14. Harold L. Wilensky, *The Welfare State and Equality* (Berkeley: University of California Press, 1975), pp. 3–7.
15. Parti Socialiste, *Libérer l'Ecole,* p. 39.
16. Alain Mingat, "Aptitudes et Classes Sociales: Accès et Succès dans l'Enseignement Supérieur," *Population,* 36: 2 (March–April, 1981), pp. 337–359; Jean-Claude Eicher and Alain Mingat, "Education et Egalité," in O.E.C.D., *Education, Inequality and Life Chances,* Vol. I (Paris: OECD, 1975), pp. 202–292; Christopher Jencks, *Inequality, a Reassessment of the Effect of Family and Schooling in America* (New York: Basic Books, 1972).
17. Dominique Paty, *12 Collèges en France* (Paris: Centre National de la Recherche Scientifique and Documentation Française, 1980); and *Le Monde de l'Education,* No. 84 (June 1982).
18. Jean Binon and MEN, "La Réforme dans les Collèges: Situation en 1979–1980," Report of the Inspectorate General, as reported in *Le*

Monde de l'Education, No. 84 (June 1982), p. 14.

19. Parti Socialiste, *Changer le Vie, Libérer l'Ecole,* and *Manifeste* of Party Congress, January 24, 1981, as printed in *Le Poing et la Rose,* February 1981, pp. 9–15.
20. MEN, *Tableaux des Enseignements et de la Formation* (Paris: Service Central des Statistiques et Sondages, 1976), p. 15; and MEN, *Statistiques des Enseignements, Tableaux et Informations,* No. 1.1, 1980 (Paris: Service Central des Statistiques et Sondages, 1980), p. 5.
21. Press Statement, May 1, 1981.
22. Ezra Suleiman, *Elites in French Society: The Politics of Survival* (Princeton, N.J.: Princeton University Press, 1978).
23. Benoit Millot, "Social Differentiation and Higher Education: The French Case," *Comparative Education Review,* 25: 3 (October 1981), p. 363; and Grignon and Passeron, p. 74.
24. Parti Socialiste, *Libérer l'Ecole,* pp. 12, 160–161.
25. Parti Socialiste, *Changer la Vie,* pp. 154–155.
26. Yves Agnès, "L'Administration dans le Changement: Vers l'Etat P.S.?" *Le Monde,* June 29, 1982.
27. Ezra Suleiman, *Politics, Power and Bureaucracy in France* (Princeton, N.J.: Princeton University Press, 1974), Chapter 13.
28. *Le Monde,* November 12, 1981, p. 6.
29. *Lettre de Matignon,* No. 3, March 1, 1982; and *Le Monde,* October 2, 1982.
30. Serge Bolloch, "Les deçus de la rentrée," *Le Monde,* October 6, 1982, and National Assembly debate on education budget, November 5, 1982, reported in *Journal Officiel, Ass. Natle., Débats,* for that date.
31. These figures are from Commission du Bilan, pp. 138, 142, 143, and MEN, *Note d'Information,* 82.09, pp. 2–3.
32. MEN, *Etudes et Documents,* 1975: No. 31, pp. 20 and 34; and MEN, *Note d'Information,* No. 76-40, November 19, 1976, p. 3.
33. MEN, "Dossier: les zones prioritaires. Une politique de lutte contre les inégalites sociales," *Cahiers de l'Education Nationale,* No. 1, January 1982, pp. 8–10.
34. Figures supplied by MEN, Service des études informatiques et statistiques, 58, Bd. du Lycee, Vanves.
35. *Le Monde,* January 25, 1983, p. 12.
36. *Le Monde,* January 25, 1983, p. 12.
37. *Le Monde de l'Education,* No. 92, March 1983, pp. 6–7.
38. *Le Monde,* February 3, 1983.
39. *Le Monde,* February 8, 1983.
40. Christian Beullac, "Quai des Brumes," *Le Monde,* February 11, 1983.
41. *Le Monde,* December 21, 1982, p. 10.
42. MEN, *Note d'Information,* 81-08 and 82-12.
43. Charles Vial, "Guerre ou paix pour l'école privée?" *Le Monde,* March 20 and 21–22, 1982.
44. *Le Nouvel Observateur,* May 15–21, 1982, p. 46.
45. Among the 277 deputies from metropolitan France elected as Socialists or Radicals of the Left (MRG), the professions listed in the candidates' official declaration of candidacy give the following totals: 25 university professors, 94 secondary school teachers, and 13 elementary school teachers. *Les Elections Législatives de Juin 1981, Le Monde, Dossiers et Documents,* June 1981, p. 84.
46. *Le Monde,* December 21, 1982.

47. *Le Monde,* December 23, 1982.
48. Interview with Charles Vial, *Le Monde,* December 29, 1982.
49. *Le Monde,* January 11, 1983.
50. *L'Unité,* November, 1977.
51. John S. Ambler, "Politicization of Higher Education in Britain and France," *Policy Studies Journal,* 10: 1 (September 1981), 136–149.
52. For an excellent analysis of this phenomenon, see Gianni Statera, *Death of a Utopia: The Development and Decline of Student Organizations in Europe* (New York: Oxford University Press, 1975).
53. See, for example, *Le Point,* May 31, 1976.
54. *Le Monde,* October 14, 1980.
55. *Le Monde,* October 2, 1981.
56. Evelyne Fallot, "Les Universités sur la paille," *L'Express* No. 1648 (February 11, 1983), pp. 49–51; and *Le Monde,* October 16, 1982, and February 3, 1983.
57. Quoted in *Le Monde,* November 27, 1982.
58. *Le Monde,* November 27, 1982.
59. *Le Monde,* July 1, 1983.
60. The *autonomes* were unrepresented on this committee, having boycotted the election of faculty representatives on the ground that all ranks were thrown together, with no representatives to be chosen by senior faculty.
61. Alain Savary, "Enseignement supérieur: les motifs et les tâches," Part II, *Le Monde,* January 27, 1983.
62. Savary, "Enseignement Supérieur."
63. Serge Bolloch and Charles Vial, "Errance," *Le Monde,* May 2, 1983.
64. *Le Monde,* October 7, 1982.
65. *Le Monde,* December 3, 1969.
66. John S. Ambler, "Neocorporatism and the Politics of French Education," a paper presented to the annual meeting of the American Political Science Association, September 1983.
67. Jean-Marie Donegani and Marc Sadoun, "La Réforme de l'enseignement secondaire en France depuis 1945. Analyse d'une non-décision," *Revue française de science politique,* 26:6 (December 1976), 1125–1146; and Paul Gerbod, *Les Enseignants et la Politique* (Paris: Presses Universitaires de France, 1976), Chapters 3 and 4.
68. Commission du Bilan, pp. 178–188.
69. André de Peretti and the Commission on *La Formation des Personnels de l'Education Nationale* (Paris: La Documentation Française, 1982); and SNES, *L'Université Syndicaliste,* March 19, 1982.
70. This view was expressed in interviews with the author by Jean-Louis Piednoir, *Chef de la Délégation National à l'Education,* Parti Socialiste, June 2, 1982, and various officials in the *Ministère de l'Education Nationale,* June, 1982.
71. Interview with Didier Chouat, Deputy, Parti Socialiste, June 30, 1982.
72. John S. Ambler, "The Politics of French University Reform: Ten Years after May," *Contemporary French Civilization,* Fall 1978, pp. 11–27.
73. Interview with Michel Alliot, July 19, 1976.
74. Mail survey of university *Secrétaires généraux,* conducted by the author, with 45 of 72 responding.
75. Raymond Boudon, *Education, Opportunity, and Social Inequality* (New York: Wiley, 1974).

6

Decentralizing France

DOUGLAS E. ASHFORD

The political and administrative uncertainties of massive local reform make it a formidable and unwelcome task for any modern democratic government. There have been several global reorganizations of local government systems in Europe such as those in Scandinavian countries and Britain,[1] but they have often fallen short of expectations. The main reason for these difficulties has been the close relationship between national and local government in the modern welfare state. France is no exception. The rapid social and economic development of France over the past 30 years has created an intricate pattern of administrative interdependence and a well-entrenched system of reciprocal political rewards and benefits. The network or *réseau* of mutual dependence among political and administrative officials is by no means unique to France, but it has a particularly resilient and ingenious pattern of intergovernmental relationships. It also has been the object of strong criticism from many leading French scholars.[2]

The Mitterrand government has launched numerous reforms that will affect French institutions for many years to come, but the most ambitious in terms of the potential organized resistance and the

This chapter is based on the situation of the *loi Defferre* in the French legislature as of early 1983. Details may change by the time the Senate and Assembly act and as decrees elaborate existing legislation. Some of the evaluations here are from interviews during visits to France in the summer of 1981 and in January 1982, accomplished with the assistance of the Center for International Studies at Cornell University, for which I am indebted.

145

immense administrative complexity is surely the *loi Defferre* of March 1982 and its legislative sequel. By the end of 1982 there were nine new statutes affecting various elements of the local government system as well as 21 decrees and eight circulars providing more precise directions and procedures. In 1982 some of the most controversial and complex laws were still being considered: the establishment of a local civil service, which will involve three pieces of legislation; the law on holding multiple elected office *(cumul des mandats)*; the law on local functions *(compétences)* under debate in the 1982–83 parliament; the law on local electoral reform for overseas possessions; the law on the mixed public-private local development agencies *(sociétés d'économie mixte)*; and legislation on the immensely complicated task of reforming the local tax system. If one is bewildered by the endless wave of legislation to reform the French local government system, one must also admire a government prepared to initiate such a complex and thankless task.

In fact the Socialist Party made no secret of its determination to reform the system, and the French people were well aware of the consequences of their vote in May 1981. Under the theme "decentralization" such reforms figured prominently in the negotiations producing the Common Program with the Communists in 1972. For the 1977 local elections and the 1978 legislative elections the Party produced a short book on its proposals.[3] The most detailed source on Socialist thinking was a *proposition loi* submitted to the National Assembly in 1980 and widely distributed within the Party.[4] Local reform was a major campaign promise in the 1981 presidential and legislative elections. Mitterrand appointed Gaston Defferre, one of his most powerful supporters and the city boss of the Socialist bastion of Marseilles, to head the new Ministry of the Interior and Decentralization and to shepherd the new legislation through parliament. With virtually a *carte blanche* from the president, the elderly Defferre clearly intends to make decentralization the keystone of his final, lasting contribution to French democracy. The magnitude of the political risks to the Socialist Party can be best understood by recalling that like most French parties, it is built on departmental federations of which the strongholds of Lille, under Prime Minister Mauroy, and Marseilles are the most important.

The political and parliamentary effort to achieve decentralization has high political costs in time and energy that might be devoted to the nation's other serious national and international problems. But on taking power in 1981, the Party also had real obligations to its local militants, many of them strong advocates of decentralization and self-management *(autogestion)*, which would require changes in the social and economic role of regions, departments and communes. Within the Party there was an indecisive debate on the perennial problem of whether regions or departments should predominate in the new structure.[5] Within the cabinet familiar ministerial rivalries surfaced to restrain Defferre's determined efforts to dismantle Parisian powers over localities. In short the reforms have not been easy for the Socialists even though they are uniformly committed to decentralization. As we shall see, pleasing local militants and rushing through complex legislation also produced a few political blunders that tarnish Socialist reputations. In this respect the Socialist experience with local reorganization has been no different than that of their Gaullist and Giscardian predecessors. A glance at precedents of the earlier regimes helps put the Socialist reforms in perspective.

Gaullist and Giscardian Lessons on Decentralization

Although the earlier governments of the Fifth Republic were by no means enthusiastic decentralizers, restructuring the overly articulated and inefficient French local government system was an integral, if unwelcome, part of de Gaulle's plans to modernize France. A decree of 1959 consolidating the regional field administration was among his first acts. There followed the 1964 regional reforms and the creation of a national agency devoted to regional planning and assistance (DATAR). These changes were by no means effortless, and some were bitterly resisted by the prefects.[6] But to modernize French industry and to rebuild French cities de Gaulle needed a modern urban infrastructure. This entailed the struggle between two of the elite *grands corps* wherein the *ponts et chaussées* emerged as the dominant group in allocating massive public investments to French cities.[7]

It was no easier for the Gaullists than for the Socialists to avoid the political dilemmas of rapid local change. In many respects the Gaullists were even less well equipped politically for their party had no strong local base in 1958. Their efforts to prod the communes and departments into action were no less clumsy than some of the Socialist proposals. The 1964 local election reform, for example, was clearly aimed at depriving the Communists of their local power base; but the real effect was to make the Left aware for the first time that if they were divided electorally they could be easily defeated. The first signs of effective Socialist-Communist electoral cooperation are actually to be found in the 1965 local elections. Without doubt the most serious political blunder was the 1969 referendum to reform the Senate and to create regional governments. The defeat of the referendum was orchestrated by local leaders and ultimately drove de Gaulle from office.

Although many accounts of the early Fifth Republic leave the impression that de Gaulle could easily sweep aside opposition, this was never the case in implementing local reforms. On the contrary, de Gaulle was in the uncomfortable situation of attacking his most reliable supporters, the *petite bourgeoisie,* whose attachments to outmoded forms of local governance as well as to inefficient economic and social habits were an obstacle to building an independent, competitive France. Many of the local *notables* had always distrusted de Gaulle even though they turned to him in the dark days of the Algerian revolution. Many were later to drift toward the centrist party of Giscard d'Estaing because it promised less abrupt change. The most detested of Gaullist reform efforts were the various plans to consolidate communes. Ninety percent of the communes (32,405) contain only 26 percent of the French population (about 14 million people), but the major problems of modernizing industry and commerce were in 266 cities of over 30,000 that hold two-thirds of the population. The first two efforts to consolidate this unwieldly system failed for many reasons. Finally, in 1971, the *loi Marcellin* established a cumbersome and ultimately very ineffective process to consolidate communes voluntarily.

Neither Pompidou nor Giscard were prepared to force change on local government, but their steady pressure toward improving aspects of the system helped prepare the ground for the Socialists. As with the Socialists, there was a lively debate within the Gaullist ranks over the relative merits of strengthening regions or departments. The regions, then as now, were championed by the more technocratic modernizers because they provided a more reliable way to channel public investments. Pompidou's first prime minister, Jacques Chaban-Delmas, who was himself a city boss from Bordeaux, hoped to reinforce the regions. Pompidou, who came to view Chaban-Delmas as a rival, blocked these proposals, conceding in this case, as in others, to the local *notables.* In 1970 the president took control of DATAR from his prime minister and in a well-known speech announced that the regions were to be no more than "unions of departments."[8] President Giscard d'Estaing was no more favorable than Pompidou to strong regions which would be a threat to the more traditional middle-class French citizens that he attracted to his party. Though in many respects still the most complete report on the diverse problems of French local government, the Guichard Report[9] of 1976 only provided lip-service to a highly suspected reform. Even though the Report suggested the mildest form of voluntary regrouping of communes, it received severe local criticism and was quietly put aside as the 1978 legislative elections approached.

These early reforms proved useful to the Socialists but were less dramatic and gradual. They were introduced at great effort and often at great cost to national government. The efficiency of local services was improved by an elaborate system of single and multipurpose local districts (SIVOM) that by 1982 included over 38 million French citizens. Nine metropolitan areas established reasonably effective government by forming *communautés urbaines.* For land-use and development purposes an elaborate system of plans and related development districts emerged which now involve over 10 million French citizens.[10] In effect France experienced local modernization by stealth and at great cost to national government that had no choice but to provide the financial incentives and new administrative structure to make these improvements possible. There gradually emerged an entirely new relationship between the prefects, their staffs and their areas based on a *tutelle financière.*[11] Much resented, it was in reality the only recourse of a national government that found nearly every direct approach to local reform blocked.

The path to reform prior to 1981 required enormous ingenuity and effort by national government, and now provides the base for the Socialist reforms.[12] There were elaborate negotiations and endless debates in parliament, for example, on how to modernize the antiquarian local tax system. At enormous cost (the government is estimated to have contributed about 4 billion additional francs per year in local operating subsidies) a block grant was devised and later converted by Giscard into the *donation globale de fonctionnement* (DGF). Plans were well advanced to create another block grant for investment, the *dotation globale d'équipement* (DGE). Both these policies became integral parts of the Socialist reforms. But the most important lesson learned from 20 years of struggle to reform communes was that consolidation is impossible. No less sensitive to local political interests than their predecessors, the Socialists never raised the consolidation issue.

The Socialists learned a great deal from the constant, if often discouraging, efforts of their predecessors. Much highly technical work had been done, especially on local tax reform, on block grants to localities and on property assessment. Because they arrived in power after five years of controlling most of the large French cities (154 of the 222 cities over 30,000), the Socialist leaders had an intimate knowledge of local government complexities. Moreover, decentralization seemed an opportune way to deliver on Socialist promises of increased participation.[13] Most important there was a leading Socialist politician, Gaston Defferre, who had chaffed under the frustrations of the French local government system for over 30 years, and who had developed strong ideas on how to modernize the system.

Within a month after the election of the new Socialist parliament, the basic legislation was introduced. Like the earlier efforts to pass local government legislation, the progress of the *loi Defferre* was slow and frustrating. Although given priority in a crowded parliamentary agenda, the Socialists were determined not to use parliamentary shortcuts to diminish debate. The *loi Defferre* was debated in the National Assembly for over 170 hours over a nine-month period and was subjected to some 1500 amendments, many gratefully received to clarify the law. Under pressure from the Senate, the bastion of local power-holders, the initial bill of 65 articles grew to an extensively detailed law of 108 articles. There were lengthy and useful reports from both the Senate and the Assembly.[14] Under pressure from the Constitutional Council, changes were made to clarify the powers of the prefect, now labeled the *Commissaire de la République*. The principal objections raised to the reform concerned the proposed elimination of the traditional requirement of prior national government approval for local government expenditures and its replacement by *a posteriori* budget control. Several of the more sweeping and controversial reforms, such as the reorganization of Parisian government, were postponed in order to get the *loi-cadre* over parliamentary and constitutional hurdles. The *loi Defferre*, promulgated on March 2, 1982, thus became the most important transformation of the communes, departments and regions since Napoleon put the structure in place in 1801.

Creating a Parallel Administrative System

The most critical change was undoubtedly redefining the status of the prefects. Under the *loi Defferre*, communes, departments and regions will have their own executive agents responsible to the mayors and elected councils. But the prefects do not disappear. Many feel that they will have even greater powers because the law also gives the new *Commissaires* more control over their staff, composed largely of civil servants from other Parisian ministries who have been known to pursue their own ends and programs regardless of the wishes of the prefect. The presumption that the prefects will now become ciphers in French administration is misleading. Since 1960 they have steadily developed high-level managerial skills and are sought out as executive agents in Paris as well as by local councils who value their skill in manipulating the system and want them as chief executives of important departments and large communes. The *Commissaire* retains all his state powers over law and order, the police and electoral supervision. Moreover, he will undoubtedly still be badly needed to manage the affairs of the small communes which cannot afford to hire their own executives. Article 3 of the law permits the communes to waive their new powers, thereby opening a loophole so that the thousands of poor and depopulated communes will continue to rely on the *Commissaires* to prepare their budgets and oversee disbursements, much as the prefects have always done.

Despite Socialist enthusiasm for decentralization, defining the new conditions for exercising the *a posteriori* review of local budgets remained controversial. The new *Commissaire* has two months to appeal to an administrative tribunal any local decision that violates the law.[15] If the tribunal has not decided the case in three months, it automatically moves on as a matter of urgency to the Council of State. Under previous legislation the communes brought some 2200 cases per year before the tribunals, but recourse to the courts to settle differences is as laborious and disruptive in France as in most democracies and in most instances suggests that neither national nor local officials are working well. Perhaps the most important amendment accepted by the Socialists was an elaboration of the review powers where the issue concerns public or individual liberties. In these cases the tribunal can suspend the decision within two days and the case can be directly appealed to the Council of State within two weeks.

Though difficult to write, the audit controls are probably more crucial than the judicial ones. However liberated we may think the communes are by the right to execute their budgets without prior prefectoral approval, public spending has become too large in all democracies to leave the consequences to chance. Communes are still required to have balanced budgets. Article 5 states that receipts and expenses should be evaluated in a "sincere fashion"—a remarkably frank admission of the complexities and uncertainties of budgeting in an inflationary world. Where the *Commissaire* believes the budget to be unbalanced, he notifies the local council and may submit his objections to a newly organized system of regional *Cours des Comptes,* which proposes the necessary adjustments. If these recommendations are not acted on in a month or if the adjustments are considered insufficient by the court, the *Commissaire* prepares the budget himself. The *Commissaire* also retains the power to execute the budget himself if it is not prepared by the end of March of the budget year.

The significance of this cumbersome procedure remains to be seen. The general feeling in Paris is that the process provides little protection for the state because there are no sanctions. In fact, without elaborate and rarely used proceedings, none of the inspections and decisions of the *Cours des Comptes* has ever had the force of law. To anticipate the future one must look to other countries relying on an audit system. If Britain is an acceptable example, enforcing audit decisions can only create political *causes célèbres* as the famous Poplar decision did when a steadfast local Labour council trooped off to prison amid cheering crowds after defying government spending limitations.[16] In a world of rapidly rising local costs and increasing resistance by local taxpayers, the audit is a paper tiger. Indeed the new law admits this. Where the local accountant declines to execute the budget, the mayor may override his objections (Article 10). To the applause of the opposition, Defferre so diluted the possibility of fining local councillors (Article 11) that they can only be deprived of their compensation for abuse of budgetary powers. Whatever may be the truth of the legendary pecuniary habits of the French, under the new system they are the only effective check on excessive local spending.

The realities of modern government mean that if the reformed system does not have persons of the caliber of the old prefects, they will have to be invented. More likely, as *Le Monde* noted,[17] the prefect has been made "to disappear in order to better reappear." Since their creation the prefects have been adept political animals, and all the signs suggest that these very skills will be no less indispensable in the future. The Socialists have not foregone the traditional "waltz of the prefects." By late 1982 there had been 91 changes among the 94 departments and 19 changes among the 22 regions.[18] The effect of the *loi Defferre* may well be to sharpen prefectoral political skills. The most important clue to the probable outcome is the formation of a parallel prefectoral corps composed of prefects on leave to work as local chief executives under the new law. In recognition of the new pattern, the prefectoral *grands corps* formed a new association for those employed by local governments, with the remarkable name of the *Association Amicale des Hauts Fonctionnaires du Ministère de l'Intérieur en Service auprès des Collectivités Locales et des Regions.* The group represents a new twist to the long-established habits of *service détaché* practiced by all the *grands corps.* As the prefect organizing the new group said at the inauguration of the new association, prefects will continue to exist as a body because "mobility and adaptation have always been part of their equipment *(baggage)*."[19]

The curious ultimate effect may be to make the *réseau* of the 1960s into an even more politically attuned *réseau* over the 1980s. In a pragmatic fashion the prefects have organized themselves into two groups, one working with the government of the day in their official capacities and another detached to work with politically sympathetic localities. As the electoral cycle unfolds, prefects may simply rotate between national and local jobs according to their political ambitions and political dispositions, no less secure than they have ever been and probably no less influential. Of course, this effect can be exaggerated because the large cities have had their own staffs and managers for many years. The Association of Secretary Generals is also one of the most influential local government groups and can be expected to prosper under the new system. At the other extreme, the poor communes will not be able to take advantage of the new law in order to create their own staffs. The uncertainties are greater for the intermediate-sized communes and poorer departments which will want to enjoy the autonomy offered by the new law, but do not have the experience and perhaps the resources to afford expert help. But to these known horizontal differences among the communes and departments there is now added the new dimension of an informal prefectoral corps within which localities can more easily identify politically sympathetic administrators, possibly making the old "waltz of the prefects" more like an energetic polka as elections periodically restructure central-local linkages.

To these administrative uncertainties must be added the still uncertain future of a local civil service. Very early in the history of the *loi Defferre* the Communist Minister for the Civil Service, Anicet Le Pors, extracted an agreement from Defferre that any new local civil service would enjoy the same privileges and security as the national civil service. Again the large communes have had their own bureaucracy for some time (Paris has 40,000 public employees). It is the intermediate-sized communes and poor departments where the local councils will be tempted to add public employees, perhaps encouraged by the official program of reducing unemployment by creating more public jobs. There are now about half a million local civil servants in France, but the number could easily double under the new law. The cost could be substantial because many of those to be added are the technically and managerially more skilled employees who were formerly often supplied by the national field administration or paid special fees *(primes)* by local governments in order to perform specific tasks and to prepare projects for Paris.

In any event the legal organization of the new local civil service will add to the complexity, not to mention the incentives for political manipulation, within the French local government system. The early estimate is that 15 new territorial civil service corps will be needed,[20] corresponding as they do in any country to the major functions of national government. Respect for administrative rights has not disappeared with a socialist government. Indeed, in order to avoid alienating the many socialist supports within public sector unions, the government must not appear to be jeopardizing the existing privileges of the national civil service. Moreover, socialist supporters in local government must be assured that new public employees are in no way second-class bureaucrats. The result is that the new local civil service will entail three laws: one to define the rights and obligations of the entire civil service; one to state more clearly the status of the national civil service as part of the proposed general reform of the civil service; and one to create the new territorial or local civil service. As in all modern states, the national political importance of public employees and their strong public sector unions create uncertainties whether creating these reforms will change old administrative habits.

Though more a commentary on the complexity of modern intergovernmental relations than a criticism of the Socialist administrative reforms that accompany the *loi Defferre*, it is clear that decentralization will relieve few administrative tangles and will generate new dimensions of complexity. For example, in order to persuade the *Cours des Comptes* to staff the regional *Cours*, a special *grands corps* was created. With the unofficial split of the prefectoral *grands corps* there are in effect two additional elite administrative groups added to the panoply of the higher civil service. As the communes, departments and regions expand their executive support there will be a dozen or more local civil service groups, presumably enjoying pay, privileges and security similar to the benefits of national civil servants. As the administrative system at all levels becomes more politicized, as it shows every sign of doing, there will be the added complications of a regularly rotating body of top local administrative managers and technicians as elections create new opportunities for some and cut off careers of the politically less fortunate. To all this one must add the parallel administrative network that will still extend down to the communal level. There is little reason to think that the new *réseau* will be less intricate than the old one.

Political Risks and Opportunities

The political risks and opportunities of the *loi Defferre* and its supporting legislation are not to be found solely within the new legislation itself, but in relation to the factions within the Socialist Party, its alliance with the Communist Party and its relations to the opposition. In the euphoria following the Socialist victory of May 1981, many of these problems were temporarily submerged. The Socialists themselves are beneficiaries of the remarkably localized political system. How the Socialist Party made its political calculation is not known, but the reforms present a number of difficult choices to the Socialists and have produced at least one serious political blunder that has been mercilessly exploited by the opposition.

There was little surprise in the Socialist reform of the local electoral law, although it was not nearly as unmistakably politically motivated as was the Gaullist 1964 local electoral law. Like minority parties in many democracies, the Socialists and the Left generally have felt discriminated against under the older system and hoped that some element of proportional representation would insure their full representation in elected councils. But there are important differences within the Party as to how far the Socialists should go in protecting the diminishing strength of their ally, the Communist Party, when it appears that they alone might be able to make a persuasive electoral appeal. A small sign of such internal differences appeared with the early discussion of the local electoral reform. The usual explanatory notes of the discussions by the Council of Ministers of pending legislation said nothing when the matter first reached cabinet level.[21] In addition it should be noted that the indirect method of electing departmental and regional councils worked to the advantage of the Socialists in 1981. Their sweeping victory in the 1981 legislative elections was translated into control of 13 regional governments, a gain of four. There is a familiar specter hanging over the Socialist Party for it knows very well how it acquired credibility by transforming local power into national support. There is no doubt that the opposition had the same designs during the 1983 local elections.

Given these complications, it is courageous of the Socialists not to have fashioned a local election law more openly favoring their interests. As with the administrative reforms, the new electoral law also recognizes the stratified character of the local government system and applies only to those communes with over 5000 persons (under 1500 communes representing about 32 million persons). Several provisions remove old inequities and abuses,[22] but the basic format is a modified proportional representation system retaining the old method of lists. If one list receives a majority on the first ballot, it is given a majority of seats and the remaining seats are distributed proportionally. There is no second ballot. If there is no absolute majority on the first ballot, half the seats are distributed proportionally and the remaining half in proportion to second ballot results. Parties are again permitted to merge their lists between ballots. The method of voting is designed to accommodate the multiparty system while providing some insurance that a majority will emerge in most elections.

To some extent the new electoral system responds to sentiments among local Socialist militants who feel that they were forced to make inordinate sacrifices on behalf of the Communist alliance, and much stronger feelings in a few communes where Socialists have been in a state of perpetual warfare with Communists. It is easy to forget that the Common Program was not only a dramatic national gesture, but was forged in local elections where the Party disciplined their voters to assist Communists and in a few cases permitted Communist mayors to be elected even though Socialists might have controlled the council. The law responds by providing the opportunity for local Socialist organizations to win on the first ballot without Communist support, using the reorganized second ballot as a safety measure to prevent the opposition from winning. But at the same time the new system also provides an incentive for the divided opposition to get its house in order. The widely publicized luncheon of ex-President Giscard d'Estaing and ex-Prime Minister Chirac in late 1982 was a signal that Gaullists and Giscardians meant to fight the 1983 elections in every way possible.

The Socialists persisted in their determination to democratize local politics despite somber warnings in local elections. Although the Left could benefit nationally from the proportional representation measures introduced for larger communes, their difficulties with unemployment and inflation hurt them badly in the 1982 and 1983 local elections. In the departmental elections of March 1982, the opposition took control of 58 of the 94 departments. Given the cumulative effect of the indirect electoral system for departments, they will probably also lose control of three regional councils. Because of the relentless cycle of elections in France, both the departmental and communal elections were severely nationalized. No sooner did the departmental elections end than the 1983 local election campaign began. The results confronted the Socialists with the paradoxical effects of their decentralization efforts. In much of France the implementation and the local benefits of the reforms will fall to the opposition.

The Socialists expected to suffer some losses in the 1983 local elections, but were clearly surprised by the indecision and lethargy of many previous voters on the Left. In the first ballot the Left lost 16 cities with populations over 30,000 (the results in the 220 cities in this category are generally taken as the main indication of party trends), and in the second ballot lost an additional 15 cities. The Socialist Party managed to hold on to only 31 of its 61 newly won cities from the local elections of 1977, suggesting that there was a serious drift toward the Center of many undecided voters. Control of the Left in these larger towns and cities dropped from 154 in 1977 to 120 in 1983 (63 Socialist and 57 Communist), while the opposition took 100. Of the 36 cities with populations over 100,000, which will benefit most from the new laws, the opposition in 1983 controlled 24 and the Left 12. Chirac won control of all the Parisian *arrondisements* so that his national challenge is more firmly rooted in Paris than ever before.[23] Perhaps more humiliating for the government, 10 of the 34 ministers running as mayors were defeated, and both Mauroy and Defferre were forced into second ballots in their Socialist bastions of Lille and Marseille. There is no doubt that these sobering results will moderate Socialist reforms in the future, but they in no way constituted a rejection of the Defferre reorganization proposals.

Perhaps the least welcome task of reordering the French local government system has been reforming the *cumul des mandats*. Until 1982 it was possible to hold five elected offices simultaneously, clearly a ridiculous situation as all the major parties agree. French presidents have preferred to leave the diplomacy of changing the system to their prime ministers, as Giscard did with Barre and Mitterrand did with Mauroy. The problem is slightly more difficult for the Left because the Gaullist study of the *cumul* shows that Socialists and Communists benefit slightly more than does the Right.[24] But the Socialists have always regarded the tradition as unfair, and very early in their government they encouraged ministers who held the presidencies of regional councils to leave these more demanding posts. As the task suggests, Mauroy chose a well-placed Socialist Deputy, Marcel Debarge, to conduct the new inquiry. The Debarge Report[25] suggests a complex scheme to restrict the number of elected offices: presidency of a communal, departmental or regional council is incompatible with sitting in the European parliament; being a deputy or senator is similarly incompatible with sitting in the European Parliament; the presidency of both a regional and departmental council is incompatible; and the total number of elected offices is limited to three. While hardly the strict limitation on elected offices recognized in most democracies, the changes would be a major restriction on the electoral monopoly that has choked the development of new local political leaders in France.

The most serious political blunder among the many Socialist reforms has been the reorganization of the Parisian city government. For all the efforts of earlier regimes to disperse the attractions and even the glamour of Paris, the magnetism of the capital city seems stronger than ever. Just as Giscard was annoyed to see his rival, Chirac, become mayor in 1976, so also the Socialist and Communist minority (they controlled 7 of 20 *arrondisements* in 1982) in Paris resented having such a highly visible and important office in the capable hands of the Gaullist leader. In fact Mitterrand agrees with Chirac that Parisians should not bear the burden of living in the capital and cooperated with Chirac in sharing the expenses and major investments in the capital city. The Paris budget of nearly 15 billion francs is 5 percent of all local government expenditure, and its capital budget of nearly 3 billion francs provides ample opportunity to reward supportive voters. But because there is no possibility that the Left might control Paris, the initial harsh and unworkable proposals for the reform of Parisian government appeared to be nothing but a vindictive political act. To cries of "electoral sauerkraut" from the opposition, the Socialists were forced to retract their proposals.

In effect the *avant-projet* for Paris would have created fully independent local councils in the 20 *arrondisements,* each with their own budget and their own powers to raise taxes for most of the vital functions of city government. Apparently yielding to pressure from the Socialist leader on the Paris city council, Georges Sarre, Defferre had made a major miscalculation. Soon all of Paris and much of France reacted with outrage. The opposition waged a relentless battle to extract political capital from the blunder and used it to deprive Mauroy of much needed publicity for his newly launched public works and unemployment programs. The plan was released to the press in early July 1982. By mid-month the president himself intervened to reassure the nation that Paris was not to be dismantled.[26] In a belated attempt to soften the adverse impact, the Socialists decided that the other two largest cities—Lyon and Marseilles—would also be included in the law, although the organizational differences among these cities are so great that it greatly complicates legislation.

When the revised bill was revealed in late 1982,[27] the Socialists retracted nearly every strong measure to dismantle the city. The Parisian *arrondisements* will have elected mayors wtih a small staff, but they will not acquire the full legal status of communes, be able to enact a budget or to levy taxes. Their powers extend mostly to managing local amenities such as playgrounds and parks, plus some voice in the construction of public housing in their areas. They will have no powers to hire public employees, but they can submit questions concerning the performance of Parisian government to the city council and must be consulted in land-use planning. But the political costs of this major miscalculation remained to plague the Socialists. Months after the government had conceded everything demanded by the Gaullist leader, Chirac devoted an entire city council meeting to his attack on the ill-considered proposal, clearly using the blunder to mobilize support for the approaching local elections of 1983. In those elections this blunder probably cost them the small number of seats they once held on the Paris city council.

The Ambiguities of Local Social and Economic Powers

The most severe dilemmas confronting the Socialists are how to achieve a measure of social justice and equity while adding new social and economic functions to lower level governments. This is a classic problem of decentralization. Given the political and technical problems of redistributing resources within such a highly articulated local government system, it is virtually impossible to prevent large differences in spending and tax revenues among the local units. In France such inequalities are exaggerated because local taxes are based on various forms of property and payroll taxes, while the government grant to localities is based on value-added tax paid by the locality.[28] The Giscardian government tried to reduce some of these inequities by introducing an equalization fund within the grant system, but the new provisions take effect over a decade and were severely amended by the National Assembly. To the end of 1982 the Socialists have preferred not to reopen this difficult question, and the grant system continues to function under the legislation of earlier governments.

The economic situation of localities is further complicated by other socialist policies. Roughly half of local taxes are raised by a *taxe professionel,* essentially a salary tax paid by business and commerce. The government promised to reduce this tax by 5 billion francs to encourage economic recovery. Because the government increased corporate, income and social security taxes that are calculated in very similar ways, it is difficult to ask the same taxpayers to accept large increases in local taxation. The problem is further compounded by unemployment and inflation. The Socialists have appealed to business to create new jobs and even offered incentives in reduced social security taxation for those who do. Any increase in local taxes might easily negate whatever unemployment relief comes from these national policies. From mid-1982, combating inflation also became a major national economic goal. The entire local government system costs the country roughly 300 billion francs a year, and nearly half this amount (44.9 percent of operating expenses and 67 percent of investment expense) is provided by Paris.[29] As we have seen in Britain and the United States, grants to localities are an obvious and accessible target for budget cuts. Even if the system is undisturbed there is no doubt that the Ministry of Finance will be watching closely for any sharp increase in local expenditure. It is significant that Finance

Minister Jacques Delors was in charge of writing the two laws specifying how the *a posteriori* budgetary system would work.

These problems are by no means unique to the Socialists, but in their electoral campaign the Party promised a larger local role in major economic decisions affecting localities. Indeed the haste with which the nationalization program was pressed on parliament in 1981 left little time to consult regional governments, and this neglect drew public criticism from local Socialist militants. More than most industrial democracies, France has built an elaborate system of regional planning and consultation which the Socialists have promised to continue and even to strengthen. Leaving aside the austerity which the Socialists are trying to introduce, these promises face several difficult complications. The provisional two-year plan does not make radical suggestions,[30] and Mitterrand is a less enthusiastic planner and regional advocate than many government leaders. The change of government in March 1983 suggests that any ambitious plans to expand regional government will be delayed.

The orchestration of national and local economic interests is always a difficult task, but it is clear that the strong Socialist regions of France expect to have a greater voice. In the decentralization debate Defferre noted that local economic assistance to firms would be consistent with national industrial policies, but no one knows quite how this will be accomplished. The old *tutelle financière* was clearly clumsy and inefficient, but it did manage to bring national and local objectives into focus. Whether this structure will disappear with the new investment block grant (DGE) remains to be seen, but there are reports that enterprising elite civil servants of the *ponts et chaussées,* who for many years dominated the Ministry of Infrastructure and manipulated the entire system of investment subsidies to localities, are eagerly seeking jobs in other parts of the government. In any event the DGE will be only a fraction of total local public investment. New laws are planned on urban planning, intercommunal projects and public-private development projects *(sociétés d'économie mixte)*.

There is also a large component within the Socialist Party devoted to principles of self-management *(autogestion)* and their aims received recognition in the *loi Defferre*. Article 34 provides that regions and departments may intervene in the local economy with both direct and indirect assistance for "enterprises in difficulty." What this actually means is extremely vague and will have to be worked out in practice. But there is no doubt that some Socialist strongholds want to expand their economic roles. Some initiatives had been taken in Grenoble under a strong *autogestion* advocate, Dubedout, but his defeat in the 1983 elections casts a shadow over this experiment. One regional council, Picardy, has taken a 20 percent interest in the regional bank, which suggests how intricate the potential conflict of financial and public interests could become. The Socialist leaders have not appeared eager to unleash their more militant local supporters, as revealed in the delay in appointing the new Economic and Social Committees to the regions. When the new procedures were finally announced in late 1982, there was an enlarged quotient of trade union members, but the president of the CFTD expressed his disappointment that consultation of the Committee on the national and regional plans was not made obligatory.[31] Clearly the government does not welcome the possibility that its plans to encourage industrial investment, to enlarge training programs and to reform unemployment insurance might be mired in trade union rivalries at the regional level.

The social and economic problems are of much greater importance to national officials than the transfer of new functions (*compétences*) to local government, although the latter have received more publicity. The *projet-loi* law on new functions was widely circulated over the fall of 1981 when ministries negotiated with the Ministry of the Interior to see what powers they might sacrifice to enlarge the activities of the new local government system. It is likely that few ministers voluntarily gave up important powers, and, when they did, insisted on preserving explicit supervisory powers. The results of the interministerial negotiations were significant but hardly a massive decentralization of ministerial powers. A total of 26 billion francs will be transferred to regional, departmental and communal government, the bulk of it (21.5 billion) to departments.[32] Of the 26 billion, 15 billion will come from national tax revenues to be assigned to the localities and 11 billion from grants (*dotations*) which presumably represent decreases in ministerial budgets.

The law on local functions was promulgated in January 1983 after having been declared to matter of urgency by the government. A law of 123 articles, it provides that the new local functions will be implemented in waves over three years: urban planning, public housing and job training programs in 1983; urban transportation, personal social services (*aide sociale*) and local courts in 1984; some aspects of educational and cultural programs, environmental controls and (perhaps most controversial) some local police activities in 1985. There is obviously an immense amount of planning and preparation to be done before the localities can organize the new services. Later decrees will define how responsibilities will be divided between national field services and the new offices of local governments. How effectively the ministries have protected their turf is difficult to foresee, but there was an enormous furor in the National Assembly because communes that did not have a state-approved land-use plan (POS) would still need permission from the *Commissaire* to issue construction permits.[33]

The law on functions also provides some additional information on how new resources will be provided in addition to the 26 billion in transfers from the national budget. The DGE for 1983 is 2.7 billion francs, about half going to the departments for roads and half to the communes for local roads and as a block grant for 20 percent of the old investment subsidies. A modest amount of new fiscal resources is also provided: regions will acquire a billion francs from auto registration fees *(cartes grises)*, and departments 7.7 billion from the road tax placed on all vehicles *(vignettes)*. The purpose of these additional revenues is presumably to assist the localities in paying for the new services, but the debate also alerted Socialists in parliament to the pitfalls of their own proposals. A group of Socialist deputies from departments normally run by conservative councils expressed their fears that "national aims" (meaning the influence of the Socialist national government) would be diluted with such substantial transfers of funds and functions.[34] As the 1983 elections demonstrated, much of these new revenues will be used by the opposition parties at the local level. But as in the case of the electoral changes, Defferre persevered in his determination to see important new responsibilities given to the localities.

Conclusion: Rebuilding the Intergovernmental Network

Although much remains to unfold as the *loi Defferre* is implemented with numerous decrees, circulars and interministerial confrontations over the coming years, the battery of decentralization laws will have irreversible effects on French institutions and society. The famous, and sometimes infamous, *services extérieurs* of French national administration will be divided, at least in the heavily populated and more prosperous areas of France, with a parallel administrative structure of the elected councils. Political conflict within and among the localities has always been fierce, but it can be expected to become more visible and possibly more intense, especially where the local councils of differing partisan alignment and at different levels of government must coordinate their efforts. Central-local relations are likely to become more complex because ministers who have struggled to the top of French politics are not about to relinquish their authority easily and because, as already is apparent with 58 departments and over half the regions under control of the opposition, national party rivalries will intrude on the conduct of local affairs and the design of local projects. Thus the *loi Defferre* and its sequel will be one of the most exciting experiments in transforming intergovernmental relations for many years to come.

Finally, it is interesting to speculate to what degree the *loi Defferre* represents a radical departure from the gradual change of the French local government system that has been proceeding for many years. The Socialists have learned important lessons from the Gaullist experiments with consolidation and have simply avoided the issue, even at the price of accepting one of the most fragmented local government structures in Europe. Furthermore, they have not chosen to advance with a single, global reform, but in their pragmatic fashion have understood that major change requires multiple adjustments of electoral laws, local taxation, local and national administration and numerous adjustments in legislation affecting land-use, planning and public housing. If the visible form of the new structure seems extraordinarily complex it is because the French, as they have throughout the Fifth Republic, recognize the complexity of intergovernmental decision-making. Unlike Britain, for example, the Socialists have continued to press for adjustments and redefinition of relationships throughout the entire fabric of intergovernmental politics and policy-making. Unlike nearly all the major European reorganizations of local government over the past two decades, the Socialists accepted the political risks of major reform, even when it was unpopular with their own supporters. In their acceptance of the complexity of modern government and in their determination to see that such complexity remains subject to diverse political interests and preferences, the French Socialists have reaffirmed the strengths of French democracy and have once again provided a model for vigorous local government that should be instructive for all the Western democracies.

Notes

1. For a good account of recent efforts to deal with the current problems of European local government systems, see James Sharpe, ed., *The Local Fiscal Crisis in Western Europe: Myths and Realities* (Beverly Hills, Cal.: Sage, 1981). On the historical and political development of central-local relations in Britain and France, see Douglas E. Ashford, *British Dogmatism and French Pragmatism: Central-Local Policy Making in the Welfare State* (Boston: Allen & Unwin, 1982). Consolidation has probably been the most severe in Scandinavia. See Francesco Kjellberg, "Local Government and the Scandinavian Welfare State: Structural and Functional Reforms of Local and Regional Authorities in Europe: Theory, Practice and Critical Appraisal" (Linz: Council of Europe, November 1981) No. 5–6.

2. The most complete account of the *réseau* is by Pierre Grémion, *Le pouvoir périphérique: Bureaucrats et notables dans le système politique français* Paris: Editions du seuil, 1976). The peculiar dynamic of administrative-political interdependence in France has been most completely described by Jean-Claude Thoenig, "La relation entre le centre et la périphérie en france: une analyse systémique," *Bulletin de l'IIAP*, 36 (October–December 1975) pp. 77–123, and Marie-Françoise Souchon, "Le réseaux de relations dans le système politico-administratif: Le cas des maires élus pour la première fois en mars 1971," in *Bulletin de l'IIAP*, 32 (October–December 1974) pp. 67–91.

3. See Socialist Party, *Citoyen dans sa Commune* (Paris: Flammarion, 1977).

4. Socialist Party, "Les Proposition Socialiste pour la décentralisation de l'Etat et la Réforme des collectivités locales," *Communes de France* (March 1, 1980), pp. 5–78.

5. Socialist Party, *Rapport Pisani* (Paris: May 1977).

6. On the conflict between government and the prefects over the 1960s, see Catherin Grémion, *Profession Décideurs: Pouvoirs des Hautes Fonctionnaires et Réforme de l'Etat* (Paris: Gauthiers-Villars, 1978). For a good account of the evolution of DATAR, see Sylvia Biarez, "Aménagement du Territoire in France: State Inverventionism or Regulation?" in *West European Politics*, Vol. 5, No. 3 (July 1982), pp. 270–286.

7. The classic study of this interministerial and administrative struggle is by Jean-Claude Thoenig, *L'ère des technocrates: le cas des ponts et chaussées* (Paris: Editions d'organisation, 1973).

8. François Decaumont, *La Présidence de Georges Pompidou: Essai sur le Régime Présidentialiste Française* (Paris: Economica, 1979), pp. 152–153.

9. Guichard Report, *Vivre Ensemble* (Paris: Documentation Française, 1976).

10. *Le Monde*, July 6, 1982.

11. On the development of the tutelle over the 1960s and the 1970s, see Douglas E. Ashford, "La Tutelle Financière: New Wine in Old Bottles?" in D. Ashford, ed., *National Resources and Urban Policy* (New York: Methuen, 1980), pp. 95–114.

12. See Douglas E. Ashford, *British Dogmatism and French Pragmatism*, pp. 85–125.

13. Electoral participation in French local elections is among the highest in Europe, often attracting 70 percent of the eligible voters. Nearly 80 percent of eligible voters turned out in 1983. However, the Socialist militants had hoped that there would be much more direct participation in determining local projects and local investment.

14. For the report by Senator Giraud, see *Rapport No. 33*, Sénate, First Session, 1981–1982 (October 22, 1981), 3 Vols. For the Richard Report, see *Rapport No. 697*, Assemblée Nationale Second Session 1981–1982 (January 21, 1982), 3 Vols.

15. Administrative tribunals are the court of first instance in the administrative legal system. In the past they have heard about 2000 causes a year from communes, only about 5 percent of the total caseload. In anticipation of an increase, the *loi Defferre* added 27 judges to the system. On their role and development, see *Le Monde*, August 14, 1981.

16. The best account of the incident is in Bryan Keith-Lucas and Peter G. Richards, *The History of Local Government in the Twentieth Century* (London: Allen & Unwin, 1978), pp. 65–91.

17. *Le Monde,* April 29, 1982.
18. *Le Monde,* November 25, 1982.
19. The incident precipitating the formation of the new association and no doubt offending many prefects was the appointment of Eric de Giuily as Director General for Local Government in the Ministry of the Interior. Giuily did not come from the prefectoral corps and broke the long tradition that the chief administrative official for local government should be a prefect. Giuily is actually from Conseil d'Etat and had been a personal aid for Defferre.
20. *Le Monde,* July 16, 1982.
21. *Le Monde,* May 23, 1982.
22. Two additional interesting provisions of the initial version of the law tried to rectify problems of particular significance to the Socialists. The local electoral lists were to include no more than 75 percent of persons of the same sex. In the past women held only 3 percent of the seats on communal, departmental and regional councils. The second reform relates to the manipulation of overseas votes in past elections in order to maximize their effect in marginal elections. Henceforth overseas voters can only vote in their commune of birth or of their last residence in France.
23. Jean-Marie Colombani, "Limiter les dégats," *Le Monde,* March, 15, 1983.
24. See the report prepared by the Gaullist deputy, François Neuily Léotard, "Faut-il limiter de cumul des mandats?", *Revue Politique et Parlémentaire,* Vol. 81 (November–December 1979), pp. 18–33.
25. Debarge is the leader of the Socialist Parliamentary Group in the National Assembly. See *Rapport au Premier Ministre sur le statut l'élu local, départmental et régional et la limitation du commune de fonctions et mandats électives* (Paris: National Assembly, January 22, 1982).
26. *Le Monde,* July 15, 1982.
27. *Le Monde,* September 28, 1982.
28. For more details of the past use of national subsidies and local taxation see Douglas E. Ashford, *British Dogmatism and French Pragmatism,* pp. 251–309.
29. *Les finances locales: Mémento Statisque 1982* (Paris: Director General of Local Government, 1982).
30. See *Plan Interminaire: Stratégie pour deux Ans 1982–1983* (Paris: Documentation Française, 1982).
31. *Le Monde,* November 25, 1982.
32. The distribution of these funds suggests that advocates of the department have won the preliminary skirmishes against increasing the power of regions. The figures are taken from the Ministry of Interior publication, *Démocratic Locale,* No. 22 (October 1982), p. 4.
33. French mayors of all political backgrounds have long considered the necessity of official approval of construction permits the most objectionable national constraint on local decision-making. On the debate, see *Le Monde,* December 2, 1982.
34. *Le Monde,* December 3, 1982.

7

Immigrants and Politics in France

MARTIN A. SCHAIN

Throughout this century France has maintained a large resident immigrant population. Three percent of the nation consisted of aliens before the First World War, a proportion that continued to increase to 6 percent after the war, until the mid-1930s, when unemployment and official and unofficial expulsions reduced the alien population back to about 3 percent. The vast majority of these resident aliens before the Second World War were Europeans, mostly from Italy and Eastern Europe.

After the Second World War, immigration began to increase once again, but the pattern changed (see Table 1). While the proportion of non-French European residents increased moderately, the proportion of Third World immigrants increased rapidly and substantially. During the postwar period, European residents increased by 35 percent (mostly from Portugal), while Third World residents increased by almost 600 percent (mostly from North Africa): in 1946, Third World immigrants accounted for only 0.5 percent of the French population, while in 1975 these immigrants constituted at least 2.6 percent of the population. Although they were still not a majority of resident immigrants in France (about 40 percent), in 1975 they were a minority that along with the Portuguese accounted for the growth of the immigrant population.

If we include the roughly 400,000 residents in France from the overseas departments and territories, residents from Third World coun-

166

TABLE 1. Immigration Patterns, 1911–1975

Percentage of Population	1911	1921	1931	1936	1946	1954	1962	1968	1975
From EEC	2.2	2.5	2.9	2.5	1.7	1.7	1.7	1.5	1.1
From Europe (total)	2.8	3.6	5.8	4.7	3.9	3.3	3.4	3.9	4.0
From Third World	0.2	0.3	0.8	0.6	0.5	0.9	1.3	1.5	2.6
Total Population (millions)	39.2	38.8	41.2	41.2	39.8	42.8	46.4	49.8	52.6

Source: <u>Donnes Sociales, 1981</u> (Paris: INSEE, 1982), pp. 46–47.

tries accounted for at least 3.3 percent of the population, and 46 percent of the immigrant population.

This "new" immigration is different from the older European immigration not only because of the obvious cultural differences, but also because of important differences in the patterns of linkages established between the different immigrant groups and the larger society. While the European immigrant groups have been gradually disappearing as differentiated ethnic divisions, either through naturalization or departure, the new immigrants have remained visible both because they have not been naturalized and because they have been perceived as ethnically and racially separate, whether or not they have become French citizens. Thus, for the first time, there is a large sector of the French population that is both stable and socially differentiated and that forms a basis for racial and ethnic conflict.

The question addressed in this chapter is the political impact of large concentrations of Third World immigrants and how their presence has stimulated and altered political issues, redefined and changed the range of policy choices in France. The focus is not on immigration policy, but on other issues and other policies that reflect the emergence of the ethnic/racial political issue in French political life. For our analysis citizenship status is less important than ethnic origin as a reference point for political issues and policies. Thus many of the "second generation" of Third World immigrants, and all of the Third World residents from French overseas departments and territories, are French citizens, but form part of the Third World community in France.

The political impact of the new immigration is unclear. By the 1980s the problem was clearly "how to reconcile a multicultural society with a more homogeneous tradition."[1] At least from some distance it appeared that the French had been far more successful at this enterprise than, for example, the British across the Channel, for whom racism had become an issue in electoral competition and who had experienced major urban race riots. Of course there were problems and tensions, particularly during the last 10 years. There were racial murders in Marseilles in the early 1970s, urban riots in the suburbs of Lyon during the summer of 1981, as well as protests and industrial strikes organized by North African workers.[2] However, at least at the national level, it has been argued, established institutions of the Left have acted to defuse racial tensions, and "defend themselves against the corrosive effects of intraclass conflict." Thus the strong working-class commitments of French Left elites have been the principal check on the politicization of racial tensions.[3]

The government of the Left that assumed power in May 1981 was committed to improving the conditions of foreigners living in France, while at the same time gaining greater control over the entry of new immigrants and avoiding the pitfalls of the politics of race. However, it has been at the local level that the issues and policies involving immigrant integration have been developed, particularly in localities governed by the Left. Therefore, in order to analyze the key role of the Left, we must examine their actions at this level. We have found that from this perspective Left elites have been far weaker in defending themselves against the corrosive effects of intraclass conflict and have been far more prone to define the immigrant problem in racial-ethnic terms. Nevertheless, the containment at the local level of issues involving immigrant integration has contributed to the defusion of racial and ethnic tensions. The style of local problem-solving in France—for these issues as well as many others—has been strongly apolitical and technocratic. It generally excludes broad political debate and political mobilization, and isolates local politics from the involvement of national political parties.[4] Therefore, we will argue, it is political structure and process, rather than ideologies, which have reduced racial tensions in France.

Third World Concentrations:
The View from the Local Level

Viewed from the local level, Third World immigration is an urban phenomenon: Third World communities tend to be concentrated in the largest towns and cities in France. If immigrants were 6.5 percent

TABLE 2. Cities Governed by Different Political Parties by Concentration of
          Immigrant Population

Percentage of Immigrant Population	Communist No.	%	Non-Communist Left No.	%	Center-Right No.	%
-10	33	45	62	77	49	79
10.1-20	35	47	18	22	13	21
20.1+	6	8	1	1	0	0
Mean Immigrant Population for Each Group (%)	12		7		7	

Source: Percentage of immigrants is derived from 1975 census figures. The political
breakdown is as of 1982.

of the population nationally in 1975, they comprised a mean of 8.7
percent of the population in towns and cities with greater than 30,000
population. The proportion of Algerian residents, which is 1.4 percent of the population nationally, tends to increase faster at the local
level than the proportion of immigrants in general. Thus, in cities
where the immigrant population is 10 to 20 percent, the mean Algerian population is 4 percent; in cities with immigrant population of
over 20 percent, the mean Algerian population is 9 percent. Although
there are no reports of other Third World immigrant groups broken
down by city, the concentration of Algerians (more than half the
Third World immigrants) provides us with a reasonable index of their
concentration. Moreover, the concentrations in larger towns and
cities are greatest in those towns governed by the Left, and by the
Communists in particular. The proportion of immigrants is 70 percent higher in large municipalities governed by Communists than in
those governed by other parties. In 1977, 82 percent of cities with an
immigrant population greater than 10 percent were governed by the
Left, and two-thirds of these were governed by the Communists.
While there are some important large cities with high concentrations
of immigrants that are governed by the Center-Right (including Paris
and Lyon), large resident immigrant populations are most character-
istic of cities governed by the Left (see Table 2).

Third World immigrant communities are increasingly comprised
of families rather than simply workers. Indeed the majority of immigrants residing in France (61 percent in 1978) are non-working
families of workers; because of the restrictions on immigration after
1974, the number of family members has been growing much more

rapidly than the number of workers. Among non-European immigrants, a majority (51 percent) in 1976 were not in the labor force.
During the following two years, over 95 percent of those admitted to
France from these countries were family members, increasing the
percentage even more.[5]

The proportion of children of immigrants in schools is greater
than their proportion in the general population. Thus 9.5 percent of
the primary school children in 1981–82 were immigrants, about half
of whom were non-Europeans (mostly North Africans).[6] This high
proportion, moreover, is concentrated in a few areas. Thus in Paris, it
is 24 percent, and even higher in many of the towns in the region,
according to internal reports of the Ministry of Education in 1981. In
the Paris region about half of these children are non-European. In
the Lyon region the percentage of immigrant primary school children
is a little lower (17 percent), but almost two-thirds of these children
are non-European. Similarly in the area around Nice and in the Marseilles region, the percentage of immigrant children is just above the
national average, but more than two-thirds are non-European, mostly
from North Africa.[7] In each case the proportion of both immigrant
and Third World children is growing.

The concentration of primary school children is related to housing patterns and the development of immigrant neighborhoods
within larger towns. Increasingly, in recent years, the word ghetto has
been applied to the "new" phenomenon of immigrant concentration
in France by the press and by official state agencies. Thus, in a recent
atlas of foreigners published by the French statistical services
(INSEE), a map labeled "foreigners" is captioned as follows: "foreign
workers occupy . . . sorts of ghettos in the regions of heavy industry of
the North and the East, as well as in the Paris region."[8]

In fact, since 1968, it appears that there has been a growth in the
immigrant population in public housing that has corresponded to its
increased proletarianization. Between 1968 and 1975, the percentage
of immigrants among family heads residing in public housing in the
Ile de France doubled—from 4.4 percent to 9.2 percent—and it has
continued to grow since then.[9] The immigrant proportion of total
population in public housing, however, is considerably higher, since
immigrant families, particularly the non-European, tend to be larger
than French families.[10] Moreover, they tend to be concentrated in
specific neighborhoods. In the Paris region, housing offices have sent
immigrant families to the periphery, rather than the center, to the
older, less desirable developments and to more overcrowded housing,
often in suburbs governed by the Left.[11] Although it is rare that immigrants comprise a majority of the residents in public housing de-

velopments, there are a few cases that have been noted. For example, in the Paris region:

> Certain neighborhoods have become enclaves. The 1200 inhabitants of the Cité Port Autonome in Gennevilliers . . . are all North Africans. [Of] the 3000 apartments of Rose des Vents in Aulnay-sous Bois, 80 percent are inhabited by Arabs, Blacks or Asians.[12]

In the Lyon region, one of the largest public housing developments in France is located in the working-class suburb of Venissieux. Half the population of Venissieux lives in Les Minguettes, 62 percent of which are immigrants, two-thirds, of whom are non-European.

For North African families public housing has become crucial. Compared with native Frenchmen, twice as many Algerians (29 percent), and almost three times as many Algerian women (44 percent), depended upon public housing in 1975.[13] According to the census of 1975, while less than a quarter of the French population lived in overcrowded housing, almost half the immigrant population, and two-thirds of the Third World immigrant population, lived in substandard, overcrowded housing.[14]

The evidence indicates that Third World immigrants are neither sufficiently dispersed as individuals to be "invisible" nor sufficiently concentrated on the margin of society to be isolated. They are visible as groups, rather than as individuals, that interact with the larger community. There is also evidence that concentrations of immigrants are stable and growing, despite efforts by the government since 1972 to reduce the Third World immigrant population.[15] If the Third World is in France to stay, then their presence has been related to the emergence of the issue of race in French politics. This is most evident at the local level. The focus of the remainder of this chapter is the context in which the issue has emerged and how the issue has been related to policy and the operation of political institutions.

The Political Impact of Immigrants

LOCAL ISSUES

At the local level the presence of immigrant communities has become an increasingly important issue during the past 15 years. Immigrants have been equated with Third World immigrants, and Third World immigrants—as communities—have been defined as unabsorbable. In interviews with local administrative and elected officials in cities with more than a 10 percent immigrant population in 1981 and 1982, it was clear that the policy areas that concerned them the most were housing, education and security. This was true for elected officials, even though they have only limited responsibilities in the first two areas, and virtually none in the last. The problem—or the issue—as defined by both administrative and elected officials focused on concentrations of immigrants, not as workers, but as part of the local population. The deterioration of public housing was linked to concentrations of immigrant families; the failure of the education system was linked to the large numbers of immigrant children in the schools (especially primary schools); and the rise in crime rates was related to the growth in the number of alienated immigrant youth engaged in gang violence and petty crime. Moreover, it quickly became clear that the problem was not immigrants in general, but non-European immigrants.

Thus a field representative of the Ministry of Education in Lyon explained that "there were four million immigrants before the war, and there are four million immigrants in France now. But the new ones from North Africa will not be easily integrated—and they are going to stay here." Therefore the basic problem in education today is how to deal with the high failure rate among non-European immigrant children. In Nice the failure rate is also high and is largely attributed to the children of North African immigrants: "from the point of view of the norms of the French school, it is a phenomenon of vast scope." Nationally, it has been estimated that 80 percent of immigrant children emerge from the French school system either illiterate or with great difficulties in basic skills.[16]

The failure rate among immigrant children is related to a second issue at the local level, essentially that of school integration. In France this issue has emerged out of the individual behavior of parents of European origin (not simply French). In some schools in which there are high percentages of non-European children, European parents have withdrawn their children. This accelerating process was reported by educational authorities in such diverse places as Paris, Lyon, Nice and Grenoble. In the case of Grenoble, the schools involved were in an experimental housing and school complex, Villeneuve de Grenoble, in which some effort was made to promote and facilitate integration. While the cases certainly seem to be limited, the process in these schools was used as an example to support the increasingly widespread notion that in schools (as in housing) there is a "threshold of tolerance"—a percentage of immigrant children that will drive out European children. There seems to be no evidence to support this general notion, but the existence of such a threshold is becoming a political—if not a sociological—fact in many areas.

In a primary school class, the presence of more than 20 percent of foreign children slows down the progress of all of the students. In a hospital service, problems of coexistence arise when foreigners are more than 30 percent of the patients. In a building, it is not wise to have more than 10-15 percent of the families of foreign origin, when they are not accustomed to life in a modern building.[17]

Such precise conclusions are not based on empirical research on the reaction of Frenchmen to foreign ethnic communities—"To our knowledge there exists no research in France relating actually to the general acceptance of a threshold of tolerance"—but on increasingly accepted conventional wisdom and on the limited experience of local administrative and political officials. In effect this *idée reçue* defines the issues, filters the experience of daily interactions and serves as a basis for defining policy choices.

The discussion about problems of public housing also focuses on the presence of concentrations of immigrant families. Concentration has become increasingly linked to ideas of "ghettoization," and the prevention of ghettos is an issue that has been smoldering at the local level for the last decade. This issue is connected to the "maldistribution" of immigrants that Communist municipalities began raising more than 10 years ago.

French local governments have been concerned with "excessive" concentrations of immigrants in public housing since the mid-1970s. In June 1980, the Secretary of State in charge of immigration, M. Stoleru, noted that for several years most cities had been complaining about excessive numbers of immigrants.[18] "Excessive," however, has been consistently defined politically by local authorities. A report on the problems on Les Minguettes in Venissieux, released in April 1982, observed that housing authorities were concerned about the growth in the number of empty apartments (1,917, or 25 percent of the available apartments, and in some sections more than 50 percent of the apartments), which they related to the growth in the number of immigrant households, particularly after 1977.[19]

"Problem areas" are not simply developments in which there are high concentrations of immigrants, but also sections of developments defined in this way. In an analysis of problems in another public housing project, in Villeurbanne les Buers, a local government report emphasizes:

This relatively small proportion of foreigners, and above all of North Africans, would seem not to pose any problems, but their localization in certain buildings, certain staircases, engenders zones of heavy concentration, designated as problem sectors . . . Only the oldest, least comfortable buildings have high percentages of North Africans.[20]

The definition of the problem of housing, while politically charged, has not been an issue of partisan contention in local politics. Venissieux has been governed by Communists since before World War II, but the concerns of the Communist government were similar to those of the Socialist government of Villeurbanne, also a suburb of Lyon, in 1977. A small, private housing development near the center of the city had become a North African "ghetto" as well as a center of agitation and considerable violence. One of the first concerns of the new Socialist government (headed by Charles Hernu, now Minister of Defense) was to deal with the problem of this development, Olivier de Serre, which was quickly defined as the concentration of North Africans, and the need for the suppression of the "ghetto." This definition of the problem was shared by the centrist government, which had been in power until 1977. Indeed the problem had been defined by a report commissioned by centrists and implemented by the Socialists.

Party contention has been more evident around the question of the "maldistribution" of immigrants. The issue was first raised in a declaration of Communist mayors in the Paris region in 1969. It recognized that the immigrant workers who were moving, and being encouraged to move by state housing policies, into their cities were a special class of workers—"victims of social discrimination." However, they were also special in the sense that they seek a disproportionate amount of social aid. At a time when the state is constantly reducing its credits to local governments, and when "the needs of our populations are growing unceasingly," it is no longer possible for Communist municipalities to continue to absorb large numbers of immigrants.

> In these conditions, the concentration of immigrant workers in certain cities corresponds neither to the interests of the local population, nor to those of the immigrants. Consequently, we demand an equitable distribution of immigrant workers among the different communes of the Paris region.

It is important to note that immigrants were seen as a population that was set apart ("our populations" and "the immigrants"), and when confronted with difficulties of absorption related to cutbacks in state credits, the first priority was to reduce immigrant concentrations and the second to demand additional funding: "At a time when hundreds of thousands of French families wait for housing, the financing of housing for immigrants cannot, and, in any case, must not be charged to the communal budget."[21] The Communist mayors raised the same issue again, in more or less the same terms, in 1972 and 1974. Afterwards they continued to send delegations to the prefectures to protest the distribution of immigrants among cities of different political persuasions. Although the issue of distribution was raised and defined by Communist local authorities, it was echoed by Socialist mayors in a less systematic way.[22]

Woven into the issues of immigrants in public housing and concentrations of immigrant children in schools has been the issue of rising crime rates and urban violence. Here, too, the focus has been on the presence of immigrants and the responsibility of young people of North African origin. Indeed much of the passion behind the education and housing issues derives from fears of urban violence. Thus concentrations of young people of North African origin in both schools and in housing have been generally associated with security problems at the local level.

Concentrations of Third World immigrant children have been associated with petty violence in schools in Villeneuve de Grenoble, Venissieux and in some areas of Villeurbanne, and local authorities have reported withdrawals of French (or sometimes "European") children from schools because of this violence. The director of a primary school in Venissieux reported that there was a high level of various forms of juvenile delinquency in his school:

> North African children represent around one-third of the population
> of the two Max Barel schools. . . . [There is] a development of racism on
> one side and the other. Wealthier inhabitants are leaving the neighbor-
> hood, and are going to live in the country. Beyond this, we note a flight
> to private education, perceived as more secure.[23]

There was at least one report of a student strike for the "restoration of discipline" directed against immigrant students in a secondary school in St. Etienne.[24]

Security problems, however, are most closely associated with immigrants in public housing. Thus the problem of Olivier de Serre in Villeurbanne was not simply the high concentration of immigrants, but the number of North African young people associated with violence in the early 1970s. Similarly, in Venissieux, security and violence were seen as the core problems of housing—"gangs of young North Africans," who were creating a climate of insecurity, argued the mayor in June 1980. The director of Villeneuve de Grenoble was more sympathetic to the problems of young people in Velleneuve, where half the residents are less than 20 years of age, 40 percent of whom are non-European. He, too, emphasized the importance of the security problem but saw it in terms of interaction between French and North African youth, linked to the multiple deprivations of the North Africans.

The accuracy of the associations made by local authorities, for our purposes, is less important than their perceptions and their definitions of the issues. There has been a tendency to define the core problems of education, housing and security in terms of Third World immigrants and race, rather than deprivation and class. Although there have been some incidents that have reflected racial tensions, in general issues have emerged at the local level not as a reaction to mass mobilization and mass demands, but as an anticipated response by local political and administrative elites to perceived problems. Although issues involving immigrants have emerged in towns where they are most highly concentrated, there has been close collaboration between local political officials and the representatives of the field offices of the central administration in both defining issues and elaborating policy. The solutions that have been sought and applied at the local level reflect a large area of agreement between political and administrative officials.

LOCAL POLICIES

Without much publicity, policies have been developed at the local level across the country—generally at the initiative of local authorities—to deal with the issues of immigration. Education policies have been the most confused, housing policies have been the most prejudicial, and considerations of security have been interwoven into both.

A series of reports produced by a research group in Nice have focused on the schools, rather than the children, as the source of high failure rates among immigrant children.

> Failure in school among the children of immigrant workers is, from the point of view of the norms of the French school, a phenomenon of vast scope. Although it reveals as much about the "inadaptation" of the schools to this foreign student group, as well as to a good number of French working class students, and thus is part of a similar problem, the intensity which characterizes it in the case of the immigrant students attests to the uniqueness of their position in the educational system . . . in the first place because they are trained in a context that explicitly downgrades them and makes them inferior, in the second place, because, on this basis, a process of selection and orientation has been instituted that is unique and discriminatory.[26]

The presence of immigrant children in the schools, therefore, accentuates the problem of failure rates, but also raises problems of curriculum, organization and attitudes, not only for immigrants, but for others as well.

The failure rate, however, has been defined basically in terms of

Third World immigrants, and policies that have been developed reflect this definition. Education policymaking is a highly centralized process in France. Nevertheless, local political authorities and local education administrators claim to have exerted pressure for programs that would enable them to deal more effectively with the growing populations of Third World children in their communities. While the programs appear to recognize a desire to maintain order among immigrant children, they also reflect confusion about the future of these children in French society. Thus, during the 1970s, through cooperation between local authorities and the Ministry of Education, two programs were put into place that imply two contradictory objectives: integration into French society and reaffirmation of Arab culture.

Orientation and remedial classes were established by the Ministry of Education in the early 1970s to help immigrant children better integrate into the French school system *(classes d'initiation* and *classes d'adaptation).* Although remedial classes are open to every child who's having difficulty in school, in fact such classes appear to have been established primarily in areas of immigrant concentration, at the initiative of local political and administrative authorities. It is clear that this effort has involved only a small percentage of Third World immigrant children and has not been particularly successful in checking educational failure among these children.[27] However, the stated intention of these early programs was adaptation and integration through the educational system.

In 1975 and 1976, a second program was initiated that was far more ambiguous. Two decrees provided for immigrant children to have a third of their instruction in their native languages as part of their normal curriculum, or to take special language and culture classes outside of their normal curriculum. These programs were established through agreements with the countries of origin, and the teachers were recruited by the governments themselves. Arranging such classes has been a complicated process, since they are technically outside of the French education system, and has involved considerable cooperation from French local authorities. Nevertheless, they have been strongly supported by the North African countries as a way of maintaining links with the "second generation" of their citizens in France, and encouraging their eventual return to their home countries. They have attracted almost 20 percent of foreign students and 10 percent of the Algerian students in France.[28] Thus local and national education authorities have established programs of both integration and segregation as approaches for dealing with the growing Third World population. Neither approach has been particularly successful, and the development of neither approach involved the immigrant communities themselves. In this case as in others, the representatives of the immigrant communities have been their national consulates, embassies and ministries, even in policymaking at the local level.

By the late 1970s there were signs that local authorities were initiating new policy departures that reflected greater concern with the presence of immigrant children in the school system. For example, in 1980–81, an agreement was worked out between the municipal government of Villeurbanne, which is responsible for delineating school districts, and the Ministry of Education, to redraw the boundaries for three schools. The purpose was to eliminate the "ghettoization" of one of the elementary schools that was reputed to be entirely Arab, and to disperse the immigrant population. According to the Mayor of Villeurbanne, Charles Hernu:

> I am striving to disperse them [the immigrants] throughout the city in such a way that no neighborhood surpasses a threshold of ten percent. I believe that there is a threshold that we cannot exceed without tragedy.[29]

Even before this, however, there was an attempt to limit the number of immigrant children in schools in the Rhone department (in which Lyon is located). In 1979, under pressure from local authorities, the prefect of the department reportedly issued a circular strongly recommending that new immigrants be prevented from moving into neighborhoods where 45 percent or more of the children in the local elementary school are immigrants.

At the same time, several Communist-governed municipalities were initiating specific quotas for various auxiliary school services. In 1978, in the Paris suburb of Ivry, the traditional distribution of used clothing to children of deprived families was abandoned, when it was discovered that 80 percent of those receiving clothing were immigrant children.[30] In January 1981, the same municipality announced that a quota of 15 percent would be applied to children of immigrant families for the city's summer camps (normally open to all children living in the city). Immigrant children are 28 percent of the population under the age of 16, and a much higher percentage of the children from the poorest families. The municipal authorities argued that in some summer camps immigrants comprised half the children in camp, and that the purpose of the quota was to "limit and push back the weight of immigration."[31]

If the use of quotas has been tentative in education, it has become *housing policy*

a major aspect of policy at the local level in housing. Quotas were first used in 1968 when the prefect of the Paris region was authorized to reserve 6.75 percent of new apartments in public housing for people living in slum housing (for the most part, immigrants). However, the quota proved to be difficult to apply, particularly in localities where there was strong political resistance.[32] More recently, quotas have been widely used—and applied—to limit the number of immigrants in public housing developments, neighborhoods and towns, sometimes with strange results.

In 1982, 25 percent of the apartments were empty in Les Minguettes, not because of the flight of French families, but because after 1977, "under pressure from the city, a consensus was established to refuse [apartments to] new immigrant households . . . The refusal of apartments not only to foreign households, but also to migrants of French nationality, closed even more any possibility of maneuver."[33]

The decision by the local government of Venissieux was not unique. Virtually every town in the Lyon region has made the same decision during the previous four years, reaffirming the political importance of the idea of a threshold of tolerance. Throughout the country local authorities of every political persuasion have refused to admit immigrants into public housing and have systematically refused the construction of dormitories for single workers.

The problems of Les Minguettes highlight the complexity of housing decisions in those municipalities governed by the Left that had built large public housing developments during the 1960s and early 1970s. Despite their complaints about the maldistribution of Third World immigrants, they had accepted large numbers of immigrant families into this housing, not only because of pressure from the state, but also because they were having difficulty filling existing apartments. By the late 1970s, public housing was becoming increasingly working-class. As private housing became more abundant, public housing became a refuge for the most disadvantaged working-class families, many of whom were Third World immigrants. Indeed, by 1975, many municipalities governed by the Left were beginning to cut back on their projected housing plans.[34]

The logic of limitation through quotas has been carried one step further in at least two cases—Olivier de Serre in Villeurbanne and Les Minguettes in Venissieux—where decisions have been taken to demolish housing. In Les Minguettes the decision was tentatively agreed to in 1982 by the various public and private agencies with interests in the development to demolish at least one of the large towers because of the problem of empty apartments (although the apartments were empty because of other decisions that were made in the late 1970s).

The decision to completely destroy and then rebuild Olivier de Serre was made in 1977. It was a complicated operation because the development was completely private and, therefore, was first purchased by public housing authorities in order to be destroyed. The policy of the local government was succinctly stated by the mayor: "the suppression of the 'ghetto' and the dispersal of the North African tenants of Olivier de Serre throughout the social fabric . . . geographically and socially speaking."[35]

Although in each case the decision was initiated by the local authorities, the ultimate decision involved the state, either because the state owned part of the property involved or because the state was paying for part of the operation. In each case the decision was related to an analysis that linked violence and deterioration to the concentration of immigrant families, particularly immigrant youth. The solution, however, indicates the extent to which the definition of the problem has been linked to the choice of policies.

The closed process through which these policies were decided also had an impact on the outcome. The process involved bargaining and collaboration among many agencies and levels of government, but consultation with those involved was considered only in the implementation stage. Thus, in Villeurbanne, the decision to demolish Olivier de Serre was made in 1976 but there was consultation with the residents only after the formal announcement in November 1977. Moreover, this consultation was mediated through the Algerian consulate and the Aimicale des Algeriens.

One result of the imposition of quotas in the Lyon region has been the emergence of an acute housing problem for immigrant families. When it was decided to demolish Olivier de Serre, the municipal government pledged to rehouse the residents in the area around Villeurbanne. In the end this proved to be impossible. In fact the demolition of the last building was delayed, because housing authorities were not able to find apartments for the remaining residents in the Lyon region. The problem became sufficiently acute that a group of social workers in Lyon who counsel immigrant families issue a report and a desperate plea in 1982.

> Our objective is to attract the attention of the public authorities to the multiple requests for housing made by these foreign families, to . . . resulting failure [of these requests], as well as to the impossibility for us to resolve these situations.[36]

The policy of quotas in the Lyon and Paris regions has been strengthened and tinged with racism in specific instances. Thus the mayor of Venissieux, in the summer of 1980, threatened to expel from public housing "certain families whose members are guilty of acts of violence, vandalism or aggression. We will not hesitate . . . to exclude such families from our community and from the frontiers of Venissieux."[37] A year later the threat was reinforced in a letter to residents of a public housing project that dealt with the behavior of "about 30 children and adolescents, most of North African origin":

> When the identity of those guilty is known, we will act in a way to eliminate them, and their families, from the Max Barel houses and from the neighborhood. The leases will not be renewed, and, in case of recidivism, the procedure for expulsion will be begun, whatever the situation of the family in question.[38]

In Paris, perhaps as a result of a more general Communist campaign against immigrants, several letters were sent by local housing authorities in Communist-governed suburbs, rejecting the applications of immigrants from French overseas territories (who are, of course, French citizens), specifically on racial grounds:

> . . . the administrative council has decided to house only native families . . . [because of] the saturation in our district of applications by foreign families and families from the overseas departments and territories.[39]

A second letter noted that:

> We are constrained to limit the housing of persons originating in the overseas territories. In effect, their presence in our buildings provokes numerous problems at different levels . . . their way of living—frequent and late gatherings, loud shouting and loud music.[40]

The education and housing policies developed at the local level have usually been initiated by local authorities, often with the collaboration of departmental and national administrative officials. In some cases, such as Les Minguettes and Olivier de Serre, policies emerged from real problems of intercommunal conflict or urban violence. In general, however, the education and housing policies that were initiated at the local level were not a response to mass ethnic conflict. This is particularly true of policies that have presumed the existence of some kind of general threshold of tolerance. There have been no mass demonstrations in the streets in favor of the imposition of a 15 percent limitation on housing for immigrant families, nor is there any evidence that the citizens of Ivry were marching on city hall to demand that their elected leaders limit the number of immigrant children in summer camps. With few exceptions the definition of the issues and the decisions on policies relating to issues involving immigrants were made by local elites who have seen immigrants as a problem, but who have not been under mass pressure. On the other hand, local officials have not attempted to mobilize mass support on behalf of the decisions that they have made, and until the presidential election of 1981 and the local elections of 1983, policy involving immigrants was not an important issue among contenders for political office.

Thus the volatile issues of the integration of a growing Third World population have been both nurtured and contained at the local level where they have concerned, but not sharply divided, the local elites. National discussion about immigration policy has focused on the related but less volatile problems of the entry, expulsion and general treatment of immigrant workers. During the past few years, however, the preoccupations of local politics have begun to filter into the national arena.

Third World Immigrants and National Politics

The first attempts to define a coherent national policy for immigration developed after the May crisis of 1968, and is summarized in a report written by Correntin Calvez for the Economic and Social Council in 1969. The report recognized the economic need for immigrant labor, but for the first time clearly differentiated European from non-European immigrant workers. Europeans were clearly assimilable and should be encouraged to become French citizens, argued Calvez, while non-European immigrants constituted an "unassimilable island."

> It seems desirable, therefore, more and more to give to the influx of non-European origin, and principally to the current from the Maghreb, the character of a temporary immigration for work, organized in the manner of a rapid process of introduction which would be linked as much as possible to the need for labor of the business sectors concerned and in cooperation with the country of origin.[41]

Thus efforts toward integrating Third World immigrants would be futile, and policy should be directed toward regulating their movement in and out of the labor market.

During the seventies, the government struggled to implement the main lines of the Calvez report, but it proved impossible to transform the increasingly stable Third World population into temporary immigrant workers. The opposition of the Left (including the trade unions) rallied to the defense of North African immigrants who were threatened with expulsion (the Fontanet-Marcellin *circulaires* of 1972, struck down by the Council of State in 1975), and continued to oppose similar legislation that was passed by parliament in 1980 (the Bonnet law). Confronted with mobilized opposition, the national government avoided any serious attempt to exclude the families of Third World workers in the countries. Thus, even after the ban on further non-EEC immigration in 1974, the population of Third World residents continued to increase.[42] The Left opposition, therefore, was generally successful in checking and limiting the "racist" labor market policies of the governments of the Right during the 1970s at the national level, at the same time that it was defining issues and developing integration policies at the local level that were based on similar "racist" assumptions.

Although important policy initiatives concerning integration continued to be developed at the local level throughout the decade of the seventies, after 1974 the role of the state became increasingly important as a source of finance for particular programs, particularly in housing and education. For the first time, in 1974, a Secretary of State for Immigration was appointed, and prefects were ordered to assign officials who would be responsible for immigrant problems.[43] The actions in 1974 followed a wave of racist incidents in the fall of 1973, the first during the postwar period.

The Socialist Party Manifesto in 1981 promised to alter the situation of immigrants in France in several ways. Discrimination against them would be dealt with, undocumented workers would be more carefully controlled at the frontiers, and legal rights for immigrant workers would be reinforced and expanded. In general these promises have been kept. Like governments before them, the Mitterrand government has continued to focus on the labor market problem of entry, expulsion and treatment of workers. The Chairman of the National Assembly Committee, presenting the new legislation in 1981, explained that:

> the two considerations consist of tightening entry controls at the frontiers, but to give greater juridical stability to the situation of foreigners residing regularly on the national territory; the principle resides in attenuating the risk of arbitrariness by seeing that decisions concerning foreigners are taken, from now on, through juridical or quasi-juridical means, and no longer by administrative authority.[44]

Conditions of entry have been tightened, family reunification (the main source of growth in the foreign population) has been limited somewhat more, and sanctions against both illegal immigrants and those who employ them have been authorized. At the same time the regularization of the situation of illegal immigrants who are now employed has been facilitated, and the wave of expulsions, threatened by the 1980 *loi Bonnet,* has been temporarily halted. Nevertheless, although more limited by juridical safeguards, the authority of the state to expel immigrants has also been reaffirmed. Perhaps the most important long-term change is that for the first time since 1939 foreigners have the right to establish their own associations. Thus the government has "strived to reconcile humanitarian preoccupations and economic imperatives."[45]

Increasingly, however, it has become more difficult for Socialists to avoid responsibility for dealing with the issues and policies of integration. In a number of important ways the government has expanded the national-local partnership initiated during the 1970s, and has developed policies at the national level to support initiatives taken at the local level during the past decade. In education, for example, one of the first acts of the new government was to recognize the failure rate in the education system as a national problem by setting up zones of educational priority (ZEPs). Such a designation for a school district means additional funds, teachers and the possibility of experimental educational programs.[46] The criteria for such a designation are complex, but the most important is the percentage of immigrant children in particular schools. On one hand, the new program appears to recognize the special problems of ethnic concentrations in the schools; on the other, from the description of proposed initiatives in Les Minguettes, it also appears that the ZEPs are meant to give additional support to programs already begun by local educational authorities.

The government has also recognized that urban deterioration is a national problem, and quickly established several commissions that involve the mayors of the larger cities, the most important of which are the Interministerial Commission for the Social Development of Neighborhoods and the Commission of Mayors on Security. The initial reports of these commissions appeared to reaffirm the definitions of problems developed at the local level. Thus one of the first acts of the Neighborhood Commission was to authorize the demolition of a section of Les Minguettes as an initial solution to the urban problems of Venissieux, emphasizing the link between immigrant concentration and urban decline. Similarly, after meeting with the mayors of the nine communes in the eastern suburbs of Lyon to review problems of urban decay and security, an advisor to the prime minister reported, in January 1983, that the mayors seemed more sensitive to the necessity of long-term programs for integrating the large immigrant population. Nevertheless, the mayors appeared to support the system of quotas in public housing.[47]

The emergence of the discussion of integration policies from the local into the national policy arena has also stimulated the consideration of a broader view. In its report to the prime minister in January 1983, the Neighborhoods Commission emphasized the broad view that urban problems in France were related to the emergence of a multi-ethnic society:

> The development of intolerance, of rejection, of racism leaves deep marks in a society already undermined by the crisis. The increase of a feeling of insecurity without objective justification is a disturbing sign. If the present policy does not demonstrate its effectiveness, the way of authoritarianism will be desired by a majority of citizens.[48]

The discussion of the role of immigrants in education, housing, urban deterioration and urban crime is at the core of the analysis of these problems, and the proposed solutions all involve the Third World immigrant communities. In this way the government has begun to deal with immigrants as a social, rather than simply a labor, issue.

Given the narrow, incoherent policy consequences of the containment of integration issues at the local level, the national discussion and the active role of the national government may prove useful. However, such involvement may also broaden and intensify political conflict based upon racial issues. France was treated to a taste of such conflict during the presidential election campaign of 1981 when, for the first time, a major political party attempted to use integration issues to mobilize support for its presidential candidate. The Communist candidate, Georges Marchais, expressed support for a series of actions in Communist-governed towns against immigrants. The most dramatic of these actions occurred in a suburb of Paris (Vitry), where the mayor led a group of municipal councillors, together with a crowd of irate citizens in a march against a newly installed immigrant workers' dormitory. The municipal authorities attacked the dormitory with a bulldozer, cut off the supply of water and electricity, and demanded that the (Malian) workers go back to the town from which they had been sent. It quickly became apparent that the incident was part of a broad Communist offensive against non-European immigrants, as well as policies of the (Center-Right) government. The Communist actions and the reactions of others were inseparable from the presidential campaign.

The actions of the Communist local authorities were widely condemned, but not universally. The Socialist group in the city of Vitry, for example, supported what had been done, and the Socialist mayor of Epinay-sur-Seine commented that "The concentration of immigrant workers in working-class housing developments, beyond a certain threshold, leads inevitably to difficulties . . . It is easy to cry racism when you live far from this ghetto housing."[49] Almost every side of the debate accepted the definition of the issue—if not the solution—of the Communists, that immigrant concentration posed problems of racial/ethnic conflict.[50]

If the Communist campaign was meant to mobilize votes for the Marchais campaign, it was not particularly successful. Only a bare majority of declared Communist voters, and only 24 percent of the electorate approved of the position of the party.[51] Moreover, in the election, Marchais ran poorly in those towns that were the focus of the campaign. In fact the social issue was raised in national politics at a time when opposition to immigrants appeared to be declining in public opinion.[52]

By 1983, however, it was clear that the Communist campaign had served to legitimize thinly disguised racist rhetoric that proved to be an effective tool for mobilizing the conservative electorate. In local election campaigns that year, the Right opposition was able to link immigrants to high unemployment and fears of crime and urban insecurity. The campaign was spearheaded by Jean-Marie Le Pen and his fascist National Front. Le Pen's electoral success (and that of his party in local by-elections) has forced leaders of the established Right to support many of his anti-immigrant positions. Thus, in 1983, the opening created by the Communists in 1981 was successfully exploited by the rightists against both the Communists and the Socialists.[53]

Conclusion

For at least a decade, immigrants have been a major issue in local politics. Local officials have defined issues and developed policies that have been based upon presumptions of ethnic divisions. In general they have not reacted to mass conflict and mass pressure. Despite continued conflict between Frenchmen and non-European immigrants, and reaction in public opinion, there has been remarkably little mobilized, organized intercommunal conflict. Instead local authorities have generally operated on the basis of anticipated ethnic conflict. At least until 1980, contending political forces at the local level did not attempt to use the immigrant issue to mobilize political support.

The absence of mass political pressure is one reason that the issue has been contained at the local level for so long. There are, however, other reasons. Perhaps the most important is the tendency toward political consensus at the local level, the absence of continuous, institutionalized political conflict. In this kind of environment it was easier to generate political issues and policies without mass mobilization. French local governments also tend to develop policy through administrative, rather than political contacts, a process that serves to separate issues at the local level from those at the national level. Thus, for many years, local elected officials have raised numerous issues involving immigrants at the local level that have been more or less ignored by national political parties.

Finally, the issue has been contained at the local level because it has concerned, disproportionately, those municipalities governed by the Left. With little real access to the political system, representatives in these cities before 1981 had great difficulty raising issues with which they had been preoccupied.

On the other hand, the containment of the integration issue at the local level may well have limited the scope of political pressure around racial issues. Gary Freeman has argued that the refusal (at least until 1981) of organizations of the Left "to blame migrants for the failures of French capitalism" has been a major factor in defusing racial politics in France.[54] While this may be true at the national level, clearly governments of the Left at the local level have increasingly regarded immigrant workers and their families in much the same way as the Calvez report of 1969. Nevertheless, because of the dynamics of local policymaking, and the general lack of political opposition and competition at the local level, local Left elites did not act to mobilize their constituencies around anti-alien hysteria.

Nevertheless, the policies that emerged from the local arena have frequently treated immigrant residents as objects rather than participants, and have emphasized social control rather than integration. Moreover, several changes have developed that are making local containment more difficult. First, the resources of localities are increasingly insufficient to deal with the severe problems of integration and policy coordination. Also, growing public concern with crime and the identification of immigrants with these concerns have made it more difficult for the state to avoid dealing with integration issues. Finally, the victory of the Left in 1981 has meant that Socialist and Communist mayors have gained greater access to the government and the state, and that the issues that they have been nurturing at the local level for a decade are beginning to emerge in Paris. The establishment of a national government of the Left has also provided a scapegoat for the Right opposition to blame for the tensions of integration. By 1984, the issue of immigrants and integration became politicized as an important vehicle for mobilizing the conservative electorate of France.

Notes

1. Douglas Ashford, *Policy and Politics in France* (Philadelphia: Temple University Press, 1982), p. 284. In theory, children born in France from foreign parents can become French citizens at the age of majority, if they have resided more than five years in France. These provisions, however, are not always applied. Algerians born in France after January 1, 1963, are French citizens. Algeria, however, does not recognize these provisions of the Evian Accords, and considers these children Algerian citizens. See Catherine Wihtol de Wenden, "La Seconde Géneration," *Projet* No. 171–172, January–February 1983, p. 104. V. O. Key, in *Southern Politics* (New York: Vintage Books, 1949), pp. 666–71, emphasized the political importance of blacks in the southern United States, even during a period when they were deprived of citizenship rights.

2. Ashford, pp. 226–85. Surveys taken in the early 1970s showed that the French estimated the foreign population at twice its actual size. In 1981, President Giscard d'Estaing estimated the number of non-European immigrants at 1,490,000, almost twice the actual number. See George Tapinos, *L'Immigration étrangère en France* (Paris: PUF, 1975), p. 66; and *Le Monde*, March 12, 1981.

3. Gary Freeman, "Immigrant Labor and Working Class Politics," *Comparative Politics*, October 1978, pp. 38–39.

4. On this question, see Mark Kesselman, *The Ambiguous Consensus* (New York: Knopf, 1967); Jeanne Becquart-Leclerq, *Paradoxes du pouvoir local* (Paris: Presses de la FNSP, 1977); and Sidney Tarrow, *Between Center and Periphery: Grassroots Politicians in Italy and France* (New Haven: Yale University Press, 1977).

5. *La Situation demographique en 1977 et 1978* (Paris: Collection de L'INSEE, serie D, No. 77 1980), p. 85. For the 1976 figures on non-European immigrants, see *Mesure de la presence étrangère en France* (Paris: Rapport remis au Ministre du Travail, 1979), Annexe III. For tables on immigrant families, see *Données Sociales, 1981* (Paris: INSEE, 1982), pp. 59–64.

6. Ministère de l'Education, service des études informatiques et statistiques, *Note d'information*, May 1982.

7. We should note that Third World immigrant population is younger than the general population and younger than the population of European immigrants. See *Données Sociales, 1981*, p. 53.

8. *Activité et Habit* (Paris: INSEE, 1981), cited by Veronique de Rudder, "La Crise de l'habitat social ou naissance des ghettos?" Paper presented at "Le Logement des Immigres en France," Lille, May 13–14, 1982, p. 1.

9. *Activité et Habitat*, p. 4.

10. Michel Pincon, *Les Immigrés et les HLM* (Paris: Centre de sociologie urbaine, 1981), p. 61.

11. de Rudder, "La Crise de l'habitat . . . " p. 6, and de Rudder "L'Exclusion

n'est pas le ghetto," *Projet,* No. 171–172, January–February 1983, pp. 80–91.

12. *L'Express,* November 22, 1980, p. 41.

13. Pincon, p. 59.

14. Données Sociales 1981, p. 68.

15. See the report by Anicet Le Pors, *Le Monde,* June 19–20, 1977. This report argues that immigrant workers are, and are likely to remain, an integral part of the workforce. It is supported by the conclusions of a report of the National Assembly in September 1981 (*Rapport fait au nom de la commission des affaires culturelles, familiales et sociales* No. 388, p. 4). About 37,000 immigrants were expelled from France between 1974 and 1981, and others left voluntarily, but more than that number of dependents took their place. A study by the National Office of Immigration in 1980 showed that very few jobs were "liberated" for Frenchmen when immigrant workers left. See *L'Expansion,* June 20–July 3, 1980.

16. Jean-Pierre Zirotti, "Les Effets de la scholarisation sur les strategies des emigrés," paper presented at "Crises en Europe et Emigration Maghrebine," Algiers, March 28–29, 1981, p. 2. See Catherine Wihtol de Wenden, p. 105; and James Marange and Andre Lebon, *L'Insertion des Jeunes d'origine étrangère dans la societé francaise, rapport au Ministre du Travail* (Paris: Documentation Française, 1982).

17. Michel Massenet, "Communication a l'Academie des Sciences Morales et Politiques," in *Vivre en France,* No. 8, 1970, cited by Veronique de Rudder-Paurd, "La Tolerance s'arrête au seuil," *Pluriel,* No. 21, 1980, p. 3. Massenet's ideas, and the widespread acceptance of the notion of threshold of tolerance, are analyzed in Gary Freeman, *Immigrant Labor and Racial Conflict in Industrial Societies* (Princeton, N.J.: Princeton University Press, 1979), pp. 157–60.

18. Reported in Jean-Pierre Dumont, "Le racism du Voisin," *Le Monde,* February 14, 1981, p. 9.

19. *Les Minguettes,* rapport présenté à la Commission Pour le Developpement Social des Quartiers (Lyon: COURLY-Ville de Venissieux, 1982), p. 44.

20. *Habitat et vie sociale, une operation de rehabilitation pour les Buers* (Lyon: COURLY-Ville de Villeurbanne, 1981), p. 12. This report was a reaction to major urban disturbances in les Buers, as well as in other suburbs east of Lyon, during the summer of 1981.

21. The 1969 statement, together with a second declaration in 1972, is reprinted in Andre Vieuguet, *Français et immigrés: le combat du PCF* (Paris: Editions sociales, 1975).

22. For example, the Mayor of Villeurbanne, in a press conference on October 24, 1977, referred to the obligation of the municipal government to counteract the national and regional policy of the government, which is "nonsense." The mayor of Epinay-sur-Seine, in 1980, supported the positions taken by the Communist mayors, particularly with regard to the maldistribution of immigrant families. See *Le Monde,* December 30, 1980.

23. Testimony of the director of the Max Barel Schools, in the mayor's report on security, May 11, 1982, from the municipal archives of Venissieux.

24. Paul-Henry Hansen Catta, "Malgré nos profs, nous voulons de la discipline," *Figaro Magazine,* May 30, 1982.
25. *Le Monde,* June 14–15, 1980.
26. Zirotti, pp. 2–3.
27. de Wenden, p. 106.
28. *Le Monde,* June 2, 1981.
29. Veronique de Rudder, "Sous les quotas, les hommes," *Différences,* April, 1981, p. 16.
30. Dumont, "Le racism du Voisin."
31. de Rudder, "Sous les quotas," p. 15.
32. Dumont, "Le racism du Voisin."
33. *Les Minguettes,* p. 44.
34. de Rudder, "La Crise de l'habitat. . . . ," p. 3.
35. Press conference of the Mayor of Villeurbanne, October 24, 1977.
36. *Problème du relogement des familles immigrées* (Lyon: Centre Medico-sociale, 1981).
37. Le Monde, August 21, 1980.
38. Letter from the mayor as director of the company that owns the project, September 18, 1981, from the municipal archives of Venissieux.
39. Letter from the Office of Public Housing at St. Denis, November 28, 1980.
40. Letter from the Office of Public Housing of Nanterre, September 20, 1980.
41. Correntin Calvez, "Le Problème des travailleurs étrangers," *Journal Officiel de la Republique Française, Avis et Rapports du Conseil Economique et Social,* March 27, 1969, p. 315.
42. See Ashford, pp. 280–81.
43. Freeman, "Immigration and Racial Conflict," p. 97.
44. *Le Monde,* October 2, 1981.
45. For a summary of the new legislation, see the reports of the *Service d'information et de diffussion,* September 6, 1981 and November 3, 1981. The most complete review of the actions taken by the Socialist government is an unpublished document by Jacqueline Costa-Lascoux, "Les Nouvelles orientations de la politique migratoire en France," November 1982. On new expulsions, see *Liberation,* July 4, 1983.
46. See *Les Minguettes,* pp. 125–30.
47. *Le Monde,* January 9–10, 1983.
48. *Le Monde,* January 21, 1983.
49. *Le Monde,* December 30, 1980, p. 23.
50. See Catherine Wihtol de Wenden-Didier, "Les Immigrées et le discours politique municipal," Colloque GRECO, Marseilles, February 18–20, 1981.
51. *L'Express,* April 11, 1981.
52. *L'Express,* October 18, 1980.
53. See Martin A. Schain, "The 1983 Local Elections: Race and Politics in Socialist France," *Conference Group on French Politics Newsletter,* March 1984.
54. Freeman, "Immigrant Labor and Working Class Politics," pp. 38–39.

8

French Socialism in Comparative Perspective

JOHN S. AMBLER

The picture of socialist France that emerges from the preceding chapters is clear: a government committed to the creation of a new kind of society based on the principles of equality, solidarity and self-management proceeded rapidly to implement a wide range of new policies, but soon found itself forced into the role which it had vowed to avoid, that of managing the economic crisis. A number of socialist policy innovations are likely to endure, notably the increase of leisure time and rights for workers and at least some of the newly nationalized industries. A SOFRES poll taken in March 1982, indicated strong public support for the wealth-tax (74 percent) and for the fifth week paid vacation (72 percent) and at least plurality support for workers' right and the 1981 nationalizations. Only the abolition of the death penalty, at a time of rising concern with crime, was judged negatively (56 percent).[1] Yet as Mitterrand entered his third year of office, the polls also showed that those who were dissatisfied with his performance and that of his government greatly outnumbered those who were satisfied.[2] In such policy areas as income redistribution, economic growth, agriculture, social security, education and the treatment of immigrants, the obstacles to the accomplishment of socialist goals have been formidable.

One set of constraints has been economic and financial. France's economic growth rate surpassed that of most OECD countries in the first socialist year before the vulnerability of "socialism in one country" became apparent. Having rejected autarky, Mitterand was left only with the Delors alternative of austerity, designed to reduce imports and inflation, even at the cost of halting growth and increasing unemployment. The proponents of economic nationalism on the Party's left wing viewed with alarm this decision to tie the fate of French socialism to a hope of restoring the confidence of the national and international business communities.

A general increase in purchasing power from 1981 to 1982 did not produce as much redistribution of income as the government had hoped. A study by the *Centre d'Etudes des Revenus et des Coûts,* published in early 1983, showed that from 1981 to 1982, while physicians suffered a 1 to 7 percent decline in income and some shopkeepers (especially butchers and bakers) enjoyed increases of 4 to 17 percent, the monthly income of workers rose only 0.1 percent despite sharp increases in the minimum wage.[3] Inflation coupled with the work-sharing objective of much of the early social legislation (the 39-hour week and the 5-week vacation) produced higher hourly wages but essentially no increase in monthly income in constant francs. Economic constraints also were instrumental in decisions to delay reforms intended to increase quality of condition in social security (Freeman's Type I reforms), agriculture (subsidies to small farmers) and education (smaller class size and massive support for weaker students).

While there can be no doubt that the weakening international position of the French economy and the subsequent austerity policy seriously undermined reform efforts and contributed to growing dissatisfaction with the government, some of the most serious obstacles to reform were not economic at all. No less important were policy constraints imposed by vested interests like the FNSEA, which blocked agricultural reform; the *patronnat,* which warned of the dire consequences of self-management in particular and socialism in general; teachers' associations, which quarreled over status and workload; privileged workers, who helped block unification of social security benefits; and local governments, which defined immigrant policy in a way that appeared to clash with socialist ideals. While political hostility to the Left reinforced the defense of corporatist interests in the case of farmers, employers, doctors, private schools and law students, the government also met resistance from elements of its own clientele. Trade unions and teachers' associations, which generally refrained from challenging the government in massive street demonstrations, were active and effective opponents of change in social security and secondary education. Municipalities governed by the Left were a force to be reckoned with on immigration policy and decentralization.

The Mitterrand government clearly accomplished less than it had hoped in the first two years in office. Its experience raised again the question of when—or if—democratic socialism can succeed. As was shown in Chapter 1, French governments of the Left prior to 1981 were so restricted by their unstable coalitional base and by the brevity of their tenure in office that they offer no conclusive evidence regarding the potential for socialist reform within an environment dominated primarily by market forces. The experience of other European democracies may suggest conditions under which democratic socialist parties can avoid a forced choice between electoral defeat and the abandonment of reformist objectives. We will first review the quantitative evidence on the policy impact of leftist electoral strength, then examine more closely the socialist experience of Britain and Sweden.

Do Parties and Elections Matter?

The policy impact of socialist parties in power is one piece of the broader question of whether the policies of liberal democracies generally are shaped by election results. If in fact policies are shaped by forces other than elections and parties, it would be unrealistic to expect great changes from a French socialist government. A growing body of literature in the field of comparative public policy offers mixed evidence on this question. Clearly in extreme cases such as the desertion of democratic parties by German voters in 1932, the plurality election of Allende in Chile in 1970, and the defeat of Indira Gandhi in 1977, elections have dramatic, if not always predictable, outcomes. In less dramatic circumstances they determine who shall govern when one party or candidate wins an absolute majority and at least limit the alternatives among coalitions in multiparty systems.[4] But do they shape policy?

Classical Marxists are not alone in believing that economic forces are more powerful than political ones.[5] American political scientists discovered in the 1960s, somewhat to their surprise, that levels of state spending for social services were more closely associated with the wealth of the state than with the extent of political competition.[6] Wilensky and others have produced similar findings in cross-national studies. The wealthier a nation, regardless of its ideology or political regime type, the larger the proportion of its GNP it is likely to spend on social security programs.[7] Highly urbanized and industrialized societies have similar problems of social insecurity, as well as the resources to spend dealing with them. If politics also makes its contribution to levels of social spending, as will be shown later, it remains true that all wealthy states are welfare states, and poor states—whatever their ideology—can afford only modest programs.

In Western democracies generally as in France, limitation of financial resources is only one of the realities that inhibit the realization of party goals.[8] These constraints, which are particularly severe for governments pledged to fundamental change, may be categorized as political, economic, corporatist and bureaucratic. All democratic leaders are constrained by the need to hold together their party or coalition majority and by the inevitability of a coming election. Certain options which would alienate supporters needed to win elections, provoke a revolt from within after the party has achieved power, or take longer to produce results than the time remaining before the next critical election, are usually excluded. As Ross and Jenson have shown, Mitterrand's dependence on PCF and CERES support encouraged him to adapt a platform and initial policy well to the left of the Socialist center of gravity. When policy subsequently shifted to the Center, the government paid the political cost of strident criticism from its own left wing.

Those economic constraints which have plagued French governments of the Left—inflation, which encourages imports, undermines the exchange value of the currency and nullifies increases in purchasing power; a suspicious private sector which seeks incentives and guarantees before it invests; international business cycles, which disturb the most carefully drawn plans for the domestic economy; and foreign trade partners, whose certain retaliation against protectionism would eliminate jobs—all of these are familiar as well to socialist governments in Britain, Greece, and even Sweden. So too are the demands and resistance of a host of interest groups, including the trade unions, which expect that under socialist leadership wages should rise, working conditions improve and union influence expand. Lastly, a reformist government must overcome resistance to change from within the state bureaucracy. Even where the civil service has a strong tradition of political neutrality, as in Britain, a new crusading minister may encounter resistance like that described by Barbara Castles, who was Minister of Transport in the British Labor government in the 1960s: "I wasn't in a political caucus at all. I was faced by departmental enemies."[9] Edith Cresson, as Minister of Agriculture under Mitterrand, and Anne Gorsuch, as Director of the Environmental Protection Agency in the Reagan administration, must have felt the same way on assuming office in 1981. When a disgruntled department bureaucracy can obtain the support of powerful interest groups and political allies, the party in power either adapts its policy or risks defeat.

In view of these constraints, and the similarity of the problems which confront the industrialized liberal democracies, it is not surprising that the policies of the Left and the Right when in power are closer together than their ideologies. Yet wealthy democracies do in fact differ among themselves, and over time within individual countries, with respect to the percentage of GNP which they spend on social security, the degree of inequality in income distribution and the extent of government intervention in the functioning of the economy. Among researchers on these subjects, the majority view—but hardly the unanimous view—is that the political complexion of the government does matter. Let us review the evidence.

SOCIAL WELFARE EXPENDITURE

Researchers using diffierent time periods, country sets and modes of categorizing and coding the political complexion of governments have reached a bewildering variety of conclusions regarding the relationship between the ideology of governing parties and the proportion of GNP which they spend for social welfare programs such as income maintenance, health and education. A few studies have found leftism to be a highly significant predictor of social expenditure.[10] In contrast Wilensky finds that "cumulative left power has had no effect on welfare effort or output," but finds that the strength of Catholic parties does have a significant positive impact.[11] Midway between these poles is the study by Francis Castles, who examined OECD data on percentage of GNP spent on education, health and income maintenance in 18 industrialized democracies (Table 1) and compared these social welfare expenditure levels with the political complexion of each nation's legislature and cabinet over the 10 years prior to the date of the expenditure data.[12] For the mid-1970s he found a modest positive correlation ($r = .34$) between total welfare expenditure and the average percentage of cabinet seats held by socialist parties.[13] The best predictor of levels of social welfare spending was not the relative strength of socialist as opposed to non-socialist parties, but the relative strength of conservative as opposed to non-conservative parties. Jurgen Kohl reaches the same conclusion after examining similar OECD data.[14] Both Castles and Kohl conclude that governments of the Right tend to slow down the growth of social expenditures, while centrist coalitions, like those which typically control the Dutch government, tend to spend for social welfare programs almost as generously as socialist governments.

TABLE 1. Public Welfare Expenditure (Excluding Housing) in the OECD Area

	Early 1960s				Mid-1970s				Total "Welfare" Expenditure Elasticity With Respect to GDP
	Education	Income Maintenance Expenditure	Health	Total "Welfare"	Education	Income Maintenance Expenditure	Health	Total "Welfare"	
Australia	2.4	4.7	2.5	9.6	3.8	4.0	5.0	12.8	1.33
Austria	2.6	14.1	2.9	19.6	4.0	15.3	3.7	23.0	1.17
Belgium	3.8	11.7	3.1	18.6	4.9	14.1	4.2	23.2	1.25
Canada	3.5	5.4	2.5	11.4	6.5	7.3	5.1	18.9	1.66
Denmark	(4.0)	6.5	3.7	14.2	(7.0)	9.9	6.5	23.4	1.65
Finland	4.8	6.7	2.5	14.0	5.6	9.9	5.5	21.0	1.50
France	2.1	11.8	3.1	17.0	3.2	12.4	5.3	20.9	1.13
Germany	2.1	11.9	2.5	16.5	3.0	12.4	5.2	20.6	1.25
Greece	(1.7)	6.0	1.8	9.5	(2.3)	7.1	2.3	11.7	1.23
Ireland	(3.0)	5.3	2.8	11.1	(4.9)	6.4	5.4	16.7	1.50
Italy	3.2	7.5	2.9	13.6	4.0	10.4	5.2	19.6	1.44
Japan	3.0	2.1	1.9	7.0	2.6	2.8	3.5	8.9	1.28
Netherlands	(2.8)	8.6	2.8	(14.2)	5.9	19.1	5.1	29.1	2.04
New Zealand	2.8	7.6	3.3	13.7	4.4	6.5	4.2	15.1	1.10
Norway	4.1	5.1	2.5	11.7	4.9	9.8	5.3	20.0	1.72
Sweden	4.0	6.0	3.6	13.6	5.9	9.3	6.7	21.9	1.61
United Kingdom	3.7	4.4	3.2	12.6	4.4	7.7	4.6	16.7	1.33
United States	3.6	5.5	1.2	10.3	5.3	7.4	3.0	15.7	1.52
OECD average (unweighted)	3.2	7.3	2.7	13.2	4.9	9.5	4.9	18.8	1.42

Source: OECD Studies in Resource Allocation, No. 5, Public Expenditure Trends (Paris: OECD, 1978), p. 25. Percent of GDP is given in current prices.

Jens Alber's examination of a whole century of social welfare development suggests that the disparities in these findings are due not only to differences in methodology, but also to the changing impact of parties over time. He finds that authoritarian regimes took the lead until the turn of the century, followed by liberal parties in parliamentary democracies from 1900 to 1915, giving way in turn to social democratic parties in the interwar years.[15] In the postwar period he finds that when socialists controlled or participated in European cabinets, social expenditures rose at an above average rate in the 1950s and 1960s, but not in the 1970s.[16] In sum, most studies have shown that while social expenditures have risen in all wealthy democracies, they have tended to rise less rapidly in countries controlled by conservatives than in those controlled by the Left or Center. The evidence is mixed and inconclusive as to whether socialist governments have been more generous than centrist coalition governments. Indeed, as seen in Table 1, some of the highest social expenditure levels are found in countries like the Netherlands, Belgium and Austria, which have been governed for much of the postwar periods by coalitions which include religious parties, and which have developed a corporatist pattern of policymaking with centralized unions and peak business associations participating directly with the government in shaping social policy.[17]

INCOME DISTRIBUTION

If socialist strength has only modest and uncertain consequences for the level of social expenditures, is it more effective in increasing economic equality? Again the evidence is mixed but points toward a qualified affirmative answer. After examining income distribution in 25 industrialized nations, Hewitt concluded that "Socialism is consistently and positively related to government redistribution and to a lowering of the share of the top income groups, regardless of the economic control being considered."[18] In other studies restricted to wealthy democracies, Cameron, Tufte, Dryzek, Stephens, and Borg and Castles all generally support this conclusion.[19] Robert Jackman, however, while agreeing that the income share of the wealthiest 20 percent of the population is lower in countries where socialists are strong, finds that it is the middle and upper middle income groups in the income hierarchy (from the 40th to the 80th percentile) which benefit, rather than the poorest 40 percent of the population.[20] Jackman measures socialist strength by the percentage of legislative seats held by parties of the non-communist Left over the period 1945–70 and compares this with two data sets on income distribution, includ-

TABLE 2. Size Distribution of Post-Tax Income: Quintile Share of Household Income

	Year	1 (poorest 20%)	2	3	4	5 (wealthiest 20%)	Gini Coefficient of Inequality*	Decile Ratio (10/1)*
Sweden	1972	6.6	13.1	18.5	24.8	37.0	.302	9.68
Norway	1970	6.3	12.9	18.8	24.7	37.3	.307	9.65
Australia	1966-67	6.6	13.5	17.8	23.4	38.8	.312	11.29
Japan†	1969	7.9	13.1	16.8	21.2	41.0	.316	9.07
United Kingdom†	1973	6.3	12.6	18.4	23.9	38.7	.318	9.40
Netherlands	1967	6.5	11.6	16.4	22.7	42.9	.354	10.65
Canada	1969	5.0	11.8	17.9	24.3	41.0	.354	16.73
Spain	1973-74	6.0	11.8	16.9	23.1	42.3	.355	12.71
Germany	1973	6.5	10.3	15.0	21.9	46.1	.383	10.82
United States†	1972	4.5	10.7	17.3	24.7	42.9	.381	17.73
Italy	1969	5.1	10.5	16.2	21.7	46.5	.398	18.18
France†	1970	4.3	9.8	16.3	22.7	46.9	.414	21.70
Average		5.9	11.8	17.2	23.3	41.8	.350	12.52

* The decile ratio is the income share of the wealthiest ten percent divided by the income share of the poorest ten percent.
The Gini coefficient is a measure of the divergence of income distribution from absolute equality. It can vary from zero
for complete equality to one for extreme inequality.
† Figures estimated from pre-tax distributions by Malcolm Sawyer.

Source: Compiled from Malcolm Sawyer, "Income Distribution in OECD Countries," OECD Economic Outlook: Occasional Studies,
July 1976, pp. 14 and 17.

TABLE 3. Correlations Between Political Variables and Inequality of Income After
Taxes and Transfers

Measure of Inequality of Income	LR	LL	CR	CL	GAPS	UN
Gini	.46	−.60*	.17	−.38	−.51*	−.51*
Theil	.49*	−.59*	.23	−.40	−.59*	−.54*
Decile (10/1)	.61*	−.51*	.47*	−.51*	−.86*	−.68*
10/(3+4+5)	.52*	−.50*	.33	−.42	−.77*	−.62*

* Significant at 5% level.

Key: LR – The average percentage of seats in the legislature held by the selected
          party of the Right over a period of 10 years.
       LL – Same for the selected party of the Left.
       CR – The average percentage of cabinet seats held by the selected party of
          the Right over a period of 10 years.
       CL – Same for the selected party of the Left.
     GAPS – A rank-order scale derived from the political complexion of governments
          and political systems. This scale is based on a 10-year period and in-
          dicates strength of the Left versus that of the Right.
       UN – Labor union membership as a percentage of the non-agricultural labor
          force.

Source: Adapted from J. Corina M. van Arnhem and Guert J. Schotsman, "Do Parties
Affect the Distribution of Incomes? The Case of Advanced Capitalist Democracies,"
in Francis Castles, ed., The Impact of Parties (Beverly Hills, Cal.: Sage, 1982),
pp. 315 and 324.

ing one collected by Malcolm Sawyer and shown in Table 2. Considering these data from a different perspective, in the three countries in which socialist or labor parties had the most important governing role from 1945 to 1970—Sweden, Norway and the United Kingdom—the two poorest quintiles had an average post-tax income share of 19.3 percent, as compared to 17.3 percent in the other eight countries.[21] The most striking exception in Table 2 is Japan, where the poorest two quintiles had 21 percent of the total income, or more than in any other country in this study, despite the opposition status of the Socialist Party. It should be noted that Table 2 does not reflect the trend in France toward greater income equality in the 1970s, as discussed in Chapter 1.

Van Arnem and Schotsman, in one of the most interesting studies in this field, find a relatively strong correlation between socialist strength and equality in income distribution in 14 OECD countries, as shown in Table 3.[22] Except in Sweden, where social programs and a progressive tax structure make a real difference, this relationship is due principally to differences in *primary* income distribution, before taxes and transfer payments; hence "These findings suggest that the Right is more successful in curbing the equalizing character of the redistributive system than the Left is in accentuating it."[23] Van Arnhem and Schotsman speculate that the relatively egalitarian pattern of income distribution in the more socialist democracies is due less to differences in tax structure and social policy than to the presence of strong, centralized unions, which bargain directly with employers' associations in corporatist fashion within "a leftist or egalitarian tradition and milieu."[24]

These and other studies suggest that income distribution patterns tend to be more egalitarian where socialist parties are strong, but with only slight benefit for people at the bottom end of the hierarchy.[25] Those in low-income groups may be more secure under socialist leadership, but not necessarily any richer. Government subsidies in kind (the British health service and government housing), which are not included in these studies, may improve slightly the real income share of the less affluent, particularly in Britain and Sweden.

ECONOMIC POLICY

There is some evidence to suggest that in the 1950s and 1960s governments of the Left were more attentive than were conservative governments to the problem of unemployment and more inclined to intervene in the economy with a variety of macroeconomic policy instruments.[26] More recent studies on the recessionary 1970s do not reveal any systematic difference.[27] Interestingly enough there seems to be little relationship between socialist strength and the extent of public ownership of industry. As shown in Table 4, the public sector is relatively modest in Sweden, where the socialists governed, with one brief interlude, from 1932 to 1976, but quite extensive in Italy, where its origins and development are linked much more to fascism and clientelism than to socialism. The most striking contrast, and one related to the extent of support for collectivism as opposed to economic liberalism, is between Europe and America.

The traditional linkage between socialist parties and public ownership weakened greatly in the prosperous decades of the 1950s and 1960s as socialists in Britain, Sweden, Germany and elsewhere began to doubt the political feasibility—and even the desirability—of further nationalization, and conservative governments that replaced leftist ones were content to manage firms already in the public sector. At least until the 1980s, when the Thatcher government began planning for extensive "privatisation," British steel and road haulage were

TABLE 4. Ownership of Economic Firms

Economic Firm	France	Italy	Britain	Sweden	West Germany	Canada	United States
Transportation							
highways	G	G	G	G	G	G	G
railroads	G	G	G	M/G	G	M/G	M/P
airlines	M/G	G	M/G	M/G	M/P	M/G	P
auto manufacturing	M/G=P	M/P	M/P	P	M/P	P	P
Communications							
radio/television	G	G	M/G	M/G=P	G	M/P	P
telephones	G	G	G	G	G	M/P	P
postal service	G	G	G	G	G	G	M/G
Power Industries							
gas	G	M/G	G	M/G=P	G	P	P
electricity	G	M/G	G	M/G=P	M/G	M/G	M/P
coal	M/G	M/G	G	M/P	P	P	P
oil	M/G=P	M/G	M/P	M/G=P	M/P	P	P
steel	M/G	M/G	G	M/G	M/P	P	P
Banks	G*	G	M/P	M/P	M/P	M/P	P

Key: G - Ownership by the government, either central or local
      P - Private ownership
      M/G - Mixed, with government ownership predominating
      M/G=P - Balance between government and private ownership
      M/P - Mixed with private ownership predominating

* All domestic banks have been nationalized. Foreign banks remain private.

Source: Charles Andrain, <u>Politics and Economic Policy in Western Democracies</u> (North Scituate, Mass.: Duxbury, 1980), Table 2.5, p. 23, updated for France. Based originally upon Anthony King, "Ideas, Constitutions and the Policies of Governments: A Comparative Analysis, Parts I and II," <u>British Journal of Political Science</u>, 3:3 (July 1973), p. 296.

among the rare European cases of denationalization. To revisionist socialist theorists like Anthony Crossland it seemed that Keynesian economics, coupled with appropriate regulation, taxation and welfare policies, would allow a reformist party to steer the economy and redistribute wealth without more extensive public ownership.[28] Public enterprises appeared to have no advantage of efficiency and to offer no unique solution to the problem of worker alienation. When used extensively as levers for government steering of the economy they tended to become a drain on the treasury.[29] The international economic crisis beginning in the mid-1970s, and the inadequacy of Keynesian formulas in the face of high rates of inflation and unemployment, rekindled the debate over public ownership, even in Sweden where the issue once seemed dead. But with the exception of France in 1981–82, since the immediate postwar period no socialist government has so far taken important steps to extend public ownership.[30]

There are a few cases, notably Scandinavia and Austria, where socialist leadership has produced broader social programs and a more egalitarian income distribution than prevail in most countries under non-socialist government.[31] Yet looking across all of the industrialized democracies, the strength of socialist parties is only modestly associated with achievement of the typical socialist objectives of security, equality and public ownership of industry. It seems likely that statistical analysis underestimates the socialist contribution to growth of the welfare state. In Britain and in France the new programs established after the Second World War by leftist governments generally became popular and were extended by the conservative governments that followed. Competition from the Left, either anticipated or actual, no doubt has contributed to the generosity of conservatives and moderates from Bismarck to Giscard d'Estaing and the contemporary Christian Democratic parties.[32]

The experience of governments led by the British Labour Party and by the Swedish Social Democratic Party is particularly interesting for the clues which it offers to the extent and conditions of success of democratic socialism. In parallel to the French governments of the Left of 1945 and 1981, the British Labour government of 1945–51 rapidly implemented a broad program of social and economic change, then struggled to control inflation and defend the pound. In the 1960s and 1970s, Labour—like the Conservatives—proved incapable of halting a relative decline in Britain's economic productivity and prosperity. In sharp contrast the Swedish Social Democrats, proceeding at a deliberate pace over a period of four decades, were able to create a developed welfare state while Sweden's relative wealth and productivity continued to rise. Yet the Swedish socialists have not yet collectivized industrial ownership. Moreover, they enjoy advantages which may make their example irreplicable in France.

Britain Under Labour Party Leadership

When the Labour Party emerged from the 1945 elections with a clear majority for the first time in its history, it was equipped with a broad program inspired, not by Marxism (which had made few inroads into a working class drawn more to Methodism than to revolution), but by the Fabian Society's version of evolutionary socialism. The Party's election manifesto, entitled "Let Us Face the Future," laid out a host of economic and social objectives, including public ownership of the Bank of England, the fuel and power industries, inland transport and the iron and steel industry, as well as extension of social services, full employment and "taxation which bears less heavily on the lower income groups." Samuel Beer reviews the record of the next five years and concludes, "It is no exaggeration to say that for every paragraph of pledges one finds a corresponding statute."[33] Here is one of the most striking examples in any of the liberal democracies of an election which established a broad program of new policies for years to come.

This reformist government was a success in the sense that, as in France after 1947, the institutions and policies which it created largely endured its passing. The popularity of the National Health Service was so great that the Tories later claimed credit, on grounds that the original planning was done under Winston Churchill's wartime coalition government.[34] With the two exceptions already noted, the public enterprises remained public. The income of the working class rose, both absolutely and in comparison with the middle and upper classes.[35] Labour was markedly less successful at commanding electoral support, slipping from a 73-seat majority in 1945 to a short-lived 3-seat majority in 1950, before losing to the Conservatives by ever-increasing margins in the next three elections in 1951, 1955 and 1959. The causes of Labour's electoral problems were similar to those which plagued the French Left: economic disappointments (particularly inflation), internal divisions and the subsequent prosperity of the 1950s, for which the Conservatives took credit.

Labour initially attempted to guide the economy by retaining many wartime physical controls: import licensing, building licensing, production controls, materials allocation, consumer rationing and price controls on numerous items. Inflationary pressures and resistance from the unions to manpower controls persuaded Labour to move progressively away from physical planning and toward reliance on Keynesian techniques of budgetary fiscal control.[36] The result, to the regret of the "Keep Left" group within the Labour Party, was acceptance of the market as the basic mechanism for allocating resources. This in turn reduced the importance of public ownership and increased Labour's reliance on a general pursuit of economic self-interest, at the expense of the traditional socialist values of public service, cooperation and fellowship.[37] The Tory fifties were a period of centrist politics in which both major parties accepted the welfare state within a mixed economy.

Labour returned to office in 1964, just as the bloom of prosperity was fading and the fundamental problem of declining relative productivity was beginning to emerge. Elected on platforms which called for expansion of the welfare state, the Labour governments of 1964–70 and 1974–79 quickly fell victim to Richard Rose's dictum, "Where votes count, resources decide."[38] In the mid-1960s the United Kingdom had a per capita Gross National Product of $1500, only slightly below that of France's $1540. By 1978 Britain's per capita GNP stood at $5,030, now only 61 percent of the French figure of $8,260 and 53 percent of Germany's $9,580.[39] It is not surprising that by the mid-1970s, as was seen in Table 1, Britain, in comparison with most other European countries, was spending a smaller proportion of a smaller GNP for social welfare. Labour governments found themselves, like the Tories, defending the pound and attempting to control wage increases, rather than fulfilling a socialist vision.[40] Labour still represented the interests of lower-income groups more vigorously than did the Tories, for example, on public housing, on fees for use of the health service and on land speculation taxes (which were removed three times by the Conservatives and twice replaced by Labour); yet from 1952 to 1973 the average increase in overall public spending was no greater under Labour than under the Conservatives.[41] While Britain remains a relatively egalitarian society, Labour's inability to deal with the "British disease" of economic stagnation contributed to the Party's defeat in 1979, its move toward the Left and the consequent secession of the new Social Democratic Party.[42]

The Labour Party has been more successful at the polls than the French Left, but in office it has followed a similar course. First it produced new social programs along with increased purchasing power, especially for lower and middle income groups. Then came inflation and greater nervousness in the domestic and international business communities. In Britain in 1951 as in France in 1938 and 1947, the next stage was the collapse of the leftist government, by election in Britain and by defection in France. Labour came back with the inevitable swing of Britain's political pendulum, but was ineffective in accomplishing its objectives in the sixties and seventies. The inability of Labour to deal effectively with trade union pressures under a policy of austerity in those years is reminiscent of the problems faced by the French Left in 1947 and again beginning in 1982. The British experience under Labour demonstrates the costs for social programs of neglecting productivity. The Mitterrand government, although equally fearful of unemployment, has shown a somewhat greater sensitivity to this problem, as we shall see.

Sweden: Socialist Compromise

The Social Democratic era in Sweden, which can be dated from 1917 (when the Social Democratic Party first entered the cabinet) or from 1932 (when it began a phenomenal stretch of nearly 44 years of incumbency), differs in three important ways from periods of socialist government in Britain or France.[43] First, in Sweden there have been no dramatic bursts of reformist activity. The development of one of the world's most complete welfare state systems and one of the West's most egalitarian societies has been an extended, gradual process. Until the 1960s, the Party's major efforts were devoted to guaranteeing full employment, building a floor of social security programs and spurring economic growth, at the cost of restraining wage increases. In the 1960s and 1970s, the Party sought to increase equality, as in the democratization of a highly elitist educational system and the expansion of workplace democracy. Second, accompanying gradualism has been a continual search for consensus through compromise with all major social and economic groups.[44] The Social Democratic Party's initial Marxist belief in class struggle was abandoned, first in the practice of coalition government in the 1920's, then in theory as well.[45] Sweden offers a particularly striking example of the "moving consensus" which supports the welfare state to some degree in all European democracies. Two years after the electoral defeat of the Social Democrats in 1976, years in which public spending continued to expand, the leader of the Liberal Party, one of the three new governing parties, noted with pride that "We've succeeded in killing the myth that the welfare state is based on the Social Democrats."[46] The adversarial relationship between the Left and the Right, which jeopardizes the durability of socialist policies in Britain and France, is less pronounced in Sweden.

A third feature which distinguishes Swedish socialism is its reliance in the past on private ownership of industry. Unlike the Left in France and Britain, the Swedish socialists decided in the 1930s, before attempting nationalization, that public ownership was unnecessary to the achievement of the central goals of security and equality. In 1980, 94 percent of industrial capacity was still under private ownership.[47] More than their French and British brethren, Swedish socialists came to feel that as the natural governing party in a friendly environment, time was on their side. This state of mind is well expressed in a statement of Social Democratic theory written in 1967:

> According to our constitutions the king still has equally as much formal power as a hundred years ago, but in reality we have undressed him of all his power functions so that today he is in fact powerless. We have done this without dangerous and disruptive internal fights. Let us in the same manner avoid the even more dangerous contests which are unavoidable if we enter the road of formal socialization. Let us instead strip and divest our present capitalists of one after another of their ownership functions.[48]

This serene patience, born of confidence in the future, was supported for four decades by economic growth which by the 1970s made Sweden the second wealthiest country in Europe, after Switzerland. The economic turmoil of the 1970s—when Sweden, like the rest of Europe, was shaken by rising oil prices and competition from the newly industrialized nations—demonstrated the importance of sustained prosperity to consensual politics. The legendary cooperation between labor and mangement broke down with a series of strikes, and the Social Democrats were defeated by the "bourgeois" parties in 1976. The Party modified its view of private ownership, noting that although income was distributed in a relatively egalitarian fashion, government policies which encouraged reinvestment had actually increased the concentration of wealth in the hands of a few families. When the Social Democrats returned to power in September 1982, they were committed to the gradual elimination of the very core of capitalism: private ownership. The plan proposed by Rudolf Meidner, the research director of the Confederation of Swedish Trade Unions (LO), and adopted by the Social Democrats, calls for the placement of a portion of each firm's domestic profits in a fund to be controlled by the union. Within a generation this plan could give the unions majority control in all Swedish industries now under private ownership.[49] If it survives, the Meidner Plan will offer a test of the yet unproven hypothesis of evolutionary socialism that collectivization of all major firms can be achieved before the withdrawal of the cooperation of business causes economic crisis and the electoral defeat of the socialists. It could be the case that acceptance of private ownership has been one of the necessary costs of Social Democratic success in other areas.

The Swedish Social Democrats no longer appear invincible, yet they enjoy advantages which clearly distinguish them from parties of the Left in most European countries. Primary among these is a long record of accomplishment. More than British Labour or the French Socialists, the Swedish Social Democrats have been the principal architects and engineers of the society which they govern. After the September 1982 elections, as Olaf Palme, the Social Democratic leader, prepared to reclaim the prime ministership, he was asked if his remedies to the economic-crisis would be more successful than Mitterrand's. He replied,

> Mitterrand came to power after a long period of bourgeois government, and he was forced to respond to his constituents' pent-up desire for consumer goods. So he stimulated demand and ran into trouble. Things are different here—we have had almost fifty years of socialism, and we have no great gaps between the working class and others. We have a far better chance to stimulate savings and investment, which is what Western economies need.[50]

Back in office, Palme proceeded directly—and with union support—to the implementation of an austerity program, including a temporary reduction in real income for wage earners.

The longevity of Swedish Social Democratic rule has been based on the essential unity of the Left, the absence of religious cleavages which might weaken working-class unity at the polls (despite some decline in class voting in the 1970s), extremely high levels of unionization, and the weakness and division of conservative parties.[51] The Social Democratic policy of gradual reform through compromise has been successful in large measure because of the low intensity of social and political conflict in Swedish society and the willingness of Swedes in different social or political groups to trust each other.

In France these conditions are either absent entirely or present to a much lesser degree. The French Left has been plagued by internal conflicts. The French Communist Party, even with 16.2 percent of the vote in the parliamentary elections of June 1981, remains a far more potent rival to the Socialists than does the Swedish Communist Party, which drew only 5.5 percent of the vote in September 1982. The traditional cleavage between French Catholics and anticlericals continues to undermine the solidarity of the working-class vote. Although class voting has risen since the 1950s, frequency of church attendance remains a better predictor of voting choices than occupation or income.[52] Less than a quarter of French industrial workers belong to a trade union, compared to some 80 percent in Sweden. Moreover, the largest French trade union is under Communist, not Socialist, control. If rivalry between Gaullists and Republicans contributed to the victory of the Left in 1981, centrists and conservatives have found sufficient common cause to dominate French politics for most of the postwar period. Lastly, animosities between the Left and the Right and between unions and employers, while less intense than in the 1930s or even the 1950s, still appear to be strong enough to frustrate any attempt to replicate the Swedish policy process based on compromise and mutual trust.

The Swedish model is particularly appealing for socialists who are willing to forego public ownership of industry for the welfare state and longevity in office. It offers the useful lesson that gradual change, where it is possible, increases the likelihood that new policies will be incorporated into the moving consensus. Yet in terms of levels of social and political conflict, France has more in common with Britain than with Sweden. Like British Labour governments, French governments of the Left know that they have a limited time in office and are more likely to attempt rapid reforms. While some of these will

endure, more than in Sweden will be repealed by successor governments, or, in the case of publicly owned industries, turned to other
purposes. If the Swedish lesson of gradualism where possible is positive, the British lesson is more negative: democratic socialism (like
Marx's original conception) assumes prosperity and hence requires
attention to economic efficiency.

Conclusion

Statistical analysis, as we have seen, reveals only a small direct association between socialist party strength in industrialized democracies
and levels of social expenditure, income redistribution, public
ownership of industry and economic security for workers. To return
to the question posed in the first chapter, does the evidence support
the classical Marxist view that the state in capitalist society can serve
none other than bourgois interests? The answer would seem to be
that reformers of the Left have indeed contributed to the survival of
capitalism, but only by helping to transform it. The socialist parties of
Europe have whetted the popular appetite for expansion of the welfare state, prodding conservative governments into action even when
the socialists themselves remain in opposition. The Swedish example
demonstrates that under certain circumstances socialist leadership
can fashion a society which approximates the egalitarian ideal.

The French Left has contributed in important ways to expansion
of social services and growth of the public sector. Why has it had such
trouble dealing effectively with economic issues and maintaining itself
in power? One piece of the answer is to be found in the constraints
imposed by a capitalist international environment. The Mitterrand
government, even with a much stronger political base than the leftist
governments of 1936 and 1945, was unable to avoid allowing international economic forces to shape its policies.

The French Socialist experiment offers a poignant example of
the dilemma of the democratic Left in an era when Keynesian economics ceases to work, when efforts to reduce unemployment and
spur growth by increased consumption produce instead inflation,
trade deficits, and mounting international debt.[53] It is a dilemma already acutely familiar to the British Labour governments of the sixties and seventies. The French Communist Party and the left wing of
the Socialist Party view this dilemma as a perverse result of international capitalism. Pierre Mauroy took this position in a meeting of
leaders of seven socialist governments in May 1983 when he noted
that the recession "is the crisis of a system that is not ours—it is the
crisis of the capitalist system."[54] Yet the Mitterrand government is

aware that France owes its considerable prosperity to its integration—and success—within a basically capitalist international community. Short of converting Britain, Germany, Japan and the United States to socialism, France has only two options: to attempt to reduce inflation and trade deficits with deflationary policies, or to insulate the French economy with protectionist measures. The first option divides the Left and alienates those groups like the trade unions which expected higher wages and social reforms from the new government, rather than more appeals for sacrifice. The protectionist option might reduce the trade deficit; but a country in which a quarter of the GNP is tied to foreign trade is highly vulnerable to retaliation from trading partners. The large farm subsidies which France (as a net exporter of agricultural produce) receives from Germany and Britain (both net importers) are contingent upon continued French membership in the Common Market. Given France's dependence on imported oil, she must export or eventually exhaust her sources of international credit.

The economic interdependence of Western nations leaves national governments some margin for variation in policy, as seen in the recession beginning in the 1970s, when the United Kingdom chose to pare back the welfare state and allow unemployment to rise, while Sweden gave high priority to limiting unemployment. Even under Gaullist and Giscardian leadership, the state intervened much more forcefully in France than in Britain or the United States to promote industrial modernization, encourage mergers, develop selected firms as "national champions" and facilitate the marketing and financing of French exports. In the Fifth Republic French foreign economic policy has had strongly mercantilist characteristics, placing it closer to the Japanese model than to the American or British.[55]

France has discovered the limits of this relative autonomy. Inflation rates well above those in other major countries and persistently high trade deficits exhaust foreign reserves, force increased borrowing, weaken French influence in international affairs and even threaten to subject a proud nation to the ultimate humiliation of supervision by the International Monetary Fund. The limits imposed by economic interdependence probably are narrower for a militant socialist government than for one more sympathetic to private enterprise. In the first year of socialist leadership, France's budget deficit represented 3 percent of GNP, a lower percentage than in any other OECD country except Japan.[56] In fiscal year 1983 the U.S. budget deficit as a percentage of GNP turned out to be approximately double that of the French, yet socialist rhetoric heightened the suspicions and antagonism of businessmen, both at home and abroad. Currency speculators expected a decline in value of the franc and helped to

bring it about, even before Mitterrand took office. At home an inflation psychology made its contribution to the rise in prices, along with
higher taxes on employers and increased purchasing power. Investment rates, which had begun to decline before May 1981, continued
to drop off as capital sought more congenial havens. These problems
were compounded by what the French Left viewed as an example of
American economic hegemony. High American interest rates (due in
part to record budget deficits), forced France as well to maintain high
interest rates, drove up the value of the dollar, and hence increased
the cost of oil imports calculated in dollars.

As Ross and Jenson have shown in Chapter 2, what the Socialists
sought to do in 1981 probably was impossible under the circumstances. The reflationary policy was based partly on an unrealistic
expectation of rapid recovery in other countries, particularly in the
United States, and partly on strong commitments to impatient supporters. The Common Program was written in 1972, when Japanese-
level growth was thought to be possible in France. It was implemented
in 1981 in a no-growth international environment.

If the Mitterrand government was naive in its expectation of
rapid economic recovery, it was far more aware than was Léon Blum
that one of the keys to growth is productivity. Nationalization was
viewed as a method of increasing investment and productivity. Mitterrand has insisted repeatedly upon the importance of research and the
strengthening of high-technology industries. The government has
continued to encourage mergers to equip French firms to compete
with multinationals based elsewhere. One of the key objectives of
educational reform has been more and better professional training to
meet the needs of the economy. The government's most important
and daring contribution to productivity was the policy, emerging
clearly in late 1983 and early 1984, of supporting the reduction of the
work force in overstaffed and declining industries, notably automobiles, steel, coal and shipbuilding. The predictable results of this
official acceptance of increased unemployment were serious labor
unrest and greater tension between the moderates in power and their
critics further to the left.

Yet for purposes of limiting unemployment and satisfying its
clientele, the government adopted another set of policies which
undermine productivity. Like the 40-hour week in the Popular Front
era, the 39-hour week and the five-week vacation increase labor costs
without creating a substantial number of new jobs. The reduction of
the normal retirement age to 60, at a time when the growing population beyond retirement age already is imposing enormous burdens on
the social security system, may help to relieve unemployment in the

short term, but at the long-term cost of depressing the standard of living for all. Two policies announced in May 1983—one prohibiting banks from cutting off credit to firms in financial trouble and another revising bankruptcy laws to prevent foreclosures—may save jobs, but at the cost of inhibiting the flow of capital to efficient firms. While the government was well aware of the importance of savings, efficient investment and productivity, it felt compelled by prior commitments and the demands of its supporters to adopt policies which undermine these objectives. The lesson of British Labour governments of the 1960s and 1970s has not been fully applied.

Not all of the obstacles to the accomplishment of socialist goals are economic, nor are they all attributable to a small and wealthy capitalist class. One of the recurring themes of the preceding chapters has been the vigor with which a wide variety of vested interests resist change. Social democracy has been successful in Sweden partially because of broad acceptance in that society of equality as a value. It is not clear that either equality or socialism is so highly valued in France, at least below the level of symbolism. The victory of the Left came at a time of international recession when voters throughout the democratic world were turning out incumbents, whether of the Left or Right. In a SOFRES poll after the presidential election, the respondents were offered a list of possible reasons why Mitterrand won: 42 percent replied that it was because he "wished to bring great changes in French society," but 29 percent felt that "it was the only way to get rid of M. Giscard d'Estaing."[57] This poll, like those cited earlier on nationalization and increased leisure time, demonstrates the desire for change in 1981, perceived differently by different voters, no doubt. It also suggests that negative voters gave Mitterrand his 52 percent majority. One would expect that they have little desire to sacrifice for the eventual building of socialism.

Whatever the meaning of the 1981 mandate, it is absolutely clear that no government can be elected with the sole support of manual workers, who make up approximately 37 percent of the total work force. Almost a third of them, particularly practicing Catholics and those at the lowest income level, still vote conservative. Approximately half of the votes needed to compose an absolute electoral majority must come from occupational groups other than manual workers. When the socialists run against the communists, they are even more dependent on white-collar votes. According to the post-election SOFRES poll, in the first ballot of the 1981 presidential election, Mitterrand drew 14 percent of the votes of small businessmen, 19 percent of the votes of business executives and members of the liberal professions, 29 percent of the votes of clerical and administrative employees, and 33 percent of the votes of manual workers. An electoral appeal based on class struggle is likely to be successful only if state employees and white-collar workers with low and moderate incomes—many of whom are women—can be mobilized *en masse* into the new proletariat. Except in Sweden, white-collar workers have been notoriously difficult to organize. In the absence of such mobilization, which would represent the development of a new class consciousness, a socialist rhetoric of class conflict and policy innovations designed to effect rapid income redistribution risk alienating voters whose support is critical to the government's survival.

If the Mitterrand government succeeds in restoring economic prosperity and renews its efforts to reform French society, it still will confront a multitude of groups well accustomed to trench warfare, in a variety of forms, in defense of their interests. Decentralization and self-management represent too dangerous a delegation of power and, in a society accustomed to central arbitration, too novel a form of conflict-resolution to offer a likely solution to the problem of social change. Austerity has revived the French Left's traditional problem of internal division to the point where there is no agreement on the desired pace of change nor even on the appropriate direction. When Georges Marchais announced in May 1983 that the Government's austerity plan was not that of the Community Party, the Socialists had to be aware that without the support of voters still loyal to the Communist Party there would be no Mitterrand government.[58] Today as for more than half a century, the Socialists are impotent without the Communists, but restricted in their options when in alliance. It was the Communist presence that helped tip the balance within the government toward a program of rapid change which proved overly ambitious. It is the Communist presence, among other forces, which inhibits a shift of strategy toward Swedish gradualism and accommodation to the middle class.

What finally can be said about the possibility of democratic socialism, as a general phenomenon and in France? In the complex and value-laden world of social science analysis there is no answer to this question which will satisfy all observers. The evidence seems to suggest that socialist parties, directly through control of government or indirectly through competitive pressure, have moved their societies closer to the socialist vision of justice. They have nowhere created wholly socialist economies. Economic interdependence in a capitalist-oriented international environment may place clear limits on such a development.

As for France, the Socialists who launched their experiment in 1981 enjoyed political control unprecedented for a French government of the Left, an established *étatiste* tradition of government intervention in the economy, a sizable public sector, a lingering revolutionary tradition of equality and fraternity, and a widespread sentiment that change was overdue in the hierarchical and elitist structure of French society. Although they marshalled their forces for a rapid and impressive barrage of reform legislation, the Socialists had the misfortune to attain power at a time of deepening international economic crisis, when the potential for redistributive programs was severely limited. Most Frenchmen were still living too comfortably in May 1981 to be caught up in the mood of despair and openness to new alternatives which facilitated the task, for example, of Franklin Delano Roosevelt in the United States in 1933. The disappointing economic performance of the Mitterrand government did nothing to alter the established public image of the French Left: strong on social reform and weak on management of the economy. Austerity, when it came, simply exacerbated the tendency of French interests to cling to their *droits aquis*. The contrasting experiences of the Swedish and British socialists suggest that social welfare and redistribution fare best in a growing economy, where the pain of losers is partially allayed by expansion of national income as a whole. As the Socialist Party leadership is well aware, the future of French socialism depends upon its ability to demonstrate that social justice and prosperity are compatible goals.

Notes

1. SOFRES sample survey of 1000 respondents, reported in *L'Expansion*, May 6, 1983.
2. For example, see the IFOP poll in *Le Journal du Dimanche*, May 22, 1983, which found that the difference between the number of people who were dissatisfied with the performance of the President (50 percent) and those who were satisfied (33 percent) was greater than ever before in the Fifth Republic.
3. Centre d'Etude des Revenus et des Coûts, *Constat de l'evolution recente des revenus en France* (Paris: CERC, 1983).
4. On the impact of elections upon the formation of governments, see Donald E. Stokes, "What Decides Elections?" in David Butler, Howard R. Penniman and Austin Ranney, eds., *Democracy at the Polls: A Comparative Study of Competitive National Elections* (Washington, D.C.: American Enterprise Institute, 1981), especially pp. 283–292 and 295–300.
5. For a Marxist view, see Ralph Milliband, *The State in Capitalist Society* (London: Weidenfeld & Nicholson, 1969).
6. Richard Dawson and James Robinson, "The Relation between Public Policy and Some Structural and Environmental Variables in the American States," *Journal of Politics*, 25:2 (May 1963), pp. 265–289; and Thom-

as R. Dye, *Politics, Economics, and the Public* (Chicago: Rand McNally, 1966).

7. Harold L. Wilensky, *The Welfare State and Equality: Structural and Ideological Roots of Public Expenditures* (Berkeley: University of California Press, 1975); Frederick Pryor, *Public Expenditures in Communist and Capitalist Nations* (London: Allen & Unwin, 1968); Robert W. Jackman, *Politics and Social Equality: A Comparative Analysis* (New York: Wiley, 1975); and Philip Cutright, "Political Structure, Economic Development and National Social Security Programs," *American Journal of Sociology*, 70:5 (March 1965), pp. 537–550.

8. On constraints upon policymakers, particularly in Britain, see Richard Rose, *Do Parties Make a Difference?* (Chatham, N.J.: Chatham House, 1980), especially Chapter 8.

9. Rose, p. 149.

10. See Jerald Hage and Robert A. Hanneman, "The Growth of the Welfare State in Britain, France, Germany and Italy: A Comparison of Three Paradigms," in Richard F. Tomasson, ed., *Comparative Social Research*, Vol. 3 (Greenwich, Conn.: JAI Press, 1980), pp. 45–70, especially p. 62. Cameron also finds socialist strength to be associated with size of the public sector, but argues that the underlying cause is the openness of the economy, with an open economy leading to concentration of industry, unionization and socialist strength. See David Cameron, "The Expansion of the Public Economy: A Comparative Analysis," *American Political Science Review*, 72:4 (December 1978), pp. 1243–1261.

11. Harold Wilensky, "Leftism, Catholicism, and Democratic Corporatism: The Role of Political Parties in Recent Welfare State Development," in Peter Flora and Arnold J. Heidenheimer, eds., *The Development of Welfare States in Europe and America* (New Brunswick, N.J.: Transaction Books, 1981), pp. 345–382. This study is based exclusively on affluent democracies, unlike Wilensky's earlier study, *The Welfare State and Equality*, which reaches the same conclusion on this point (pp. 42–47), but is based upon data from a mixed set of wealthy and less wealthy countries, a mixture which favors economic over political variables.

12. Francis G. Castles, ed., *The Impact of Parties: Politics and Policies in Democratic Capitalist States* (Beverly Hills, Cal.: Sage, 1982), pp. 21–96. See also Francis G. Castles, *The Social Democratic Image of Society* (London: Routledge & Kegan Paul, 1978), Chapter 2; and Francis G. Castles and R. McKinlay, "Does Politics Matter? An Analaysis of the Public Welfare Commitment in Advanced Democratic States," *European Journal of Political Research*, 7:2 (June 1979), pp. 169–186.

13. Castles, *The Impact of Parties*, Table 7, p. 63.

14. Jurgen Kohl, "Trends and Problems in Postwar Public Expenditure Development in Western Europe and North America," in Flora and Heidenheimer, *The Development of Welfare States*, pp. 322–327.

15. Jens Alber, "The Growth of Social Insurance in Western Europe: Has Social Democracy Made a Difference?" Paper presented to the International Political Science Association, Moscow, 1979.

16. Jens Alber, "Some Causes and Consequences of Social Security Expenditure Development in Western Europe, 1949–1977." Paper presented to the International Political Science Association, Rio de Janeiro, 1982.

17. On the positive relationship between corporatism and social expenditure, see Harold L. Wilensky, *The "New Corporatism," Centralization, and the Welfare State* (Beverly Hills, Cal.: Sage, 1976).

18. C. Hewitt, "The Effect of Political Democracy and Social Democracy on Equality in Industrialized Societies: A Cross-National Comparison," *American Sociological Review*, 42:3 (June 1977), p. 460.

19. David Cameron, "Inequality and the State, a Political-Economic Comparison," paper prepared for the annual meeting of the American Political Science Association, Chicago, September 1976; Edward R. Tufte, *Political Control of the Economy* (Princeton, N.J.: Princeton University Press, 1978), pp. 94–97; John Dryzek, "Politics, Economics and Inequality: A Cross-National Analysis," *European Journal of Political Research*, Vol. 6 (1978), pp. 399–410; J. D. Stephens, *The Transition from Capitalism to Socialism* (London: Macmillan, 1979); and S. G. Borg and F. G. Castles, "The Influence of the Political Right on Public Income Maintenance Expenditure and Equality," *Political Studies*, 29:4 (December 1981), pp. 604–621.

20. Robert Jackman, "Socialist Parties and Income Inequality in Western Industrial Societies," *The Journal of Politics*, Vol. 42 (1980), pp. 135–149. Jackman's earlier book, *Politics and Social Equality: A Comparative Analysis* (New York: Wiley, 1975), which shows no effect of socialism upon income distribution, is less persuasive since it is based on an analysis of a mixed sample of wealthy and poorer countries, leaving unclear the independent impact of ideology. See Castles, *The Impact of Politics*, p. 85.

21. See Malcolm Sawyer, "Income Distribution in OECD Countries," *OECD Economic Outlook: Occasional Studies*, July 1976, pp. 14 and 17.

22. J. Corina M. van Arnhem and Geurt J. Schotsman, "Do Parties Affect the Distribution of Incomes? The Case of Advanced Capitalist Democracies," in Castles, *The Impact of Politics*, pp. 283–364.

23. Van Arnhem and Schotsman, p. 327.

24. Van Arnhem and Schotsman, p. 356. The ability of unions to produce overall gains for the working class would appear to depend upon at least two conditions: (1) very high levels of unionization, so that union gains do not simply increase the disparity between unionized and nonunionized workers; and (2) increased efficiency, through union cooperation, to prevent reduction in profits and capital flight. See Harry G. Johnson and Peter Mieszkowski, "The Effects of Unionization on the Distribution of Income: A General Equilibrium Approach," *The Quarterly Journal of Economics*, 84:4 (November 1970), pp. 539–561; and Richard B. Freeman and James L. Medoff, "The Two Faces of Unionism," *The Public Interest*, No. 57 (Fall 1977), pp. 69–93).

25. A few neo-Marxist scholars, like Frank Parkin, argue that there is no greater income equality under socialist parties than under conservative parties. Parkin takes Sweden as a case in point and uses primary income data from about 1960. Hence he misses the expansion of the Swedish welfare state in the 1960s and 1970s and the accompanying redistribution through transfer payments. See Frank Parkin, *Class Inequality and Political Order: Social Stratification in Capitalist and Communist Societies* (London: MacGibbon & Kee, 1971), pp. 103–136.

26. Douglas A. Hibbs, Jr., "Political Parties and Macroeconomic Policy," *American Political Science Review*, 71:4 (December 1977), pp. 1467–87;

and Andrew Cowart, "The Economic Policies of European Governments," *British Journal of Political Science,* 8:3 and 4 (July and October, 1978), pp. 285–312 and 425–440.

27.   See Manfred G. Schmidt, "The Welfare State and the Economy in Periods of Economic Crisis: A Comparative Study of Twenty-Three OECD Nations," *European Journal of Political Research,* 11:1 (March 1983), pp. 1–26; Manfred G. Schmidt, "The Politics of Domestic Reform in the Federal Republic of Germany," *Politics and Society,* 8:2 (1978), pp. 131–164; and the exchange between James Payne and Douglas Hibbs in *American Political Science Review,* 73:1 (March 1979), pp. 181–190).

28.   C. A. R. Crossland, *The Future of Socialism* (New York: Schocken, 1963), pp. 312–327.

29.   On the perceived costs of nationalization, see Richard Lowenthal, "The Postwar Transformation of European Social Democracy," in Bogdan Denitch, ed., *Democratic Socialism: The Mass Left in Advanced Industrial Societies* (Totowa, N.J.: Allanheld, Osmun, 1981), pp. 20–35.

30.   Ironically, several of the nationalizations that occurred in the 1970s in Britain (firms threatened with failure like Rolls Royce and Upper Clyde Shipbuilders), France (acquisition of private firms by state-owned firms) and Sweden (to prevent business failure) took place or were prepared (Upper Clyde) under conservative governments. See Peter Maunder, ed., *Government Intervention in the Developed Economy* (New York: Praeger, 1979), pp. 125–26, 147.

31.   On Austria, see Karl R. Stadler, "The Kreisky Phenomenon," *West European Politics,* 4:1 (January 1981), pp. 5–18.

32.   Wilensky finds that the reverse also is true—that socialist governments spend more for social programs when spurred by competition from Catholic parties. See Flora and Heidenheimer, *The Development of Welfare States,* pp. 345–382.

33.   Samuel H. Beer, *British Politics in the Collectivist Age* (New York: Knopf, 1965), p. 180. See also Robert Brady, *Crisis in Britain: Plans and Achievements of the Labour Government* (Berkeley: University of California Press, 1950).

34.   On the National Health Service, see Harry Eckstein, *The English Health Service* (Cambridge, Mass.: Harvard University Press, 1964); and Howard M. Leichter, *A Comparative Approach to Policy Analysis: Health Care Policy in Four Nations* (London: Cambridge University Press, 1979), pp. 157–199.

35.   Beer, p. 210.

36.   Beer, pp. 189–202; and Trevor Smith, "Britain" in Jack Hayward and Michael Watson, eds., *Planning, Politics and Public Policy: The British, French and Italian Experience* (London: Cambridge University Press, 1975), pp. 52–69.

37.   Beer, pp. 199–200.

38.   Richard Rose, *Do Parties Make a Difference?* (Chatham, N.J.: Chatham House, 1980), p. 146.

39.   *World Bank Atlas of Per Capita Product and Population* (Washington, D.C.: World Bank, 1966); and *World Development Report, 1980* (Washington, D.C.: World Bank, 1980), pp. 110–111.

40.   Stephen Blank, "Britain: The Politics of Foreign Economic Policy, the Domestic Economy, and the Problem of Pluralistic Stagnation," *International Organization,* 31:4 (Autumn 1977), pp. 673–722.

41. On fluctuations in British housing policy as party control changed (in contrast to the greater continuity and lower political salience of French housing policy), see Roger H. Duclaud-Williams, *The Politics of Housing in Britain and France* (London: Heinemann, 1978). On land speculation policy, see Arnold J. Heidenheimer, Hugh Heclo and Carolyn Teich Adams, *Comparative Public Policy: The Politics of Social Choice in Europe and America* (New York: St. Martin's, 1983), pp. 253–254. On public spending, see Rudolf Klein, "The Politics of Public Expenditure: American Theory and British Practice," *British Journal of Political Science*, Vol. 6 (1976), pp. 401–432.
42. For two not unrelated analyses of the problems in British policymaking in the 1960s and 1970s, see Samuel Beer, *Britain Against Itself: The Political Contradictions of Collectivism* (New York: Norton, 1982); and Douglas E. Ashford, *Policy and Politics in Britain: The Limits of Consensus* (Philadelphia: Temple University Press, 1981), especially Chapter 8.
43. On Swedish social democracy, see Francis G. Castles, *The Social Democratic Image of Society: A Study of the Achievements and Origins of Scandinavian Social Democracy in Comparative Perspective* (London: Routledge & Kegan Paul, 1978); Herbert Tingsten, *The Swedish Social Democrats* (Totowa, N.J.: Bedminster, 1973); Donald Hancock, *Sweden, The Politics of Postindustrial Change* (Hinsdale, Ill.: Dryden Press, 1972); Ulf Himmelstrand, "Sweden: Paradise in Trouble," in Bogdan Denitch, *Democratic Socialism;* and Olaf Palme, "Democratizing the Economy," in Nancy Lieber, ed., *Eurosocialism and America: Political Economy for the 1980s* (Philadelphia: Temple University Press, 1982), pp. 219–234.
44. Dankwart Rustow aptly entitled his excellent book on Sweden *The Politics of Compromise* (Princeton, N.J.: Princeton University Press, 1955).
45. The theme of Herbert Tingsten's *The Swedish Social Democrats* is the dissolution of Marxist ideology, which he views as unsuited to Swedish conditions. See especially his conclusion, pp. 695–719.
46. Ola Ullsten, as quoted in The *New York Times,* March 25, 1978, p. 2.
47. Himmelstrand, "Sweden: Paradise in Trouble," p. 149.
48. Gunnar Adler-Karlsson, *Functional Socialism: A Swedish Theory for Democratic Socialization* (Stockholm, Bokförlaget Prisma, 1967), pp. 101–102, as quoted by Francis G. Castles, "Swedish Social Democracy: The Conditions of Success," *The Political Quarterly,* 46:2 (April–June 1975), pp. 171–185.
49. On the Meidner Plan, see Mark Kesselman, "Prospects for Democratic Socialism in Advanced Capitalism: Class Struggle and Compromise in Sweden and France," *Politics and Society,* 11:4 (1982), pp. 397–438; Rudolf Meidner, "A Swedish Union Proposal for Collective Capital Sharing," Lieber, *Eurosocialism and America,* pp. 25–34; M. Donald Hancock, "Sweden's Emerging Labor Socialism," in Bernard E. Brown, ed., *Eurocommunism and Eurosocialism: The Left Confronts Modernity* (New York: Cyrco, 1979), pp. 316–338; and M. Donald Hancock, "Productivity, Welfare, and Participation in Sweden and West Germany: A Comparison of Social Democratic Reform Prospects," *Comparative Politics,* 11:1 (October 1978), pp. 4–23.
50. *New York Times,* September 21, 1982.
51. Francis Castles argues persuasively that the weakness of conservatism in Scandinavia is related to the inability of urban-based aristocracies to

develop support in rural areas. On the decline of class voting, see Ulf Lindstrom, "The Changing Scandinavian Voter," *European Journal of Political Research*, 10:3 (September 1982), p. 326.

52. An index of religious voting, based upon the percentage of practicing Catholics voting for Mitterrand in the 1974 presidential runoff, minus the percentage of nonbelievers and nonpracticing Catholics who voted for him, was approximately 42, as compared to an index of class voting (manual workers voting for Mitterrand minus nonmanual workers voting for Mitterrand) of approximately 28 in the same election (up from about 20 in the 1950s). Estimated from Alain Lancelot, "Opinion Polls and the Presidential Election, May 1974," in Howard R. Penniman, ed., *France at the Polls: The Presidential Election of 1974* (Washington, D.C.: American Enterprise Institute, 1975), Table 6–7, 202–203. See also G. Michelat and M. Simon, *Classe, Religion, et Politique* (Paris: Presses de la Fondation Nationale des Sciences Politiques and Editions Sociales, 1977).

53. On this theme, see Adam Przeworski and Michael Wallerstein, "Democratic Capitalism at the Crossroads," *Democracy*, 2:1 (July 1982), pp. 52–68.

54. *New York Times*, May 20, 1983.

55. On this theme, see Peter Katzenstein, in *International Organization* (Autumn 1977), especially his Introduction and Conclusion, and "The French State in the International Economy" by John Zysman.

56. Janice McCormick, "Thorns Among the Roses: A Year of the Socialist Experiment in France," *West European Politics*, 6:1 (January 1983), p. 60.

57. Other possible responses were: "He had the support of all of the parties of the Left" (34 percent); "He seemed most capable of lowering unemployment" (20 percent); and "He seemed more than M. Giscard d'Estaing to have the stuff a President is made from" (2 percent). Multiple responses were allowed. "Comment la France a basculé," in *Le Nouvel Observateur*, June 1–7, 1981, p. 40.

58. *Le Monde*, May 17, 1983.

Index